WHEN
MONSTERS
SPEAK

ASTERISK: Gender, Trans-, and All That Comes After
A series edited by Susan Stryker, Eliza Steinbock, and Jian Neo Chen

DUKE UNIVERSITY PRESS   *Durham and London*   2024

A SUSAN STRYKER READER

WHEN
MONSTERS
SPEAK

SUSAN STRYKER / Edited by McKenzie Wark

Project Editor: Bird Williams
Designed by Courtney Leigh Richardson
Typeset in Minion Pro and Futura Std by Copperline
Book Services

Library of Congress Cataloging-in-Publication Data
Names: Stryker, Susan, author. | Wark, McKenzie, [date] editor.
Title: When monsters speak : a Susan Stryker reader /
Susan Stryker ; edited by McKenzie Wark.
Other titles: Susan Stryker reader | Asterisk
(Duke University Press)
Description: Durham : Duke University Press, 2024. | Series:
Asterisk | Includes bibliographical references and index.
Identifiers: LCCN 2023040704 (print)
LCCN 2023040705 (ebook)
ISBN 9781478030478 (paperback)
ISBN N 9781478026259 (hardcover)
ISBN 9781478059462 (ebook)
Subjects: LCSH: Transgender people—Study and teaching. |
Gender identity—Political aspects—California—San Francisco. |
Sexual minority culture—California—San Francisco. |
Transgender artists—California—San Francisco. | Queer theory. |
Feminist theory. | BISAC: SOCIAL SCIENCE / LGBTQ Studies /
Transgender Studies
Classification: LCCN HQ77.9 .S78 2024 (print)
LCC HQ77.9 (ebook)
DDC 306.76/80979461—dc23/eng/20240124
LC record available at https://lccn.loc.gov/2023040704
LC ebook record available at https://lccn.loc.gov/2023040705

Cover art: Portrait of Susan Stryker by Loren Rex Cameron,
reproduced with permission of the Carl A. Kroch Library, Cornell
University. From the Loren Rex Cameron Papers box 1, file 10.

Contents

PART II. TRANS THEORY AS GENDER THEORY

PART III. WHEN MONSTERS SPEAK

INTRODUCTION

MCKENZIE WARK

The Nineties

I was a little nervous about meeting Susan Stryker for the first time. It was a cool October morning in New York City. We sat outside at the Hungarian pastry shop on the Upper West Side. I needn't have worried. It was a delightful conversation ranging from the medicinal uses of ketamine to John Lilly's experiments in dolphin communication. And, of course, we talked about transgender stuff.

In transgender time one has at least two ages: the number of spirals around the sun since birth, and another, younger age, since coming out. Meeting Susan, I was a newly hatched trans woman meeting a revered elder. And not just any elder. She literally wrote the book, *Transgender History*. And she coedited *The Transgender Studies Reader*. And she cofounded the journal, *TSQ: Transgender Studies Quarterly*.[1]

At the same time, I was meeting a contemporary. We were both born in 1961. For all I know, I might be a month or two older. We both grew up in the mass broadcast age, finding hints of who we could be through popular media, whether it was Bugs Bunny cross-dressing as Brunhilda or imagining ourselves as "tall and tan and young and lovely" in Astrud Gilberto's "Girl from Ipanema."[2]

For both of us, our thirties were in the nineties, and as writers we were shaped by and responded to the nineties as a world-historical context: The Soviet Union collapsed. China took the capitalist road. The anti-Apartheid movement in South Africa prevailed. The United States went to war in the Persian Gulf. In the nineties, we learned new acronyms like NAFTA and WTO. The internet was still fun, but its commercialization was gathering speed.

Since we are talking about queer people, the nineties needs a soundtrack: the sounds drifting from car stereos from Sydney to San Francisco were Madonna and Prince, Janet Jackson and Whitney Houston. In classically American segregated fashion, there was both gangsta rap and grunge. In the gay clubs there was house music, and in the more forward-leaning straight(ish) ones, techno—both of which you might get on a compilation CD. By the end of the nineties, Napster would suggest a whole other model of media consumption. Meanwhile, talk shows were all the rage on cable TV and featured repeated segments about trans people, mostly awful.

Our more local contexts ran in parallel, too. For much of the nineties, Stryker was in San Francisco, and I was in Sydney, two of the gayest towns on the Pacific rim. Both had lively urban enclaves of the kind one used to call "bohemian," where people gathered to shape their lives around self-creation and to invent new collective modes of being.[3] Rising rents had not yet driven us out of our playgrounds. The start of the AIDS pandemic had hit both cities hard, but at least by the mid-nineties the antiretroviral drug "cocktail" started working for people living with AIDS.[4]

I mention this by way of situating how I read the writing that I have selected and arranged here. This writing is anchored in a time I know well, as Stryker's contemporary and as a writer also formed by the nineties in a bohemian milieu. And yet, at the same time, it is writing that I approach in trans time: as that of an elder speaking of an era I missed. I didn't come out until the 2010s. In trans time, I'm very green.

Like many trans people, I absorbed the language and perspectives of those who had transitioned just before me and were my teachers, mentors, and guides. In my case, mostly millennial trans women. Trans sensibilities are constantly remaking themselves. For example, we will see how the word *transgender* became important for Stryker for defining a way of being that took some distance from the older language of the *transvestite* and *transsexual*. By contrast, I came up in an era when, at least in my Brooklyn milieu, we started calling ourselves *transsexuals* again, investing the term with different meanings, and using the term as a way of distinguishing a sensibility different from what *transgender* came to mean as a liberal institutional marker. Trans people, not unlike other tiny minorities, have only tactics in and against the languages applied to us by dominant cultures and institutions.

As a trans woman, I'm a product of 2010s-era discourse.[5] But as a writer and theorist, I started working in my own voice in the 1990s—as did Susan Stryker. I think she asked me to edit this collection in part because we share that moment. We both witnessed how languages, ways of being, forms of alternate life, were appropriated into dominant cultures and institutions, including higher education. And we both have a sense that what the selective tradition retained from those times of creation has narrowed.[6]

I don't think either of us is interested in nostalgia. Rather, it's a matter of rewinding to find some less familiar sounds to sample in order to fast-forward somewhere else. Maybe there are possibilities, ways of being queer, of being sexual, of being trans, of being a writer or artist, of living one's life as collective creation that were left behind. Maybe there are possibilities also for adding some textures and colors to the kinds of academic discourses that institutionalize the memory and teaching of such ways of life.

This is where my other perspective comes into play: not just a veteran of the nineties but a participant-observer in this much more recent trans milieu. One reason I stayed in the closet throughout the eighties and nineties is that it was unthinkable to me that, if I came out, I could get any sort of job that would be part of intellectual life—in academia or the media or anywhere. I thought the choice was to stay closeted so I could get work and write, or to come out and do survival sex work.[7] This was a fair estimation, although the life and work of Susan Stryker is the counterfactual. I could not have done what she did, though. If I tried it, I don't think I'd have made it. I imagine I'd be dead.

The situation for trans people can't be said to have improved all that much, frankly. Particularly for trans people of color, or whose family rejects them, or who are deprived of education and community support, or get caught up in the carceral system. I'm not a liberal optimist. And yet for that tiny sliver of educated and supported trans people, there's at least some slim possibility of working professionally and having some version of a middle-class life. Or there would be, were it not for the casualization and proletarianization of so many formerly "middle-class" trades, including academia.

I see this among the millennial trans people who are my contemporaries in trans time. Thanks to the struggles won and work created by Stryker and others, some things are different. Queer and trans studies have a toehold in the academy. All sorts of social and cultural institutions now feel obliged to at least acknowledge that we have a right to work and live in the world of formal liberal equality. The chances of living and working in general are under continual downward pressure, although there's some irony in that the one industry in which trans people have carved out new possibilities for financially stable lives is tech.

One of the most powerful tendencies to emerge from the nineties, and largely in the San Francisco Bay Area, was the commodification of the internet. It is now transforming the whole of the economy and rendering a lot of intellectual labor precarious and casual. There are other drivers, but the internet is one of the sources of the adjunctification of the university. Just when trans intellectuals might get their chance to have a niche in the academy, the academy itself is reneging on its commitment to sustainable intellectual lives within its doors.

At the same time, several generations of trans people have discovered each other, and themselves, via the internet. Access to the internet was so restricted for so long, that the ability to express and negotiate trans-ness, and to organize, was skewed toward the sensibilities of affluent, white trans people.[8] Traces of this linger in today's era of far more generalized social media. Meanwhile, there are certainly still queer and trans bohemian milieux to be found—I am living in one here in Brooklyn, New York. These milieux have a different texture now that so much of our existence is mediated through online social media rather than zines and newsletters.

I was there for the online world of gender play and community of the nineties.[9] But unlike Stryker, I missed the formation of a trans version of queer everyday life. When I came out, I found an everyday life already shaped both by the trans avant-garde to which Stryker belonged and by decades of online culture. I hear Stryker's voice in stereo, then: as a contemporary and an elder. And I listen through both channels when selecting and editing the texts for this book.

I wanted to make a book rather than just a collection of pieces. Each of the three parts can be read through in order and has its own story to tell. The parts are each more-or-less sequential within themselves, but each operates on its own timeline—rather like trans time itself. What follows is a guide to further points of interest.

Part 1, "Trans SanFrisco," puts into sequence texts that emerged out of the Bay Area queer and trans milieu, particularly its s/m culture.[10] Part 2, "Trans Theory as Gender Theory," builds on the practices and languages developed in the Bay Area, and it tackles questions of the politics of knowledge, memory, and inter- and intra-community alliance. I held back Stryker's best-known piece, "My Words to Victor Frankenstein," until the last arc, part 3,

"When Monsters Speak." I want the reader to become familiar, first, with the milieu from which it emerged and, second, with the kinds of patient political negotiations that came after—before confronting trans rage. We then follow that text's career across twenty years through Stryker's commentaries on it.

Trans SanFrisco

In part 1, I have grouped together Stryker's writings that emerged mostly out of the Bay Area, starting in the nineties. The space of the city appears as one for the possibility of reinventing what everyday life could be like.[11] It is hard to overestimate how traumatizing the start of the HIV/AIDS pandemic was, particularly in places that had high concentrations of gay people, trans people, sex workers, and intravenous drug users. A whole generation—mine, Susan's— who had been sexually active before anyone knew what AIDS was had to confront the loss of many loved ones in an atmosphere of panic, stigma, and isolation.[12]

The HIV/AIDS pandemic never ended. What changed in the nineties was the reconstitution of ways of life that, for want of a better term, I'm calling *bohemian*. Styrker emerges from the milieu of Trans SanFrisco as a trans woman who refuses to accept trans-ness as a mental illness or a medical diagnosis. She looks for other practices and other languages. The language of transition can instead be aesthetic or spiritual. One might learn how to become transgender through sexual or artistic practices.

We start with the short story "Trick Dive." It's set in an archetypal waterfront dive bar. Being from a port town, I can confirm that such places used to exist and contained people not unlike these characters. The story is told from the point of view of a trans sex worker confronting a man who wants something from her—*knowledge*. The knowledge he will pay for might just be whether she still has a dick or not. And it might be something more. "Trick Dive" sets up a major theme of this book: What knowledge might the trans person have?

"The Surgeon Haunts My Dreams" is writing one might now imagine as autofiction: the narrator seems close to the author, although it's not the confessional voice of autobiography.[13] It's more speculative. The trans woman's body appears here via two regimes of knowledge. One is that of the surgeon. Far from being a benevolent Man of Science, he has his own desires. Perversity, if that's what it is, belongs not only on the side of the body under the knife. The other regime of knowledge is that of the sado-masochistic practices encountered in "Trick Dive." What can a body come to know viscerally by taking the knife into its own hand?

The piece also has a masturbation scene in which the narrator has to find a way to extract pleasure from what one might think of as her dick, although the word is hardly adequate. Here and elsewhere in these autofictional pieces, Stryker is less interested in psychoanalytic language, with its assumptions about gendered bodies, than in exploring the phenomenology of the ambiguities of the trans body and its "many-handed hunger."[14]

"Renaissance and Apocalypse" sets the scene for the emergence of distinctively trans artists and art practices within a wider queer culture. Renaissance implies rebirth, and the essay hints at pasts in which something like what we now call transgender people may have had forms of cultural continuity and a place in the culture at large. The nineties was not the first, nor the last, "tipping point" for trans people, where we might begin again to make our own art after our own desires, and where that work might start attracting the attention of a wider audience.[15] Stryker is already warning of the dangers of sanding off the edges of our experiences for wider cultural consumption.

Stryker points to the structural homology between the slave narrative and trans autobiography. It's a parallel one would not want to draw out too far. A reparative reading might start from how the struggle to build a sustainable and cumulative trans existence has both political and cultural dimensions and connecting both is the problem of pluralizing the kinds of narratives we get to have.[16] There's a hope, in many ways fulfilled, that if our struggle for liberation makes any headway, it both enables and draws upon trans creative expression in new forms, which is something these autofictional pieces are already doing: finding a form for writing that can hew closer to the experiences of the trans body in the world when thought outside of our "medical colonization."

"Across the Border," cowritten with Kathy High, proposes just such a work of art—an unrealized creative project documenting an orchiectomy.[17] The class and race dimensions of orchiectomy as a transition path are noted, as removing the testicles is cheaper and simpler than vaginoplasty. It also makes a unique kind of body: distinctively trans.[18] "Renaissance and Apocalypse" experimented with a religious language for trans culture. Here we are in the language of contemporary art. High's contributions note the formal problems of making visual art about the trans body, Such art, when not voyeurism, can become surveillance. The problem of the *cis gaze* has arrived.[19]

"Los Angeles at Night" is my favorite piece of Stryker's. It pulls together beautifully an autofictional style of narrative while allowing concepts to emerge organically out of situation and story. Autofiction becomes autotheory.[20] Stryker takes the blade back from the surgeon as a tool for practicing presence in the flesh as a kind of art, or ritual. What s/m and trans-ness might have in common is that the body can't be ignored, but neither is it simply given. The "language of the body," as Kathy Acker called it, can be felt through an art that gives it occasion to speak.[21] Besides its beauty as a piece of s/m writing, "Los Angeles at Night" also asks what a trans erotics would be like if made not only about us but by us and for us.

"Dungeon Intimacies," like "Renaissance and Apocalypse," pulls out to give us a wider view, but now of a Trans SanFrisco that is disappearing. It stresses the agency of the local as something more than merely reactive to globalization. It documents the s/m scene of the time and its innovations in forms of corporeal becoming-together. Stryker learns the language of *queer*, *transgender*, and *genderqueer* in the chill-out moments on the scene.

Here knowledge merges with and emerges from avant-garde practices within a bohemian psychogeography nestled within the larger urban possibilities and constraints of the Bay Area.[22] Stryker draws from a phenomenology of experimental corporeal experience rather than relying on psychoanalysis, which takes gender categories as given. Through practices, of which s/m is only one example, bodies emerge from the ambiguity of being into a language all their own.[23] Or so it was in Trans SanFrisco, for a time. Before the tech boom changed the city and before its sexual avant-gardes became the raw material for an internet porn industry.[24]

"Perfect Day" brackets the nineties in a longer arc, ending in a more settled life of kids, partners, blended families, and all that. It starts by winding back to Stryker's teen years. "Living as a man was nonconsensual," she writes of her teenage self. Looking for knowledge about gender, the library didn't help. I had the same experience with that. The only books I could find talked about whatever was going on with my gender and sexuality in terms of medical diseases and mental illnesses, when all I wanted was a pointer to where I could find people like me to befriend.

Pre-transition trans women who love women are sometimes good at sex. We pay very close attention. But we are maybe not great at it.[25] It is hard for us to be in our own bodies. We can be attractive because we are "not like other guys." But also frustrating to our partners—because not like other guys. "Perfect Day" steps nimbly through many of these tensions, making a valuable contribution to the conversations trans women have about our sexualities.

This section concludes with two appreciations of younger artists, Charlotte Prodger and Cooper Lee Bombardier. The key to the former is the art of modified embodiment.[26] Ketamine was one of the things Susan and I discussed when we first met. I'm "out" as a recreational user but was also low-key jealous that her K is on prescription. Its dissociative, out-of-body qualities might be especially appealing to trans women.[27] "Ketamine Journal" uses diary entries as a mediating form between body and text, as Stryker does elsewhere.

I chose to end this section with Stryker's introduction to Bombardier's *Pass with Care*.[28] It registers the formation of the next generation of trans writers and artists in Trans SanFrisco. There's an intimation here that trans culture might begin to be cumulative rather than always fugitive.

Trans Theory as Gender Theory

In part 2, the story moves away from the Trans SanFrisco milieu. It deals less with cultural or spiritual or sexual languages for trans existence and more with the political and academic "micropolitical practices through which the radical implications of transgender knowledges can become marginalized." "Trans Theory as Gender Theory" tells a story about negotiating with the power of normative institutions of gender, sexuality, and history.

We start with Stryker's tribute to Gayle Rubin. Appropriately enough, they met at a queer fundraiser at the Eagle, a gay leather bar. Rubin is important as an example of a scholar whose work is "grounded in her own bodily acts." Stryker presents Rubin not only as a role model but also as one of those invaluable people who has written letters of recommendation and in other ways enabled out trans and queer people to get toeholds in academia.

Like many feminists, Rubin was interested in the conceptual double of sex and gender; only for Rubin this was a historical and institutional structure.[29] Rubin was one of those feminists who stood apart from the dominant tendency to reify and dehistoricize the category of "woman." Her intervention in the famous, or perhaps infamous, Barnard conference of 1982 was to stick up for the feminism potentials of s/m practices, sex work, and porn against the rise of "good-girl feminism."[30] This was the text by Rubin that seized my attention in the mid-eighties, when I was an undergrad minoring in women's studies. (I know, that should have told me something.)

Since "trannies were lumped in with all the other perverts" in the moralistic strain of feminism, the lines of alliance for Stryker were clear—even if Rubin was not always particularly helpful on trans stuff in her influential early writings. Even for writers coming at trans-ness sympathetically, the perspective of queer sexualities tended to see trans-ness as if it was another kind of kink. They kept the structural association of trans with deviance, then flipped the value of deviance from bad to good—and us with it. While some of us—Stryker and myself included—experience trans-ness in part through a deep connection to sexuality, many do not.

Trans-ness is not reducible to sexuality, and indeed, the sexualization, particularly of trans women, can be part of the problem. Still, the path toward trans studies was clear. Second wave feminism that took the "natural" sexed body as a given was not adequate for dealing with queer sexuality, and so queer studies had to strike out from its maternal feminist home. Further, to imagine the figure of the trans person independently from sexuality, trans studies had to take a little distance from queer studies—how much is still up for debate.[31]

Once we posit trans embodiment as its own distinctive kind of politics, knowledge, and politics of knowledge, then we can work through its consequences for feminism. Trans makes the category of "woman" more interesting and might even "queer the woman question." Gender might no longer be just a mimetic double of sex as a "biological" given—as it has become in much of Trans-Exclusionary Radical Feminist (TERF) discourse. Instead, we might all practice nonmimetic ways of experiencing and conceiving our becomings. Stryker experimented with both gender as lived, and genre as written.

Interestingly, for Stryker, the concept of trans-ness is not limited to trans people. It is present as that which the sex/gender system controls. Whether in gay or straight life, there are sanctions for doing gender "wrong." One of the agents of control of trans-ness ended up being a certain kind of feminism that set itself up as the police of good womanhood. It treats the "biological" body, or rather a fantasy of it, as if it were a "natural" given that could ground a politics and a culture of womanhood across time and space.[32] In doing so, this trans-exclusionary feminism bought into colonial formations of knowledge and power through which white women became the agents of "proper" gender expression, both in the colonies and against working-class women at home.[33] An influential strand of second wave feminism repeated the patriarchal notion of woman as close to nature and simply reversed its value, making this the source of the good, the beautiful, and the true. This conceit of naturalism was then treated as the reason for rather than against the agency of women in public life.

Third wave feminism brought a much-needed critique of the essentialism and Eurocentrism of this project as well as new concepts such as the *performativity* of gender, which in Judith Butler's view retroactively produces the fiction of embodied sex as its origin.[34] And yet transsexuality often appears in both second and third wave feminism as a kind of allegorical point of concentration for thinking about everything but the trans body itself. Despite its claims to progress, even in third wave feminism, a long-standing tradition of transsexuality as allegory for modernity finds itself repeated somewhat uncritically in academic drag.[35] Trans-ness is the sign of "gender trouble" or—one might even say—of "sex trouble."

Trans feminism makes trans-ness its own experiential site rather than a mere allegory for other people's gender anxieties.[36] Trans feminism might nevertheless connect to struggles other than around trans-ness. Drawing on her own experiences, Stryker points toward a range of social struggles around disability, mental health, undocumented labor, workplace discrimination, privacy, access to health care and housing, policing, and mass incarceration. Stryker: "How we each live our bodies in the world is a vital source of knowledge."

Trans-ness also troubles queerness. *Homonormativity*, or what Jasbir Puar will later call *homonationalism*, might be concepts describing how certain ways of being a gay man or lesbian are incorporated into models of the good citizen and consumer.[37] Homonormativity might also mean the ways in which gay and lesbian communities and organizations themselves police the boundaries of queerness against other expressions of it, particularly gender-variant and trans ones. It's disappointing, to say the least, when queer people accept the straight world's models of gender. Hence re-emergence of "LGB without the T" politics and sensibilities. The move to sever us is not without a certain perverse logic. Trans-ness is not an equivalent identity category to being a gay man, or a lesbian, or bisexual. Trans people can be any of those things, or be "straight." In the sensibility of liberal identity politics, the T functions more as a supplement, or as the "containment mechanism for gender trouble."

Leslie Feinberg popularized the idea of *transgender* as a kind of political umbrella category that could include transsexuals, transvestites, and other gender-variant or gender-expansive people, including what in more recent language one might call nonbinary and agender people.[38] Across much of Stryker's writing the term *transgender* has that valence. Now that transgender has become a liberal political identity category, I venture that one might even speak of a kind of *transnormativity*. In moments of transnormativity, certain expressions of trans-ness appear as acceptable and redeemable. This respectable trans-ness is then worthy of consideration as the basis for rights-bearing subjects. Not surprisingly the face of transnormativity is often white, or at least well-spoken, not publicly sexual, and at some remove from sex work.[39]

There are now even sanctioned historical narratives of trans-ness, which highlight certain figures and moments as formative struggles that endow certain trans people with the potential to claim to be rights-bearing subjects. Stryker reminds us that Nietzsche once dissected historical thought into three kinds: antiquarian, monumental, and critical.[40] Antiquarian history gives us a lineage and connection. Monumental history seeks heroic stories to inspire great things. Critical history is more steely-eyed and focuses on past injustices. Now that Marsha P. Johnson has a waterside park named after her, it's timely to revisit this intervention into questions of what kind of histories serve what purpose for trans people today.

How are we to remember the moment of August 1966 at Compton's Cafeteria in the Tenderloin district of San Francisco? Was it a riot or a revolt? How does it relate to what happened at Stonewall a few years later? What are we to remember: That we suffered? That we struggled? Or that we endured? Who exactly is that "we"? Stryker did much to bring Compton's into focus as a moment in trans history—to the extent that in the 2019 version of the miniseries *Tales of the City* (based on the characters from Armistead Maupin's much-loved books), Compton's becomes the key to the backstory of the central character Anna Madrigal.

The general concept of *normativity* emerges as a key theme across these texts. Whereas the writings in part I attempt to find a form outside of normative literary forms, those in part 2 take on normativity, particularly that of feminists, gays, and lesbians, as a topic. At the level of form, they also question normativity in historical studies. Historical writing that centers the body of the writer, as trans writing sometimes must, can find itself relegated to the margins by a *normativizing disciplinarity*. Scholarship that insists on a subjective neutrality as a way of simulating objectivity is for trans people part of the problem. It is exactly this epistemology that handed power over our lives to medical and psychiatric Dr. Frankensteins.

One of the most fraught kinds of normativity for trans women to negotiate is lesbian culture. As Stryker puts it, we are neither its object nor subject but often its *abject*: that which is pushed aside with disgust.[41] She asks, provocatively, what it would mean to think lesbian feminism as structured around its transphobia. Lesbian feminism, like second wave feminism, is too often a version of Eurocentric modernization discourse. It is a certain model of womanhood, posed as the most liberated, most advanced, most befitting of the claim to rights. It's critical attention turned against other women. That can include working-class butch and femme dykes, women of color, trans women, or trans men—all of whom supposedly perpetuate oppressive gender roles.[42] The personal is political, but the political can also get very, very personal.

What's striking to me about the essays I grouped together under "Trans Theory" is Stryker's patient and controlled tone. She shows the contributions trans people can make by drawing on the knowledge gained from encountering the world through our particular bodies. And at the same time, she shows how those to whom we appealed for solidarity and support did not always have our backs.

When Monsters Speak

I've arranged the book so that we start with the formative experiences of cultural and political knowledge-making in "Trans SanFrisco," followed by the application of that knowledge to the politics of institutional alliances in "Trans Theory," before returning, in part 3, to Stryker's most famous piece: "My Words to Victor Frankenstein above the Village of Chamounix: Performing Transgender Rage." Hopefully, those to whom the depth and breadth of transgender rage seemed opaque will now have some sense of what it feels like.

Another context for this text, highlighted maybe a little more than in some of the others, is transgender political organizing. It deals with the politics of emotions and the emotions of politics. Here the affinity with queer experience and organizing, whatever our tensions with it, is worth stressing. Trans politics, like queer politics, might entail the recognition that certain emotions are not private, isolated experiences. That shame, fear, despair, and rage are social and political.[43]

At the same time, the piece works through aesthetic questions as to what trans writing might become. Sandy Stone had already shown the limits of the conventional trans memoir, where transition is the culmination of a personal journey facilitated by doctors.[44] The concluding emotion of transition is supposed to be living happily ever after in one's "real" gender. Stryker imagines transition otherwise: as an art of the body, which of necessity is also a politics of the body, due to the infuriating obstacles put in the path of our individual and collective self-transformation. She creates, out of parts, a genre for this theory and practice of gender. The raging tone feels akin to that of ACT-UP, with all its survival-driven urgency.[45]

The structuring conceit of Stryker's text is the unnaturalness of the trans body. All human bodies are in some way unnatural, in the sense that they all require some kind of technics to endure and thrive.[46] But some have to be held as abject—as unassimilable, as other—to sustain the fiction of the normative body as natural. Finding this scapegoating not just from the straight world but also from feminists, lesbians, and gay men pushes the narrator to embrace alterity, to become the "leatherdyke from hell." Gayle Rubin on steroids—but where the steroid happens to be estrogen.

But here is the risk this self-fashioning runs: How to "lay claim to the dark power of my monstrous identity without using it as a weapon against others or being wounded by it myself?" This is both personal and political work: to create ways of existing with, even drawing on, this powerful affect without self-harm. If you are trans, you have very likely lost sisters and brothers and others who died by their own hand, sometimes as much from rage as from sadness. But there's more: one also has to deflect oneself from inflicting this rage onto other trans people, something I see constantly in the community drama among the trans people around me.

When trans people create themselves, it's both a personal and communal act.[47] The theme of creation in this text draws on Mary Shelley's *Frankenstein*. Once upon a time, only God was a creator, and the best humans could do is to imitate His handiwork. A hierarchy of perfection stretches down from God, via the angels, to Man, and to his imitations as a poorly realized representation.[48]

When I first read this text, years before I could even contemplate the need to transition, I read it through Raymond Williams and what, for him, was the long history to the struggle to democratize creation.[49] A key moment is that of the romantic poets, Mary Shelley's contemporaries, for whom the poet is a special kind of human endowed with creative capacities. For Williams, the long revolution of socialism had the aim of freeing not only the labor of working peoples but their creative capacities as well.

In Mary Shelley, and in Susan Stryker, we find a complication on the way to the democratization of creation: What happens when the desire to create takes the bodies of others as its material? When Christine Jorgensen became famous in 1952 as the first celebrity trans woman, one of the things being celebrated was the creative power of the men who made her.[50] The surgeon still haunts our dreams.

The more common critical path taken in second wave feminism is to celebrate womanhood as natural, which ironically enough returns us to the archaic idea of the world as God's creation.[51] Woman is aligned with nature, purity, and the good against masculinity as the Frankensteinian will to cut the world into reasonable shape. The result is the spectacle of middle-class white women taking themselves to be the apotheosis of naturalism. And so, we arrive at health authorities issuing warnings against putting wasp's nests into vaginas.[52]

Stryker takes the other path: rather than become natural and good, become artificial and bad—become monstrous. Monsters, like angels, are messengers, not from God but from elsewhere. Perhaps from creation itself, from an entirely different conception of "nature" in which it has no author or master but is change, difference—variation itself.

On this other path, "nature" is no longer a stick with which to beat others for failing to conform to some arbitrary virtue smuggled into the conceit of being ordered by God. If "nature" still exists as a concept, it might mean something more like that which unfolds into some capacity—existing or novel—to be materially ongoing in the world. Nature is not virtue; it is the *virtual*. It's virtual in the sense Gilles Deleuze and Félix Guattari gave the word. It's not an ideal, it's real. It's just not actual. It's what is not but could actually be. It's all the things the actual could become or, rather, the capacity of their becomings.[53]

From the point of view of nature as the virtual, the other concept of nature as virtue is, ironically enough, an artifice or—less politely—a lie. It is merely the transposition of some component of a historical social order as a metaphor into a state of nature as a means to justify it. This is what Marx said happens when bourgeois economics sees the market as a natural order. Or what Haraway says happens in the primate sciences when the bourgeois family becomes a given of the natural order.[54] One way to think the Anthropocene is as the failure of such a concept when implemented as a tool of domination on a planetary scale.

Stryker is still interested in how gender saturates the world, but not along a nature/artifice binary. She makes use of a reading of Mary Shelley that distinguishes the male gaze (and cis gaze) from the auditory space as feminine. The latter is ambient, unbounded, animated, and dialogic. The former treats the world as objects that—if they can be seen—can be cataloged and controlled.[55]

Alongside a critique of visibility, what are the powers and tactics of *invisibility*, of the ambient and audible?[56] It's a theme across the Trans SanFrisco writings. For Stryker, it's the darkened spaces of the s/m club, where the visual is turned down and the array of other bodies can enter all the senses. It's the sounds of quivering flesh, or dialogues in the chill-out space, where other talk comes into play. Tactics that can be very selectively deployed in the light of day to talk back to power. Capacities I was finding, at that time, on the other side of the Pacific—in raves.[57]

Talking back is, among other things, a trans power of survival in the street, when we fail to register as "natural" bodies to the cis gaze. The derogatory term among trans women for a sister who doesn't pass is a *brick*. For many, the only tactic that seems to offer any safety is to mimic cis womanhood, to *pass*, to be *unclockable*, to accept the codes of gender as given as if they were a natural order, which in the parlance of trans women is to be *fish*.

In 2021, at least fifty trans people were murdered in the United States, mostly trans women of color.[58] No wonder many trans people modify and present their bodies as cis-passing. This is gender as more than *performative*, given that it takes more than negotiating dominant language-like codes to pull it off. One had to cut and temper flesh itself. All to appear in the visual field—just so—in a way that accepts the lie of nature rather than challenging it. Many trans people do not have the luxury of queer gender play. Stryker rescues even these transsexual bodies from abjection. They too seize the powers of creation. That might matter more than the style in which the gender of the body is then fashioned.

In "My Words to Victor Frankenstein," Stryker issues a trans challenge to "nature" itself. The piece opens with a description of appearances that intentionally presents the bad object to the controlling gaze, which is itself revealed to be a gaze that is shared not only by men but also by many women who think they are feminists, and by many queer viewers who think they are somehow radical. And then this anomalous vision speaks of what it knows, of what it not only sees but also senses.

"My Words" speak—in the plural—back to the sciences that made transsexual bodies possible but did so out of weird unacknowledged desires and with a controlling instinct. They also speak back to both feminist and queer communities who have not heard the challenges trans-ness poses to the worldview that seeks to make us in their image through their fantasies of mastery. "My Words" propose an alternate queer ecology[59]—or better—a trans ecology, in which we will not be that terrifying image of what we are to all the Dr. Frankensteins: a body without a mouth.[60]

Ten years after "My Words," Stryker reflects on them in "Queer Theory's Evil Twin." Like Frankenstein's monster, the evil twin is a common narrative trope found everywhere from daytime soaps to Pier Paolo Pasolini.[61] As queer theory's evil twin, transgender studies brings trouble into the family. Stryker names three writers with whom she is in dialogue—Judith Butler, Sandy Stone, and Leslie Feinberg—for whom trans-ness is already a kind of gender trouble, needling at some corner or other of what is not yet ready to be named *cis normativity*.

Out of those texts, Stryker draws possibilities for "enacting a new narrative," and in that, she is writing in parallel to the Bay Area writers of the New Narrative movement.[62] The world of New Narrative writers is a kind of literary "family by choice," which is something akin to what Stryker wants from queer writing: a space within which trans writing can find commonality. Some years later, trans writing will start to feel the need for its own space, at some remove from queer literature and theory.[63] Just how close its relation to queerness ought to be is still up for debate.

Some twenty years after "My Words," in "Transing the Queer (In)human," Stryker offers a different kind of intertext for it, gesturing toward Gayatri Spivak on subaltern speech, Jean-François Lyotard on language games, and Michael Hardt and others on affective labor. "My Words" enacts speaking rather than being spoken to or of, crafting moves in a rigged discursive game. It vents the surplus feelings that performing all that work generates.[64] With the hindsight of twenty years, "My Words" is not only situated in multiple existing language games. It is also a key move in starting a new one—transgender studies. One might wonder, however, what other possibilities were left behind. For instance, what might it have looked like if this text was as central to a trans literature as to a trans scholarship?

Beyond that, what might be at the far horizons of what "My Words" articulated? To me, the essay speaks also to media theory and its interest in the human as a byproduct of the technical rather than as its author.[65] If the human is a special effect of technics, then it might at least be interesting to consider those versions of the body that are deemed to have failed to be human because they are too marked by technics, of which trans people are just one example.

At the twenty-five year mark, Stryker is writing in a context in which queer theory has expanded into, and linked up with, a critique of the *biopolitical*, in which forms of life are categorized, ranked, and valued—or treated as waste.[66] Against which various *new materialisms* emphasize a scaleless, interconnected universe continually in process, often charged with what looks suspiciously like old-fashioned vitalism.[67] I have written elsewhere against these kinds of contemplative worldviews that seem to forget the praxis from which any worldview extends.[68]

What I appreciate about Stryker's writings is that they are more than a merely contemplative worldview upon universal trans-ness. The texts write from their own situatedness, from moments of struggle to become. They write from practices—writerly, political, artistic, sexual—from which these particular concepts emerge. Concepts, it turns out, that have all sorts of uses beyond transgender studies, but which have their limitations as well.

In responding to Katrina Roen and Karen Barad, Stryker acknowledges these limitations, which are also those of the whiteness of the networks of trans people within which they were in part generated. More generative, perhaps, is Marquis Bey's reading of Stryker in which Blackness and trans-ness are adjacent ways of naming what was and is fugitive, unfigured, uncaptured, in racial capitalism. Scholars such as C. Riley Snorton and Jules Gill-Peterson have done much to show how in the United States and beyond, the categories of the sexed body, as they appear in that medical science (which supposedly grounds its "naturalness") have always been racialized.[69] Jian Neo Chen, micha cárdenas, Francisco Galarte, and others have brought trans of color lives, arts, and culture into the dialogue, or rather the polylog, on trans-ness, putting pressure on it as a category, even within American life.[70]

Unlike Stryker, I never felt all that strong a need to trouble queer discourse as a means to affiliate with it. I read queer theory at the time of its initial boom as if I was a cis bisexual. It bothered me for different reasons. For instance, the way that in *Volatile Bodies* Liz Grosz treated bisexuality as a vector of disease.[71] Or the way that the Sydney Gay and Lesbian Mardi Gras tried to control access to its popular annual ball by mandating that all members sign a declaration that offered only two options: lesbian or gay man. I showed up to the public debate at the Tom Mann theater with the bisexuals rather than the transsexuals to see about that.

By the time I eventually came out, queer theory, with its celebration of the ineffable, indeterminate play of gender appeared to me as one of the obstacles to my own transition. It often treated actual trans people, and trans women in particular, as the bad object for taking it all too literally (on which, see all the inexcusably bad takes on *Paris Is Burning*). By contrast, I had what Stryker did not: networks of trans people who might overlap with queer networks but did not depend on them. It must be said, however, that like everything else in America, these networks were often segregated.

I had that, in part, because of Styker's work across the nearly thirty-year period this collection covers. When monsters speak, their voices echo.

Notes

1   Stryker, *Transgender History*; Stryker and Whittle, *The Transgender Studies Reader*; Stryker and Aizura, *The Transgender Studies Reader II*.
2   On the broadcast age, see Spigel, *Make Room for TV*.
3   Lucy Sante is one of my favorite writers of bohemia. Sante, *The Other Paris*; Sante, *Low Life*.
4   See "Trans in a Time of AIDS," special issue edited by Che Gossett and Eva Hayward, *TSQ: Transgender Studies Quarterly* 7, no. 4 (2020).
5   See the fictional account of this subculture in Fitzpatrick, *The Call Out*.
6   On selective tradition, see R. Williams, *The Long Revolution*.

7   Perkins, *The Drag Queen Scene*. The late Roberta Perkins studied sociology with R. W. Connell at Macquarie University, just a few years before I did.

8   Here I'm indebted to the as-yet-unpublished work of Cass Adair.

9   To get the flavor of that, see Sullivan and Bornstein, *Nearly Roadkill*; Horn, *Cyberville*.

10 On which, see also Califia, *Macho Sluts*.

11 Compare with Tea, *Valencia*.

12 Here I know the New York accounts best: Wojnarowicz, *Close to the Knives*; Shulman, *Rat Bohemia*.

13 Gasparini, *Autofiction*.

14 Fleishmann, *Time Is the Thing a Body Moves Through*.

15 The tipping point is named after Steinmetz, "The Transgender Tipping Point." It might also include the public reception of Janet Mock's autobiography, *Redefining Realness*, and the model Geena Rocero's very public coming out in a TedTalk. See Rocero, *Horse Barbie*.

16 On reparative reading, see Sedgwick, *Touching Feeling*.

17 On the work of Kathy High, see https://www.kathyhigh.com.

18 Monir, *Napkin*.

19 A short piece by Cara Esten Hurtle got me thinking about this concept. See Wark, "The Cis Gaze and Its Others."

20 There are many versions of autotheory. See, for example, Fournier, *Autotheory as Feminist Practice*.

21 Acker, *Bodies of Work*.

22 Solnit, *Infinite City*.

23 Salamon, *Assuming a Body*.

24 On San Francisco gentrification and housing struggles, see Tracy, *Dispatches against Displacement*.

25 A point made by Peters, *Detransition, Baby*.

26 Prodger, *Selected Works*.

27 Baer, *Trans Girl Suicide Museum*.

28 Bombardier, *Pass with Care*.

29 G. Rubin, *Deviations*.

30 Vance, *Pleasure and Danger*.

31 For the case against queer theory, see Namaste, *Invisible Lives*.

32 Repo, *Biopolitics of Gender*.

33 Lugones, *Pilgrimages/Peregrinajes*; Hinchy, *Governing Gender and Sexuality*.

34 But see also Prosser, *Second Skins*.

35 Heaney, *The New Woman*. On third wave feminism, see Gillis, Howie, and Munford, *Third Wave Feminism*.

36 See "Trans/Feminisms," special issue edited by Susan Stryker and Talia M. Bettcher, *TSQ: Transgender Studies Quarterly* 3, no. 1 (2016); and "Trans/Feminisms," special issue edited by Talia Bettcher et al., *Sinister Wisdom* (Spring 2023).

37 Puar, *Terrorist Assemblages*.

38 Feinberg, *Transgender Warriors*.

39 Jean et al., *Revolution Is Love*, documents the struggle to define a practice of trans liberation outside of transnormativity. See also Meronek and Major, *Miss Major Speaks*.

40 Nietzsche, *Untimely Mediations*.

41 Kristeva, *Powers of Horror*.

42 Kendall, *Hood Feminism*.

43 Subsequent work on transgender "bad affect" includes Malatino, *Side Affects*; and Awkward Rich, *The Terrible We*.

44 Stone, "The 'Empire' Strikes Back." For selections from classic trans memoirs, see Ames, *Metamorphosis*.

45 Schulman, *Let the Record Show*.

46 Preciado, *Testo Junkie*.

47 Gleeson, "How Do Gender Transitions Happen?"

48 Wark, "Trap Metaphysics."

49 R. Williams, *The Long Revolution*.

50 See Jorgensen, *A Personal Autobiography*, with its introduction by Stryker.

51 Although here we might mention how the work of the late Rachel Pollack complicates the women's spirituality tradition. See Pollack, *The Body of the Goddess*.

52 Miller, "Why Are Women Putting Wasp Nests in Their Vaginas?"

53 Deleuze and Guattari, *Anti-Oedipus*.

54 Haraway, *Simians, Cyborgs, and Women*.

55 One could connect this to a parallel development in studies of Blackness and sound. See Weheliye, *Phonographies*.

56 Gossett, Stanley, and Burton, *Trap Door*.

57 St. John, *Technomad*.

58 Carlisle, "Anti-trans Violence and Rhetoric."

59 Wölfe Hazard, *Underflows*.

60 Vividly pictured in the Wachowskis' film *The Matrix* (1999).

61 Pasolini, *Petrolio*.

62 Killian and Bellamy, *Writers Who Love Too Much*.

63 Cugini, "The Troubled Golden Age of Trans Literature."

64 Gregg and Seigworth, *The Affect Theory Reader*.

65 Kittler, *Gramophone, Film, Typewriter*.

66 Stryker, "Biopolitics."

67 Dolphijn and van der Tuin, *New Materialism*.

68 Wark, *General Intellects*.

69 Bey, *Black Trans Feminism*; Snorton, *Black on Both Sides*; Gill-Peterson, *Histories of the Transgender Child*; Gill-Peterson, *A Short History of Trans Misogyny*.

70 Chen, *Trans Exploits*; cárdenas, *Poetic Operations*; Galarte, *Brown Trans Figurations*.

71 Grosz, *Volatile Bodies*, 197.

TRANS
SANFRISCO

I.

TRICK DIVE

The Albatross was a sea-goers' dive on the working end of San Francisco's waterfront. Years of grime grayed the derelict two-story building, so it blended easily into the fog that often masked the neighborhood from all but knowing eyes. Locked doors and boarded windows faced the street, and nothing directed the merely curious down the back alley toward the sign of the bird painted on an otherwise unmarked entrance. Inside, the few bikers and leatherdaddies cruising rough trade stood out like black islands in the sea of sex-hungry sailors who elbowed past the slumming navy boys for their chance to be hustled by one of the whores who worked the crowd. Sometimes these sailors got that chance with me.

Karl stood at the pinball machine. A row of quarters lined the glass above the plunger, a row of empty brown bottles lined the floor beneath. How long since I'd seen him—two years? Two and a half? He stopped spending nights here after Maya moved in, and I came now only when business slowed. I hung back, waiting for him to drop more of his tip money into the slot, kill his latest beer, and launch another ball before I slid my hand between his thighs to pinch his leg. I pinched harder than I intended, and he yelped angrily as he spun around.

It took him longer to make me than was good for my vanity. When recognition welled up in his eyes at last, he leaned back against the machine, working the style of every tough guy in every B-movie he'd ever seen. Coal black eyes beneath bushy brows scanned me while he fished for something impressive to say.

"Of all the gin joints in all the world," he said, finally giving up, "she walks into mine."

"She," I repeated. "That word used to stick in your throat when you talked about me."

"Just something about the way you look tonight, big guy. No offense." His lingering gaze contradicted the contempt in his voice. As his eyes raked me, I saw in them the confused anger and inarticulate need on which I loved to feed. Then he turned coolly back to his game.

I studied myself in the big mirror behind the bar to our right. My calf-length black linen dress was slit nearly to the crotch. Its neckline plunged in a deep vee to reveal the scalloped edges of my bustier. Stainless steel sheathed the toes of my stiletto-heeled black leather pumps. Nice legs, subtle make-up and miles of curling blond hair said "femme" so convincingly most people failed to notice the masculine angularity of the body.

No woman, and certainly no man, would come into the Albatross advertising like that without having something to sell. I wore my shop sign over my left breast—a discreet bar-shaped pin from which small charms dangled: a noose, a pair of tiny handcuffs, a little leather whip. A roomy pouch slung over my right shoulder harbored working versions of the jewelry.

Once in this bar some dumb fuck of a tugboat pilot thought that just because I looked pretty and seemed available he could take me without asking or paying. He grabbed me in the john, and while he groped clumsily under my bra, I pulled thirty-six inches of piano wire from beneath my belt. I left a scar around his neck he'd be explaining for the rest of his life. The dumb fucks were bad, but the smart ones were worse, especially officers. Their condescension rankled me. They assumed that if I could cheek a rubber, I'd never read a book. It never occurred to them that a person with other options could choose to live this way. Fuck 'em, I'd tell myself. They can keep their attitude. I keep their money.

I turned back to my mark and slid my hand inside Karl's pants. I throttled his limp dick and squeezed rhythmically to make it waken and pulse. I leaned into him and peered around his bulk to watch him play. Before long, his meat stood rigid in my hand, demanding more attention than his game could spare, and the last ball rolled away. His breathing was ragged, and he put no more money into the machine.

"Cut your dick off yet?" The agitation in his voice was obvious.

"Now, Karl," I cooed, dipping my head coyly to peer up at him, "what makes you think I'd tell something that personal to a lover who left me for another skirt?" When he didn't answer I dropped my voice into the male register and asked, "Besides, honey, how badly do you want to know?"

Without a word he thrust his hand into his pocket and pulled out a wad of bills. "Unless you've stopped fucking for money?"

"Of course, I'm still fucking for money, you asshole. What else would I be doing here? But tell me something, sweetie, before we do this deal. What exactly are you trying to buy?"

He became genuinely thoughtful. "Knowledge."

"Not very specific, dear. Try harder." He got huffy.

"I just want to be with you again, goddamn it, for one night. You can do whatever the fuck you want."

"Sold."

I grinned as I took what he offered. I hadn't expected this biz tonight, but I wanted something from the bastard and was pleased to think I would get it. Dropping the money into my bag, I took out a chain leash attached to a spiked choke-collar and whipped it around Karl's neck. Yanking the chain to jab the prongs into his throat without breaking the skin, I dragged him, an incarnation of sputtering rage, through the crowd and down the street to my car.

He sat stiffly in the passenger seat, hands cuffed behind him, leash locked to an eyebolt in the door. It was a quick trip to Karl's warehouse in west Oakland, but long enough for him to brew one of the unspeaking furies that always fueled our scenes. Leaving Karl cuffed and collared, I got my ropes out of the trunk, then we entered the apartment. Neither of us spoke as I slapped him down to the floor, stripped him, screwed clamps on his nipples, and readied the bondage equipment. I thought of the histories that carried us here.

We met in the Albatross, where Karl tended bar by day and stayed nights to drink his wages, shoot pinball, and spout philosophy like some improbable beat poet. When he drank, he found a voice for the intricate ideas bottled up in his head. He would rant brilliantly until the alcohol slurred his thoughts, then drift into a sullen silence that begged to be broken. I loved to break it, pierce it with clarifying pain. He screamed the loveliest things. I started our little fling mostly male, though my tits were coming in, and hustling was just beginning to seem more challenging than college. He was fresh from the sea, a working-class boho with a big hungry brain, holding down a day job and sucking up San Francisco counterculture like a thirsty sponge. Kinky went with cutting edge in his understanding of the world, and I was the most temptingly bent thing he'd ever seen. We made a striking couple. Each found in the other the smart sleaze and social mobility we'd looked for. Karl was moving up, I was moving down, and we met on common ground at the Albatross, where my fall from middle-class respectability came under my control. I made it a trick dive, falling with grace and precision.

Now I had the scene laid out. Concrete slab steps climbed the back wall of the apartment to a loft perched fifteen feet above the living area. I anchored a rope to the banister near the top of the staircase, tested its ability to bear weight, then turned my attention to Karl. He sucked air as I tore off the titclamps, but otherwise remained defiantly silent as I put him in a rope harness connected to leather ankle restraints, trussed his legs together, and tied his arms to his sides.

"All right, you motherfuckin' maggot, pay attention. Crawl first; then you're gonna fly."

I backhanded him viciously across the face, then picked up a riding crop with one hand and a switchblade with the other. A sudden torrent of blows from the crop drove him quickly toward the stairs. Karl pushed with his knees and shoulders to climb the steps and evade my aim. The rough concrete tore his skin, and the crop raised stinging welts across his back. At the top step I ordered him to stop. I had tied a rapid-release snap into the rope on the staircase, and I hooked it to his ankle restraints.

"Get up, shithead. And pray I measured right."

With the knife I snagged the underside of his scrotum and lifted, forcing him to rise precariously to his feet. I inched him back against the railing. For one second of perfect terror he balanced on tiptoe, scarlet wetness seeping around the knife point, then he toppled over the banister with a scream. The rope snapped taut and stretched under his weight. I felt the bloodlust rise in me and hurried downstairs. Karl's head swung a foot above the floor. He panted, and panic filled his eyes. The heavy smell of his sweat wrenched open in me hidden reservoirs of hate. Had he really wounded me that much? I lost myself for a while in hurting him: cat, cane, quirt, blade, like old times, his body and mind tight surfaces ripe for laceration. I raved; he surrendered; I burst him and drowned myself in his pain.

Afterward, Karl hung unconscious. Blood stained the ropes, laced his ribs and matted his hair, dripped from his shoulders and nose and pooled brightly on the bare cement floor. I checked his pulse and his breathing, and knew he needed to come down soon. But first I had to catch my breath and remember.

One night, in a playfully bitchy mood, I had tried something new with Karl, told him to kneel before his Goddess. The single malt scotch we'd worked on all night wanted out of my bladder, and my piss was too good for the toilet.

"Strip naked, dog, and open your mouth," I snarled, peeling off my gaff and lifting my skirt. Karl warily obeyed. I took him by the ears and drove his mouth down onto the soft little cock nestled between my slick thighs. He sucked it well back into his throat, and I let loose the kidney-filtered booze. He instantly started to moan and bob. I looked down to see his hand wrapped around his own stiff dick, stroking it frantically. His cum exploded onto my bare legs before I finished peeing, and he fell sobbing to the floor.

Blubbering words and raw emotion poured from him for an hour afterward as he lay curled on the floor, his head cradled in my lap. Only whores had ever done that to him, he cried, whores who pressed their stinking cunts against his face and took his money for spewing out filth, those goddamn fucking bitches. I wasn't like the rest, was I? Didn't my cock make me different? Wasn't I like him? How could I treat him the way women did? How could love be so vile?

Things quickly turned ugly between us, but some kind of sick momentum kept us fucking. One day he mounted me, his weight between my splayed legs pinning my hips to the mattress. His rod began to probe the hole between my cheeks, but it quickly drooped, and he flung himself from me.

"I don't want this anymore," he spat. "You used to be a man who could look like a woman and that was so fine. Very pure. But now you're a woman with a cock and it's all fucked up. I knew that when you pissed on me. That's what made you a woman to me. That's when you really turned into a whore. Women are whores. You're nothing I want. So you just keep fucking away from me."

"All right," I said, "I'll just keep fucking. Away from you."

The next day I rented a room in the Tenderloin and when I came back for my things, I found them in the dumpster where Maya, a college friend I had introduced to Karl, had thrown them. I watched them watch me from the window as I climbed into the cab and drove away. Fuckers. They deserved each other.

I thought that was all in the past, until I saw Karl again. But transsexual rage dies slowly, if ever at all. It's kept alive by every self-deluded prick who buys my time to cloak his homosexual desire with my petticoats, or who craves a woman and can't admit he hates and fears the smell of cunt. It threatens to explode whenever lovers, strangers, friends, or tricks try to make me something that I'm not—just a woman, just a man—or blame me for my differences, refuse to see me as a whole person, use me to avoid working out their own bullshit about themselves or the other sex. But as I swim the darkness between the shores of male and female, my rage warms me with its fires at my core. It moves me.

I was through with him. Finally. A weak moan escaped Karl's lips as I clipped a rope to his bound wrists, climbed the stairs behind him, and hauled his arms upward, bending him at the waist. I tied the rope off on the banister before slowly playing out the other line to right him, then lowered him gently to the floor. An hour later his wounds had all been cleaned and dressed, his fluids replenished, my tools put away. I flopped into a chair, and he sat wrapped in a blanket at my feet, absently stroking my legs, nursing a bottle of Gatorade. Neither of us spoke for a long while.

"I asked Maya to, you know," he mumbled, staring into space, "piss. Like that. On me."

"She did?"

"And then she left me."

"Like I 'left you'?"

The irony was lost on him. "Yeah, like you left me."

Another long pause followed, then he asked, "Would you do it to me again?"

"How? As your friend, or as your whore?"

"I don't know yet."

I pushed him onto his back and pulled a gooseneck lamp down to his face so that he saw only the blinding whiteness of electric light. I straddled him, my crotch above his mouth.

Taking my knife from the nearby bag and pressing it against his throat, I hissed, "Move, and I'll rip you up."

He held still and I felt myself let go. Piss strained through the fabric of my underwear, dribbling down on his upturned lips. His Adam's apple rose and fell as he swallowed. What would it mean to him? His eyes remained closed against the harsh light, and his face held no answers. I finished and stood up, turning away to step out of my panties.

"So," he said suddenly, "I still haven't got what I paid for. What I asked you about in the bar."

It was the trick's getting-back-on-top voice, and I knew what it meant. There's a saying in this business: piss tricks can't handle their own trips. Sad but true. Well, that was his choice; now I made mine. I picked up my bag, composed my face in a look of cruel indifference, and wheeled around to face him.

"You can't let go of your own shit, and I know how to take it out of you. That's knowledge. You wanted to be with me again, and you were. For a night. You offered me whatever the fuck I wanted, and I took it. I wanted your pain for the pain you once gave me. Sounds like you got exactly what you paid for, Karl. Was it more than you bargained for?"

"But did you cut off your dick yet?!"

"Why does it matter if I have a cock or a cunt? Will knowing that tell you if you're straight or queer? Good or bad? Clean or dirty? If that's what you really wanted, you should've said so. But that's information I'm not willing to sell."

I left Karl wiping his face, still needing to know, wondering why it made a difference, knowing only that it did. There's another saying in this business: always leave them wanting more. He'd want to see me again. I knew where to find him if I needed the money.

Notes

First published in *Taste of Latex*, no. 8 (1992): 8–11, 46.

Susan Stryker would like to thank Dani Stuchel, Samantha Bounkeua, and Muffy Koster for assistance with manuscript preparation.

THE SURGEON HAUNTS
MY DREAMS

1

I'd rather lift my hips to meet His knife as it enters me than lie there unconscious with my legs apart. I'd rather Him see in my open eyes that nothing
other than my desire brings Him here. I know it will not be that way, and it
scares me to have a need so fierce that I will let myself become completely
powerless in the hands of someone I do not completely trust.

2

I can do nothing about the fact that He is a man, and that I must deal with
Him. There are no women who do sex-reassignment surgery, not one in all
the world. There are no transsexuals who do it, either.

3

Every now and then I slip off into the fantasy of some pussy-loving amazon of
a surgeon, a bulldyke doctor who'll turn me outside-in with a welcoming smile.
"It won't be long now, dear," she'll say to me as she drops my balls into the
biohazard bin. "Next, let's flay that awkward little dick of yours, and whittle

the erectile tissue down to a reasonable size. We'll tuck it neatly into this new crevice here and dress it in this darling little hood. Your scrotal skin folds up quite delicately, and I've arranged it into such exquisite labia that I'm almost tempted to go down on you myself."

But this woman doesn't exist anywhere other than in my mind—and He is all too real. I know His name, where He works. And I know, too, that He thinks more about how deep and fuckable He can make my cunt than He does about whether I'll be able to feel anything when I rub myself against a slick, wet thigh.

4

This small dark woman's vagina fits around my fist almost as tightly as the latex glove that comes between her flesh and mine. We've drawn a circle of admirers around the waterbed at the party, who watch her writhe gracefully at the end of my dancing forearm. It's the first day of her period and she's bleeding so dramatically. Her blood runs down my forearm and drips onto the plastic sheet; I should have worn latex up to my elbow, and not just to my wrist.

The thought occurs to me that I'll bleed just once—for Him—and then no more. Will He squander the sight of it?

5

The coals in the fireplace at the end of my lover's bed glow red in the warm darkness. Before we lie naked together for the rest of the night, I pause for a moment in shy self-consciousness to push my genitals away behind me, back between my legs. When I wrap my arms around her and snuggle close, I want the curve of her ass to caress my bush—and nothing else.

The deep purple cane marks across her butt cheeks seem to radiate as much heat to the surface of my skin as the fireplace across the room does. My tits are still so tender from her clamps that it's almost too much sensation to bear when the tiniest rotation of shoulders or hips drags my nipple against the edge of a whip-welt on her back.

Her breathing is regular and relaxed now. I open my eyes and look past her to see Him watching us through the window. He scribbles His observations in a notebook, then looks in the mirror behind me to see my penis lying soft and warm against the back of my thigh. I smile at Him and He smiles back. We both know I'll give my penis to no one else but Him.

6

I listen to the click of my heels on the sidewalk, feel the hem of the short tight dress and the stockings on my freshly shaved legs, smell the delicate scent of my perfume. I usually wear jeans and T-shirts, but today I'm dressing for Him. On the way to His office, I stop and look at my reflection in a store window. I look at the make-up. I look at the hair. No, I confess, this isn't all for Him. Femme can be fun when you feel like it, sexy when it catches a woman's attention, subversive when it turns back the straight gaze, powerful when it gets you what you want.

I sit in the chair in front of His desk and pretend to listen as He moves His lips. I cross and uncross my legs. I smile at Him. If He thinks I'm the girl He wants me to be, I'm sure I'll get what I want. He tells me once more how much it will cost, and I give Him the cashiers' check. We make a date.

"Just remember," He says with a wink, "I get to use it first."

I laugh politely before I leave. How come I feel like I just turned a trick when He's the one who kept the money?

7

I'm alone in the bathtub, fucking my asshole with the two middle fingers of my left hand. My left thumb circles the spot I think of as my clit. While I work that bit of gristle against my pubic bone, my breasts sway gently in water set in motion by the movement of my hand.

For the first time since becoming a woman I feel the stirrings of an erection. The hormones make this almost impossible, but here alone, where my body does not have to be a social body, I coax the sensation along. It feels uncanny, deeply familiar and utterly strange all at the same time. I'd like to be able to touch myself anywhere and find a special pleasure there, but that ability eludes me here at this conflicted site. I don't know what to do with this thing that rises up to vex me. How can I love that which defies my ability to define myself?

I take the matter firmly in hand and struggle with it, vainly invoking different names to change its shape, but it resists all transformation. Materiality always resists the symbolic frame. I beg it, then, to throw all language off and become ungendered flesh, but language clenches this meat between its teeth in a death-grip. Words and things together taunt me. Though each downward stroke of my right hand tries to push them apart, they refuse to be unjoined. I know that I will find my pleasure in the pursuit of their estrangement, or I will not find it anywhere at all.

Finally, in my need, I call out for Him to help me. The bolted bathroom door slams open and He looks down upon me.

"You shouldn't have to think so much," He says. There is more cruelty in His voice than I have noticed before; there is a trace of threatened malice when He says, "Just lie there with your legs apart and I'll straighten out this mess."

He scares me, but I'm ready. I've been waiting for Him so long now. As He falls upon me, I see the knife glinting in His hand, and I know this water will soon be turning red. When I lift my hips to meet Him as He enters me, He will surely see that nothing other than my desire brings Him here.

Note

First published as "Preoperative," TNT: Transsexual News Telegraph (Spring 1996): 21–22. This piece was originally performed at The Illustrated Woman: The Second Annual Conference on Feminist Activism in the Arts, Yerba Buena Center for the Arts, San Francisco, California, February 1994.

RENAISSANCE AND APOCALYPSE
Notes on the Bay Area's Transsexual Arts Scene

Dishing Up San Francisco's Transsexual Arts Scene

For those of you who don't get out much, I want to make the following public
service announcement: transsexual art, literature, and attitude are the hottest
things to pop out of the San Francisco's underground since Modern Primi-
tivism entered the mainstream.

Pick up any funky-cool queerzine (like the most recent *Brat Attack*, for
instance), and you're likely to find some friendly neighborhood transsexual
pontificating about the complexity of fin-de-siècle identity. On a glossier note,
the next issue of *Deneuve*—San Francisco's slick, high-profile lesbo mag—will
include a story on dyke-identified MTFs that features a couple of Bay Area
homegirls. Local gender talent has been providing a lot of grist for the straight
national media mill, too. The *New Yorker* (yep, swankier-than-thou *New
Yorker*) is doing a piece scheduled for mid-July on female-to-male transsexuality that relies heavily on a few of the guys you're likely to bump into at the
local FTM group. *Mother Jones* ran an article on transsexuality back in May
based on Bay Area writer Richard Levine's forays into our community (and a
book by him is in the works). Closer to home, the June 15 issue of the *Guard-
ian* featured a story on the transgender liberation movement that quoted several Bay Area gender activists. It's not just schlock TV for us transies anymore.

This burst of media attention represents something more than the fact that transgenderism has become a chichi topic in fields as disparate as high fashion and academe. Increasingly, transsexuals are speaking for themselves about their own experiences, interpreting the world from their own perspectives— and nontranssexuals are listening.

A burgeoning number of local transsexual writers, artists, activists, and intellectuals are beginning to make their marks in the broader Bay Area culture— and beyond. Hard-working MTF playwright Kate Bornstein has finally hit the big-time with her latest one-woman show, *Virtually Yours*. The multimedia performance piece played to packed houses on two coasts in the spring of '94, and her new genre-busting book, *Gender Outlaw*, has men, women, and the rest of us eagerly turning pages all across the country. The ambiguously gendered (but obviously altered) body of California Academy of the Arts's Jill St. Jacques took the stage several months ago during the San Francisco run of the transgender technodrama *Umbilical Thom*. Meanwhile, at 848 Community Art Space on Divisadero, local FTM playwright David Harrison staged a trial run of his promising work-in-progress, the appropriately titled *FTM*. Also at 848, FTM photographer Loren Cameron presented his tour-de-force exhibit, *Our Vision, Our Voices: Transsexual Portraits and Nudes*. All the critics raved about it; the opening night crowd was so huge some people waited hours outside the door for their chance to get in—and inquiring minds have learned that Cameron is pursuing a book project based on his work.

Last summer another exhibit featuring transgender photographs and prose by transsexual subjects, *Crossing the Line*, opened at the now-defunct ARU Gallery on the Duboce Triangle before moving to Red Dora's Bearded Lady Cafe, the hippest boy-tolerant dyke hang-out in the known universe. Red Dora's also hosted a night of readings last August, Over and Out: Dispatches from the Gender Front by Openly Transsexual People. T-type performers appear regularly in the café/art space's cutting-edge cabaret shows, thanks largely to the trans-positive attitude of impresario extraordinaire Kris Kovic.

There's more. Sultry TS torch singer Veronica Klaus pulls in big crowds at Bay Area nightclubs with her blues and soul revue. Pop the right video by stylish German film-maker Monika Treut into your VCR and you just might find yourself staring at FTM poster boy Max Wolf. Marin County native Hank Rubin was the subject of *Trans*, a short film by Sophie Constantinou that premiered at the 1994 San Francisco International Lesbian and Gay Film Festival. I even made a few waves myself at the Illustrated Woman conference at the Yerba Buena Center for the Arts this past February, when I read a short piece of experimental prose about how a sex-change surgeon insinuates himself into all of a preoperative transsexual lesbian's erotic relationships with other women.

The list could go on. Just about any literary-minded transsexual you meet these days has notes for a novel stuffed in his/her back pocket. FTM community leader Jamison Green is currently looking for a publisher for his autobiography, while MTF Christine Beatty recently self-published her collection of sex-worker short stories and poems, *Misery Loves Company*. On July 20 at Kimo's, globe-trotting transsexual activist Anne Ogborn screened roughly edited video footage of her recent stay in a Hijra community in India, which we can only hope will reappear in a more polished form in the near future. Finally, newcomer Philippa Garner is definitely a womanoid to watch out for. In a previous incarnation she landed on the *Tonight Show* with her whimsical spoofs of American consumer culture; now that she's settling into this trans thing, we shouldn't be surprised to see something delightful from her soon.

A Renaissance?

Modern transsexual surgical techniques have been around at least since 1931. Most people have known about transsexuality since Christine Jorgensen grabbed headlines with her sex-change back in 1952. Gender clinics at major universities have been riding herd on the transsexual population since the late '60s. Oprah, Geraldo, Phil, Joan, Sally, Montel, and the rest of the talkie-tabloid pack have been functioning like a well-oiled transsexual PR machine since the mid-'80s. The numbers of transsexuals have been steadily increasing for decades. So why all this hullaballoo now?

Having spent way too many years in grad school studying American history, I start to salivate at the slightest suggestion of a long-term, multicausal explanation for anything, and have learned to draw pointed analogies between any two seemingly unrelated cultural phenomena. But such Pavlovian behaviors actually seem appropriate at this moment. Part of the answer to the question I posed above lies in everything described in the preceding paragraph—the current explosion of artistic expression is directly related to the growth, maturity, and historical development of transsexual identities and communities.

Some people in most cultures around the world and in all periods of history have "changed sex," sometimes physically altering their genitals. But transsexual surgery and hormones are unique to the twentieth century: transsexuality is a novel, historically specific way to assert an identity contrary to the one we were handed at birth. Since the practice is so distinctive, it's taken awhile for a critical mass of transsexual people to build, for transsexuals to get to know one another and start building social networks as well as start recovering our history. It's taken a while for us to begin to understand the relationship of this new identity—the transsexual—to the rest of human culture and to lay the groundwork for political mobilization. It's taken awhile to find our voices in the public arena. We are just beginning to grasp the implications of the fact that we have experiences without parallels among other kinds of people—and to insist that these differences are not best understood by labeling them a sickness. We are just now discovering transsexual pride and starting to make it self-conscious and based on our situation in the world.

This all reminds me of the Harlem Renaissance in the 1920s and '30s. After the Civil War, most of the former slaves stayed put for a few years, too poor to go elsewhere and cautiously optimistic about the prospect of achieving racial equality in a "reconstructed" South. By the late 1870s, that prospect had failed to materialize, and African Americans began leaving for the North in numbers so vast that the movement is still known as the Great Migration. It demographically transformed the old industrial cities of the Northeast, where Southern Blacks went in search of jobs. By the early twentieth century the New York City neighborhood of Harlem had become the cultural capital of African America.

Harlem in the '20s and '30s was full of young Black people whose parents had never been slaves—they had a new kind of American identity. Harlem was smack in the middle of one of the most cosmopolitan places on earth, and the people who lived there were constantly exposed to an endless variety of stimulating cultural cross-fertilizations. More importantly, Black artists, musicians, and writers began to express their understanding of their own particular experiences in a manner that succeeded both in terms of the dominant white American culture and according to their own cultural aesthetics. They had hand-me-down stories of oppression and resistance, fragments of African memory, a rich legacy of song, the multifaceted lived experiences of racial discrimination. From them, they fashioned a literature, a new kind of music, new ways of interpreting the world through dance or painting that altered the very meaning of literature, music, and art up until that point in time.

I have to wonder: Will there be a transsexual equivalent of jazz? Can we see its dim outlines today in the streets of San Francisco? Are we feeling the birth pangs of a Transsexual Renaissance?

African American literature is built upon the bedrock of the classic slave narrative, which recounts the paradigm of a uniquely African American historical experience. It begins with African freedom, includes a "middle passage" of enslavement, and culminates in a new kind of freedom after slavery. The middle passage is crucial. It is transformative; it is what separates African Americans from Africans as well as from other Americans, even while it links them inextricably with both. The middle passage is occupied by no one other than the African Americans themselves. The legacy of that occupation is part of the meaning of African American identity, but it is not the entire definition. And African American literature is more than an artistic reaction against the history of slavery; it is a powerful demonstration that the fullness of one's human experience cannot be mastered by an outside force.

Like the slave narrative, the classic transsexual autobiographical narrative has three parts: an account of pre-transitional feelings about identity, the "middle passage" of transition, and post-transitional life experiences in a new gender. And as in the slave narrative, the transsexual middle passage is the part of the story that makes it uniquely our own. Whatever myth of origins we graft that experience onto, whatever plot line we follow into the unknown future, the transition from one sex to another is the single experience that no one other than transsexuals will ever have. Having that experience makes you one of us.

The transsexual autobiographical narrative is the bedrock of our future literature, the map of our past. Almost every one of us has had to sit down with a psychological evaluation questionnaire and seriously address some version of the question, "How did you develop your sense of gender identity? Please give a brief personal statement." The very fact of our medical colonization incidentally produces a composite record of our lives. How many tens of thousands of these sketches have now been written? How many more stories are buried in case studies and other medical or psychological treatises? A handful of our autobiographies have been published, but where is the vast bulk of the raw documentary material of our culture? How are we ever to grasp the rich diversity of transsexual human experience that is our legacy if we cannot learn about the lives of our brothers and sisters?

We need to think hard, individually and collectively, about the meaning of our transitions, and ask if the stories we use to explain that life-passage are sufficient to voice the complexities of what we have experienced. Why is it that we are content to answer the questions others put to us rather than devise a story of our own? Perhaps, like Africans Americanized through slavery, we must define ourselves partly by claiming the full content of our historical experience and partly by opposing the narrative that has been imposed upon our flesh. The tale of gender dysphoria and its cure is the medical/psychiatric narrative of transsexuality. Must it also be our own? If we stop asking non-transsexuals to explain our lives and emotions to us, can we fashion the phenomenology of our experience into a radically different account of who we are, where we've been, where we're going?

We need to get beyond thinking of our desires and self-perceptions as the symptoms of a mental disorder and start thinking of them as the raw material for a new story about transsexual identity. We need to stop sanding away the rough edges of attitudes, moods, styles, opinions, and responses that don't fit somebody else's interpretation of what our lives are about. We need to become a confederate band of starry-eyed yarn-spinners. We're ripe for a Transsexual Renaissance.

Apocalypse: Fragment of a Work in Progress to Be Completed by the Reader

I have a dream that is older than heaven, keener than wisdom, more pointed than a sword of vengeance.

Seven trumpets sound; seven seals are broken, and we the shapechangers unbind our masks. We step from our prisonstriped bodysuits to launch our bioplasm against the locked drawers of psychotherapists' file cabinets. We seep through the cracks and ingest every transsexual client's file, taking upon our communal selves their every written word as the skin of our own new flesh. We leach every syllable of whispered confession from the office wallpaper and reabsorb it into our mass. We flee on a thousand legs into the desert and dance, rubbing our dung into each letter on the surface of our corporate form until we transmute into shimmering gold. We expand, our ruptured exoskeleton spilling jewels and diadems across the hot sand. We glisten in the searing sunlight, blinding all who dare approach us.

On the second day of the Anarcorporeal Dispensation we reconvene as myriad individual mammals. In this mode we maximize our spatio-political efficacy and gain control of certain areas between, as well as within, our bodies. We surround and besiege all gender clinics, psychiatric hospitals, and surgical centers. During our encampment we feast on autocastrated testicles, and warm ourselves at night with the burning fat of amputated breasts. In passing through the gate of carnal transit, we have shed the primal fear of meatification and now comprehend the full range of embodiment's usefulness. We are more resourceful than the monomorphs who would bury us in their static image. They abandon their citadels in confusion, and we gaily bedeck ourselves in the costumes of their cast-off uniforms. We take up their sober workthings as the ecstatic tools of our play.

The paired principles of homosemblance and xenogenesis shall henceforth govern the consolidation of our fluidflesh until the Chronoterminal Decree. We now disappear and reappear at will among the ankylotic ones. We shall repeat with fond attention any form that gives us pleasure, taking delight in shapeliness itself and vanishing into identity with that which we adore. Likewise, shall we unharness content from its material constraints. We shall become a menagerie bursting suddenly into sight to stop traffic on a whim with any nightmare-mocking guise. Having thus fully accomplished the twin ideals of incorporation, we announce the evening of the last day in a machine language to the bloody-throated multitudes. We shall plunge our animal tongues like justice against the barestripped bosombones of the people. The blessed plastiphiles shall receive our lips like honeywine, while all others shall be cast out—broken mirrors, swept without reflection into darkness.

Note

First published in TNT: *Transsexual News Telegraph* (Summer 1994): 14–17.

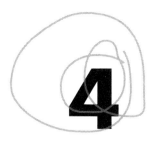

ACROSS THE BORDER
On the Anarchorporeality Project

A DISCUSSION BETWEEN KATHY HIGH
AND SUSAN STRYKER

Dear Kathy:

It was great to talk to you the other day. I'm really looking forward to working with you.

I've enclosed several items to give you a sense of what I've been up to for the last year or so of my life . . .

Project Overview

The way I envision what I've tentatively labeled the Anarchorporeality Project is as a series of transsexual surgical operations performed upon me and documented/interpreted in various media by other artists as well as by myself. I intend to accomplish several goals in undertaking this project.

The first is simply to chart the contours of contemporary transsexual experience from a transsexual perspective. Not only do I want to record the surgical procedures that most nontranssexual fixate on, I want to document the bureaucratic process of actually getting access to surgery to show how the current medical system imposes some tough choices on transsexuals about how we exercise power over our own bodies.

Second, I want this to be overtly political work—not in the sense of being didactic or moralizing, but at a more sophisticated level. Transsexuality is officially pathologized the way homosexuality was officially pathologized until 1973, and I see the project I'm undertaking as part of a broader effort to alter public perceptions of transsexuality as well as to dismantle the oppressive legal, medical, and psychiatric regime that currently regulates transsexuality. I feel this is important work not just for my own special interests but because it involves a critique of a biomedical establishment that operates coercively on most people.

The deep rationale for undertaking this project is to shift the grounds on which a transsexual project justifies itself. I've chosen to do gender politics in the arts field because I see in body performance artwork a set of precedents that can be harnessed to my broader purposes. I want to see exactly how far I can push a claim—that I'm changing the shape of my genitals and secondary sex characteristics for aesthetic and artistic reasons, not because I am eligible to receive a DSM-IIIR diagnosis of 302.5(c) gender identity disorder. I consider making a viable claim for transsexual body art to be a major step toward depathologization.

In a forthcoming essay on the photography of FTM transsexual Loren Cameron, I suggest that

> transsexuality itself increasingly needs to be considered an art form. The more we pry body-alteration technologies away from their pathologizing rationales, and the more we divorce them from futile attempts to shore up the bankrupt notion of a "true sex," the more the decision to reconfigure one's flesh relies on purely aesthetic criteria. "What's your pleasure?" rather than "What's your gender?" could well become the operant question for transsexuals in the rapidly approaching twenty-first century.

This suggests that "transsexuality" as we know it could easily become a relic of the twentieth century, a label designed to incarcerate and stigmatize the transformational potential of all human identity, as well as the capacity for its technologization. This is not to say that genital reconstruction and other surgical techniques will disappear in some imagined future of proliferated possibilities for meaningful expressions of identity; desire cannot be so easily detached from the form of one's flesh. That is why the political struggle currently being waged by the population consolidated under the transsexual sign—the so-called transgender liberation movement—is so crucial. It is but one of the initial cultural arenas in which the ability to practice consent over the technological means of our own embodiment is being fought for. Of course, pursuing this project means actually doing work of artistic and critical merit, but I am capable of that, at least as a writer and conceptualist. My lack of skill in other media is the primary motivation for wanting to collaborate with other artists. At the very least, photography, film, and video would play an important part in documenting the project's unrepeatable work in the medium of living human flesh; I imagine, however, that visual arts could play a much larger interpretive role.

Transsexuality (to my way of thinking about it) is intricately bound up with the manifestation of gender in the visual realm. Visualization and gender identification are in fact explicitly inked in several psychoanalytic theories—the gendered subject is consolidated through recognition of its projected mirror image. Through its disarticulation and redistribution of the constitutive elements of gender, transsexuality offers an opportunity to witness the temporality of this gender construction, while the visual arts—especially film and video—supply a means to investigate gender's temporal performativity through the representation and manipulation of gender's spatial display.

The project that I've envisioned would necessarily entail a critique of some contemporary body artwork that uses plastic surgery, especially that of Orlan (and especially since she is the person whose project most resembles what I propose and the person to whom I have been most pointedly compared). I want to show how the kinds of fleshly alterations Orlan undertakes uphold rather than undermine dominant standards of embodiment—she is not contesting the regulation of the most heavily policed regions of the body. My project would allow me to do precisely that.

Finally, I find the conceptual and intellectual terrain my project ventures into fascinating in its own right—the intersection of gender, sexuality, feminist politics, biomedical technology, and media. This is a terrain we all live in and contend with, and I would look forward to contributing something novel and provocative to the cultural discourses on these issues.

Stage One

The initial part of the project is, to put it as bluntly as possible, for me to cut my balls off, and to make a short film about the process that explores the issues surrounding the procedure.

Castration alone is not a routine part of male-to-female transsexual surgery for most middle-class white transsexuals; most surgeons prefer to do the orchidectomy (or orchiectomy, as it is sometimes called) at the same time they do the genital reconstruction. It is more common among transsexuals from lower socioeconomic positions because it is a relatively simple and cheap body-alteration technique that can be fairly readily obtained. Castration is also medically advised upon occasion, primarily because removal of the testes permits the administration of lower doses of estrogens (which can cause liver damage and other adverse effects after prolonged high-dosage use). I'm interested in exploring the class issues around the procedure—poorer people must often content themselves with a bodily "disfigurement" that the middle-class can afford to renaturalize and erase.

I'm also interested in looking at geography and the physical location of the body, which are always pertinent issues in the cultural construction of identities. Location profoundly affects the points at which one exercises choice about one's body, and where one loses it. In the United States, castration requires a psychiatric approval letter, a three-month waiting period, and costs upward of $3,500—but the medical care is generally quite good. There is an unlicensed clinic in Tijuana that will do castration on demand for a thousand dollars—but the quality of care is considerably less. There is also an underground circulation of pornographic home movies of castrations and thus an underground knowledge of how to do castrations outside of (or covertly within) medical settings. I want to examine the trade-offs involved in these three different routes to castration and the kinds of "border-crossings" they entail.

I would be interested, as well, in investigating the differences between acts and identities. Historically and cross-culturally, the act of castration has been associated with several different identities—the Hijra, the Galli, eunuchs, and the castrati, to name a few. What is the relationship between these historically and culturally specific identities and the late twentieth-century Western European male-to-female transsexual? What is the difference between a man castrating himself and a preoperative MTF transsexual castrating herself? What are the implications of any answers I come up with for current theorizing about the Foucauldian distinction between acts and identities in the history of sexuality?

Finally, I would be interested in the theoretical—especially poststructuralist feminist psychoanalytic—aspects of castration and its role in the formation of the gendered subject. On the one hand, "castration" functions metaphorically as the definitive gesture of consolidating a feminine subject position in the signifying economy. On the other hand, physical castration is the only surgical manipulation I can think of practiced by MTF transsexuals that deforms (rather than reconsolidates) a dominant morphology of the body—that is, transsexual surgeries are about making part of one kind of body look like a part of another kind of body rather than simply breaking a form. Theorizing from the situation of the castrated MTF transsexual body would provide an uncommon vantage point from which to examine some of the most hotly contested problems in critical theory, feminism, and cultural studies about the relationships between sex and gender, body and identity.

Practical Considerations

The bare bones of the matter is that I want to have somebody film me being castrated. How all the issues I've outlined above get addressed are open for discussion. Perhaps they, too, will be part of the film; perhaps they will be addressed in other media—lecture, photography, panel discussion, whatever. I've talked to the surgeon in Tijuana, who is fine with us doing photography/video during the procedure. I've also begun investigating the possibility of getting the surgery locally (as well as cheaply and clandestinely), through some contacts I have in the s/m community. I also have contact information for surgeons in the Bay Area and Los Angeles who require psychiatric recommendations. I do have my official diagnosis letter proclaiming me a bona fide transsexual and know psychotherapists who would write the surgery letter. If all goes well, I'd like to do the surgery in early 1995.

On the noncorporeal front, I have a public lecture scheduled for November 16, 1994, at the Art Institute of Chicago to discuss this project and am currently working on a proposal for a performance/presentation at The Lab in San Francisco for the 1995–96 season. I am also beginning to write grants and explore other means of funding the project. Finally, I am contacting other artists with whom I can collaborate.

I hope you're interested in what I've outlined above. Please let me know what you think. Feel free to use any of the material I've sent, including this letter, in any way you think might further the project.

Looking forward to seeing you in the not too distant future, and talking again before that,

Sincerely,

Susan Stryker

October 26, 1994

Dear Susan,

It was good to hear from you and to hear about this project. It brings up a lot of issues for me. I will try to explain what I am thinking about it and also how I am envisioning this project.

As I was pondering the identity of a MTF transsexual and what that actually means to me, I ran across this citation in an article by Judith Butler where she talks about the relationship of gayness to straightness:

"Imitation does not copy that which is prior but produces and inverts the very terms of priority and derivativeness. Hence, if gay identities are implicated in heterosexuality, that is not the same as claiming that they are determined or derived from heterosexuality, that is not the same as claiming that heterosexuality is the only cultural network in which they are implicated. These are, quite literally, inverted imitations, ones which invert the order of imitated and imitation, and which, in the process, expose the fundamental dependency of 'the origin' on that which it claims to produce as its secondary effect."[1]

Although this quote deals with the areas of hetero/homosexualities, and does not touch upon transsexual issues, I found it useful. I acknowledge the invisibility of transsexuality within many homosexual/bisexual contexts and am wary of the dissing and othering of transsexuals and their preferences. But, for me, the subversive/ inversive relationship between straight and gay in looking at cultural definitions of identity was useful in clarifying gender and transsexuality. So, please allow me to refer to Butler here.

Rather than an imitation of "womanness," perhaps another interpretation of woman is being produced with MTF transsexuality. Perhaps transsexuality is an inversion of the natural parts, a redoing of nature per se. What does it mean to "perform" as a woman in this culture, anyway? In your transsexual womanness I see your development of a new woman, an inverted woman. The "monster," which some may consider being created here, is much more a hybrid, a synthesis of the essence of dualisms: nature and culture perhaps. But if we step outside of those binary situatings and consider the overlaps, the combinations, as essential, I can begin to see your interpretation and mine as charged and rich for exchange. As you quote in your letter: "'What's your pleasure?' rather than 'What's your gender?'" But also, "What's your pleasure?" rather than "What's your pathology?"

I am excited about doing this project with you because it challenges me as a maker and a viewer as well. I have wanted to propose working together since we met at The Illustrated Woman conference last February. The investigation around gender and medical technologies needs to include a discussion of transsexuality. There are so few videos that look at the topic of transsexuality in a way to include recordings of MTF operations. This video could be an important inclusion in an ongoing dialogue about both transgender issues and the discourse of medical technologies or the critique of technological determinism and hierarchies. I believe your participation in this project is to define the political groundwork of the theory of gendering and transsexuality, and mine is to determine the use of the video, the politics of the "handling" of the pictures, and the choices inherent to the medium.

I have to admit I am experiencing a fair amount of resistance to the idea of taping your castration operation. I don't believe what I am experiencing is resistance to your change or to the fact that you are a male-to-female transsexual. This is something I am wary of and have thought about a lot. As you have said: "The attribution of unnatural monstrosity remains a palpable characteristic in most lesbian and gay representations of transsexuality, displaying in unnerving detail the anxious, fearful underside of the current cultural fascination with transgenderism. Because transsexuality in particular represents the prospect of destabilizing the foundational presupposition of fixed genders upon which a politics of personal identity depends, people who have invested their aspirations for social justice in identitarian movements say things about us out of sheer panic that, if said of other minorities, would see print only in the most-riddled, white supremacist, Christian fascist rags."[2]

But I believe my resistance is toward the act of cutting to alter your body. I have resistance to cutting in general (I have never had surgery and have gone to great lengths to *avoid* having it). And maybe it is the fact that you are choosing to cut off your *balls* that presents a problem for me. (And the notion of cutting off the "penis" is so closely married with the notion of castration especially in psychoanalytic associations that I tend to trip up on it all the time.) So, if that is the source of my resistance, am I ultimately resisting your choice and your change in gender identity? I can't separate it right now. Is it the *cut* or *what* is being cut? Why am I focused on this aspect? (I suspect my reactions are typical of those of a nontranssexual.) This I must examine some more with your help.

I don't see this resistance as an overwhelming problem. I think that my resistance can be used to our advantage in the tape. I suspect that other people who come to this tape will be experiencing similar resistance, and if we can successfully explore this area, we can present a shift from a judgmental viewing to one that remains open. "Just as the words 'dyke,' 'fag,' 'queer,' 'slut,' and 'whore' have been reclaimed, respectively, by lesbians and gay men, by anti-assimilationist sexual minorities, by women who pursue erotic pleasure, and by sex industry workers, words like 'creature,' 'monster,' and 'unnatural' need to be reclaimed by the transgendered."[3] I would like to work with you in your "transgender rage" to make a tape that will positively call attention to transsexuality, to make that which is presently invisible much more visible.

This notion of "heroic doctors still endeavor[ing] to triumph over nature" is intriguing to me. This notion of medical science conquering the body, mapping and charting its terrain, is a history I am familiar with critiquing. But this instance gives different possibilities. Where did this surgical practice come from? When and where was it practiced first? References to the history of transsexual surgery would be useful to include in this tape to give a context to the medical establishment's control over the genderization of the body as well as its reproductive capacities and so-called "well being."

If we do go the Tijuana route, I would like to consider the possibility of talking to the doctor before (or after) you have the surgery performed. I would like to discuss with him why he is involved in this kind of work: for the money, because of the fall-off of US clients who are, like you, skirting the regulations of the system; or is there a particular research he is interested in around genital surgery? Or perhaps there is a politic behind his practice that engages with the transsexual experience. Perhaps he only deals with a certain class of people and is committed to that socialist practice?

The surgery itself is the most challenging to consider shooting because, surgery in general is difficult to watch. I think it is a political act to show this surgery in this context. But how to present it to depathologize it, without spectacle, without sheer sensationalism sending the audience into fits of convulsions? This is my question. It seems a definitive act, but ultimately it is really only one part of the entire process for you. So, that bigger process must also be shown as well as this "act." I propose that I come to visit San Francisco and that we spend some time together. Perhaps we can map out some other ways to trace this history from your psychological involvement in your girlfriend's birthing, through the decision for your surgeries, and beyond.

To be successful, I would like to see this tape move people to understand how you have become involved in the pleasure side of the issue rather than simply the gendering. Rather than depict you "at war with nature," I would like to have you claim your gender, "constituting yourself on your own terms."[4]

I am not so concerned about shooting the surgery for myself. I know what happens to me as I shoot—I distance myself through the lens and worry about banal details like keeping things in focus and composition of the frame. Also, my viewfinder is black and white, so I will be further distanced from the color of the blood, etc. But many questions remain: How to shoot this surgery? Do we want a spectacle? Should I shoot it as a dance where I circle the surgeon and you on the table; or as a detailed microscopic shot with the lens in macro-focus; or as a unmovable still tripod shot with medium framing? What does each framing and movement within the frame suggest? How will it further distance the audience or include them in this process? Do we want them to "feel" pain, to experience nausea and discomfort? Or to be a witness and a collaborator, aligned with you, or the surgeon, or surgical assistant?

Lately, I have been really worried about the preponderance of cop shows on TV. What concerns me mostly is the identification of the camera with the cops themselves. The audience begins to adopt the position of the authority themselves, the viewer policing with the police. This psychology I would like to try and subvert and use to our advantage. I would like to identify the surgery not as an invasion, a mutation, but as an extension of your power and a transformation, much like the birth of a baby transformed from its inside world to the exterior with such force that it must be agile to survive. I want to demonstrate your agility and your survival.

To be continued and continued. When shall we get together to work some of this all out? Look forward to hearing from you soon.

Best,
Kathy High

Notes

First published in *Felix: A Journal of Media Arts and Communication* 2, no. 1 (1995): 228–36.

1　Butler, "Decking Out,"22.
2　Stryker, "My Words to Victor Frankenstein."
3　Stryker, "My Words to Victor Frankenstein."
4　Stryker, "My Words to Victor Frankenstein."

LOS ANGELES AT NIGHT

The sky's as dark as it ever gets in Los Angeles at night. His feet are spread apart, ankle restraints fastened around his biker boots and chained to the railing of the redwood deck behind the house in Silverlake I've borrowed for the weekend from a friend. He's leaning forward against the rail on his forearms, hooded, half naked, a big broad-shouldered guy with thick hairy legs but a smooth backside and clean-shaven head. The black cotton T-shirt advertising some gay leather bar is hiked up around his armpits so he can expose more target area but shyly cover the fresh scars, still too raw to show, from his mastectomies.

Trees to either side of the deck screen the neighbors' views of us, while the Ice-T tracks booming on the stereo drown out all other noise. I stand there idly puffing one of his cigarettes, holding a heavy flogger loosely in my left hand and watching his body sway absentmindedly in time with the music. I'm wearing serious play clothes—leather pants and black Docs. My shirt's off because the night's warm and I've worked up a sweat; I enjoy feeling the trickle of moisture running between my breasts. I like the pungent smell of me and the sight of him.

Beyond him I can see the fabulous City of Angels spreading out in every direction, enveloping us, creeping up hillsides encrusted with overlit houses, disappearing into the dull orange glow of early summer haze. Downtown office towers peek from behind the silhouetted palm trees and low-rise buildings that punctuate the broken horizon. I pan the city: a police helicopter hovers in the middle distance, the spotlight tracing search patterns on the ground below. He's still so lost in sensation it would be pointless to hit him again right now.

I enjoy these quiet moments in the middle of heavy scenes, when a partner's physical limits offer a contemplative respite from the concentration required for a methodical whipping. My nipples are hard, but I'm turned outward at the moment and don't really want to focus on my own sensations. I feed one nipple a short sharp twist to appease its distracting hunger and feel a jolt of electricity shoot down to my crotch.

Pleasure's never a simple thing. It always makes me stop and think—a habit that eventually gets me in trouble with tricks and lovers. As my hand returns to my breast, I pause to consider a formal question: is the link I've made so effortlessly between nipple and crotch anything other than the violent installation of a fantasy that organizes sensation for a reproductive economy? These breasts were artificially induced at a point well into my adulthood. They're prosthetic extensions of a will to translate transsexual identifications into interactions with others, generators of material effects that sustain a desired remapping of corporealized space. They have nothing to do with the physiology of milk, birth, crotch. What then is this genital-mammary connection I've made for myself if not a dream of natural womanhood carved upon my unnatural flesh? Is it the fantasy of coerced unity that arouses me, the dream of conquering unruly embodiment with an imaginary idea? Maybe it's hopelessly nostalgic, but I find pleasure in the fact that he and I can cite the forms of those fictively unified political aggregations we call "man" and "woman" even as we work to consign their current configurations to history. I take in the sweeping vistas of the city and tweak my nipple again. Fuck theory.

I return my attention to my trick's flanks and buttocks, visually slicing him into parts that matter in the moment. I can't help but dwell on the difference between my distant visual enjoyment of the scene and the overwhelming phenomenological intensities that so recently played themselves out across his skin. I have been in his position before, when the point of subjective presence flees inward from the surface with such force that it breaks down and breaks through to another space and time. Remembering such psychic implosions, desiring that sense of release and transformation for myself, trying to open him up and connect with him, I find myself wanting to literalize the experience of breakthrough. I want to cut him and turn a metaphor into something real.

Transsexuals have such emotionally loaded relations with surgical instruments. Triumph and pain, visibility and erasure, self-determination and inscription by others wrestle fitfully along the scalpel's edge. Sometimes it feels so good to take the blade firmly in your own hand.

I retrieve alcohol, latex gloves, and scalpel from the med kit waiting in the wings of the scene and begin carving a new erotogenic zone of shallow incisions along his rib cage. As if the cuts promise some fresh new avenue of escape, he returns from his inward mental journey to reencounter the volatile wonder of his own skin. The surface is lumpy, knotted with hardened lymph and discolored by subcutaneous blood. His neurons still fire frantically, relaying wild information about the energy transferred from the supple leather of my whip.

He cries out. I know this sensation too, as the painless pressure of steel slicing through flesh gives way to sting and burn. I douse his wounds with alcohol then flick open a lighter. The spark produces a magic moment of flesh and flames and blood, an abject, sacred conflagration of contraries that lasts a fleeting instant. I smother the burning alcohol quickly and watch him writhe. Fire at night is always a thing of terrible beauty. I wonder if he experiences cutting the way I usually do. Being cut forces me to confront the inescapability of my embodiment. It validates my decision to change shape as my means of continuing to live as an embodied subject, forbids me to deny the pain of the body's necessary failures, rewards me with the body's accomplishments. Cutting reminds me that I am always meat first.

He's back now, summoned to full presence by the fire and the knife like some familiar spirit. He laughs raggedly and blows air heavily through his mouth. He sighs and groans, shrugs excess energy off his shoulders, and shakes it from his fingertips before adjusting his stance. He reaches a hand to his side to smear it in blood, then settles back down with forearms flat against the railing as I start the whip swirling again in lazy figure eights. He sticks his fingers through the hood's mouth hole one by one, licking them clean, body still swaying slightly. I time the whip's circuit to the tempo of his movements and the bass line of the music, catching his ass on alternating sides with each downbeat. We haven't spoken, or needed to, for at least an hour. I'm beginning to tire, though, and decide this will be the cool-down set before we quit. I tell him so, then slow-dance the cat languidly across his haunches and let my thoughts drift.

We'd met several months earlier at some insane cocktail reception in a city neither of us called home. He was standing alone, looking out of place in the hotel lobby next to a potted fern, one hand shoved into the pocket of his tweed slacks and the other wrapped around a bourbon and water. He wasn't living as a man yet, but the combination of oxford shirt, tie, and sports coat with his platinum blond flattop and facial piercings gave him a faggish sort of flair. The way he cross-cut different styles of masculinity somehow communicated the aesthetic sensibility of a gay man rather than a butch dyke, in spite of his female form. That sophistication of presentation, leaning the eye against the grain of the visible body to express an immaterial sense of self, is what caught my attention.

I'm drawn to people who do gender with style. I don't much care what their anatomies look like, which pronouns they usually get called or which they prefer, who they tend to fuck, or how they get off. I just love a good show. He was the most provocatively gendered person in the room that evening, a female-bodied faggot who suggested economies of pleasure that existed nowhere else in sight. I felt a very queer sort of attraction for this other transgendered person—a desire making only the most perfunctory gesture toward the homo/hetero binary.

He was surveying the crowd with a look of utter boredom, clearly on the verge of leaving as soon as he finished his drink, when I walked over with a blunt announcement that I liked the way he did his gender. Soon we were deep in conversation about the semiotics of clothing and how to use the kinetic language of bodies to negotiate a public identity. He told me he was a transfag and a bottom, I described myself as a "male-to-female transsexual lesbian faghag femme top who likes to cruise FTM leather boys and very butch bottoms." Fifteen minutes later we were in his rented Ford Bronco, looking for a more congenial place to be a couple of gender queers.

We wound up at the only drag bar within driving distance, where we sat in a corner to talk and drink. A relatively good female impersonation show played on the tiny stage, but it failed to hold our attention for long. We began to compare notes on s/m: leather sex, rather than drag, was the subculture in which we had both first approached the issue of transgender identities. We both had discovered that like transsexuality, consensual s/m practice made it impossible to ignore the body: it provided exquisitely intense and intimate bodily experiences that didn't necessarily involve genital sexuality. But it had also helped each of us figure out exactly which parts of embodied subjectivity we could exercise agency over, which we could decide to live with, what we had to change. s/m, we agreed, offered a far better conceptual framework for exploring these life-changing choices than any scientific discourses on transsexuality we'd found. Changing sex is very heavy play.

By the time Patsy Cline handed the mike over to Diana Ross, we'd moved from shop talk to theory and back, flitting giddily from one critical form of reference to another. We were such intellectual perverts; we never did get around to fucking that night.

A few months later, he came to San Francisco, and we made a date. His appearance had changed now that the testosterone had started kicking in: his voice was deeper, his smell subtly funkier, his body denser. The flattop had been replaced with a buzz cut, and except for the lack of beard on someone his age, he appeared unremarkably male. The incongruously smooth face worked nicely against the severity of his biker cap, leather vest, and motorcycle chaps, giving him a kind of charming vulnerability. I was wearing a short, tight, backless black velour dress that night, with heels so high I had to take his arm to steady myself. I guessed that he might be scared beneath that cocky veneer, and I wanted to offer him the security of a masculine role in relation to my ultrafemme image.

There was no way I could know what it felt like for him, transitioning to male, but a wave of empathy, a fierce desire to connect, swept over me as I clung to his arm. I remembered what early transition had been like for me, when the hormones were first coming on like a strong dose of acid. The estrogen coded and recoded reality, sculpted flesh like putty, blurred the contours of intelligible human forms by layering one gender schema on top of another until I appeared as a shimmering moiré pattern in the eyes of others. People interacted differently with me, depending on which part of the pattern they saw at any given moment, and then grew confused or hostile when I failed to continue sending the signal they just picked up. The input from the world around me became as capricious as the shape of my own body, as if my entire life were some vast television monitor and somebody else was channel surfing. I began to think some essential part of myself might fly away into the ether, like a balloon that's slipped its string.

I'd eventually learned to play with that sort of reality hacking as one of the peculiarly compelling effects of MTF embodiment, but I remembered with clarity when it had been a frightening and out-of-control experience. His experience with testosterone was undoubtedly different from mine with estrogen, but part of my pleasure that night, I decided, would be helping this man find the channel changer for himself.

I took him to the Motherlode, a transgender dive bar in the Tenderloin where most of the women are sex workers earning their surgery money. It's a surprisingly straight-looking place in spite of the fact that all the women there used to be men and all the men want to fuck women who have dicks: you don't see much that visually contests heteronormativity. But I wanted to go there precisely because we'd be slightly out of synch with the scene and thus harder to slot into identifying categories.

Half of identity is what you put out, and half is how you're read. We were both obviously making statements, yet walking into the bar together we were damnably difficult to read. Butch-femme dykes? A drag and her daddy? A couple of straights? We stood out in the Motherlode, inviting interpretations. We could practically feel the gazes swirl around us, trying and failing to gender us. Woman/man, man/woman, woman/woman, man/man—we changed identities, orientations, and pronouns in every set of looks we exchanged with others.

I looked hard at him, wondering whether our self-identification as dyke and fag were going to bend enough for us to connect sexually this time. "Let's cut to the chase, girl," he finally whispered leaning over the table to nibble my ear. "I'm a bottom first and a faggot second. What you call yourself has no bearing on what I call myself. All I want is to get fucked. And as far as I'm concerned, I've just got three fuckholes instead of two." Grinning, I took his hand. We left the Motherlode for an s/m party South of Market, where I tied him down, beat him up, and took advantage of every orifice he had to offer.

Standing behind him again now on the deck in Silverlake, slapping my cat lazily against his thighs, I find myself replaying that previous time and wanting his cunt again. Desire, like pleasure, is never a simple thing, and like pleasure it makes me stop and think. Is my desire for him just curiosity about an exotic Other? How much am I like the trannie hawks prowling places where women like me sometimes sell our difference to strangers? Or is he the T-Bird, and I'm one of those women for him?

The endless struggle to reclaim transsexual erotics from the uses that non-transsexuals make of us angers me. But I know that sex between transsexuals is different from what happens in the Motherlode. At least neither is using the other to shore up a more normative sense of self. We've both refigured the identifications and partial objects others cobble together in ways that pass as normal. Object choice ceases to have much relevance as a concept here in this new space, because the objects at which desire might take aim have shattered into bits.

For me to enter him like this, MTF fist inside FTM vagina, is for us both to acknowledge the new reality we each locally materialize by our practice. So, it's not the partial object of his hole that I want but, rather, the excess that erupts there through his transsexual form, the surplus value of the codes that regulate gendered embodiment. His excess mirrors the archaic disarticulations from which "I" myself am fashioned and through which "I" perpetually

refashions itself. Maybe this is the transhomonarcissitic wellspring of my desire. Having traversed the territories of perversion and fetish, we have arrived
at last at a realm beyond objects, a world of phenomenal flows. The deterrito-
rialized flow itself is what I long to stick my hand in.

I am fisting his cunt hard, striving against the thin membrane of his flesh
and the distance of the stars to touch the night sky over Los Angeles. Self
crumbles here into the force that structures it, glittering shards of memory
shedding like viruses into the blackness. I'm lifting him off his feet with the
thrust of my forearm, wanting to reach beyond our bodies to grab hold of a
new space where bodies matter differently.

There's a whip dangling by its strap from a wrist, the knot at its butt end
slapping rhythmically against the crack of an ass as a fist disappears, reap-
pears, disappears. I have almost lost sight of him. I hear his labored breathing
beneath the black hood, think of the smooth-shaven head it covers. On one
of the memory shards: the platinum blond flattop he wore when we met. On
a second: Rutger Hauer in the rooftop scene in *Blade Runner*, in another fantasy of Los Angeles at night. I watch Hauer morph into Daryl Hannah before
the two cinematic cyborg bodies merge with his and mine. Media-saturated
memory fragments combine. They achieve ambience with our corporealized
present and project us into a desired future produced through this very process of subjective transformation.

It is too often impossible to be transsexual in this world, too easy to be
worn away by all the petty stigmata of daily living. Elsewhere, on the horizon, another prospect hovers at the vanishing point. Straying into the City of
Night, hip-hop sex music carrying us from Sunset Strip to Times Square to
the Tenderloin, each of us as tangible and phantasmatic as the urban dream-
scape spread before us, we pause only long enough to spray-paint our names
on the walls of the sensorium before we disappear into the darkness.

Somewhere, smooth muscle spasms around my fist, and I'm happy. I have
no idea what made him come. He reaches for a postcoital cigarette, smoke
rising into the night in a parody of movie clichés. I bask in his glow. In the
distance, more police helicopters are circling, watching the horizon. It's almost time to go.

Note

First published in *Opposite Sex: Gay Men on Lesbians, Lesbians on Gay Men*, edited by Sara Miles and Eric Rofes (New York: New York University Press, 1998),
252–62.

DUNGEON INTIMACIES
The Poetics of Transsexual Sadomasochism

Site Survey

From Bernal Heights, the city of San Francisco spreads north and west, a slow-moving accretion in steel and glass, brick, and concrete, of the human desire unleashed and focused upon this terrain by the gold rush of 1848—an alchemical transformation of precious metal into philosopher's stone upon which I sit and think.

Ian sits behind me on the grassy slope, his fingers anchored into my shoulders, his thumb expertly digging at the lump of knotted muscle between shoulder blade and spine where my keystroking and mousing actions accumulate. We've scarcely seen each other these past fifteen years and never known each other well in the ways that conventionally count as knowing someone well. But since he's been back, we've fallen into a practical familiarity with one another's bodies, rooted in our shared history of a particular subculture at a particular place and time that I think of as our "dungeon intimacy."

The physical landscape is made of memories. Over there, to the right, a few hundred feet away, Del shot Cooper for the cover of *The Drag King Book*.[1] Extending my line of sight past that point toward the city's eastern bay shore, I see the place by the abandoned steel foundry where Texas Tomboy and Monika Treut filmed some scenes for *Gendernauts*.[2] Turning my head counterclockwise, I see the live-work lofts near the Bay Bridge, where Ian and I once watched Raelyn pierce and cut Cathy Opie for one of her bloody self-portraits. There's my house, down at the foot of Bernal Hill, where my partner and I now live. Ian, after years in New York, now lives with his family over there in Marin, north across the Golden Gate. We point out to each other various places we've each lived since the 1980s: around Berkeley and Oakland in the East Bay; Potrero Hill and half a dozen places in the Mission District here in the city. He says he sat in this very spot before, smoking pot with our friend Edward, back when he helped him run the LINKS S/M play parties, which I attended regularly for several years.

Off in the middle distance, west of downtown and south of Market Street, stands a large brick building—a fortress, really—built in Moorish Revival style, complete with crenelated turrets and deeply recessed apertures in the thick walls, from which cannons and rifles could be fired. It is the old San Francisco National Guard armory on Mission Street at 14th.[3] We are both historians, Ian and I, who have been taught to encounter the space around us in four dimensions, extending our observations into patterns longer than our lived experience. There is Mission Dolores, established by Spanish priests in 1776, and its counterpart, the Presidio, a garrison farther to the west, near the mouth of the bay where the ships come in from the sea. Together they formed the original instruments of California's conquest and colonization, one housing church, and the other, army. Behind us, at the crest of Bernal Hill, is a small military telecommunications facility, a nondescript little cinderblock building sprouting metal appurtenances, humming low behind a chain-link fence and padlocked gate. It forms part of the current martial occupation and organization of the space we now inhabit.

The armory occupies an intermediate timespace framed and inflected by these maximal and minimal fixed points in temporal distance within the present built environment; it is the materialized remnant of its own distinctive meshwork of force relations, its own constitutive logics of movement, investment, and territory.[4] Constructed in the years just prior to World War I, the structure addressed itself to the labor upheavals of late nineteenth-century industrial capitalism, to a tradition of urban mass protests, and to lingering memories of civil war. In housing troops and weapons whose function was to suppress popular insurrection and maintain government control over city streets, the armory enacted a shift in military attention—management of domestic populations supplanted the threat of coastal invasion. Its massive battlements point back in time toward the Presidio, but its placement in the mixed residential-commercial working-class neighborhood surrounding Mission Dolores anticipated the contemporary biopolitical surveillance state.

A block and a half up 14th Street from the armory is the House of the Golden Bull, where the LINKS play parties took place, starting in 1989. The armory itself had been vacant since 1976, and its state of disrepair mirrored the surrounding neighborhood. Multistory houses built for multigenerational families around the turn of the last century had gone derelict in the post–World War II flight to the suburbs, and some, like the Golden Bull, had been snatched up by gay men with an eye for abandoned architecture. The Mission District abutted the homocentric Castro neighborhood and functioned, in its northwesterly extremes, as a spillover zone for populations marginal to the gay male society that had rooted there in the 1960s. A women's enclave had formed in the Mission in the 1970s, a few blocks southeast of the armory, around Valencia Street between 18th and 22nd, while the epicenter of the city's leather scene had been on the armory's northern side, in the south of the Market District along Folsom Street's "Miracle Mile." By the early 1990s, three decades of competition for land closer to downtown had driven the leather zone southwesterly, toward the Mission. The Catacombs, one of the city's most storied dungeon spaces, had been located a few blocks south of the armory on Shotwell at 17th. The Catacomb's sudden closure in 1989 contributed to the rise of the Golden Bull as an s/m party venue.[5]

The Golden Bull occupied the geographical margins of three urban zones, each characterized by distinct sexual subcultural formations and social movements—homosexuality and gay liberation, the women's movement and lesbian feminism, and the *ars erotica* of consensual sadomasochism. The property valuations of its physical site reflected the fallowness of its location in the overarching ecology of the city. The view from the back deck overlooked a disintegrating public housing project; its immediate neighbors were an edgy gay-owned art gallery, the dyke-run Black and Blue Tattoo, and Red Dora's Bearded Lady Cafe, where underground performance artist Harry Dodge and the lesbian punk band Tribe 8 held court. Pioneers of the pierced and tatted subcultural aesthetic shared street space (and sometimes substance-use habits and job descriptions) with the neighborhood's many junkies and sex-workers. The LINKS parties occupied a slice of time as precisely sited as their real estate. The AIDS pandemic was in full swing in those years before the antiviral cocktails, and s/m seemed situated at the very crux of the crisis—its precepts of negotiation and consent, its panoply of techniques for eliciting bodily sensation without exchanging bodily fluids, its meticulous disarticulations of erotics from genital sexuality, all promised a viable future.

It was to dungeons such as the Golden Bull that Michel Foucault referred when he noted that, "you find emerging in places like San Francisco and New York what might be called laboratories of sexual experimentation."[6] The dungeon, I'll suggest, in the pages that follow, is indeed just such a productive and transformative space as a laboratory—a space not merely for the discovery of an existing objective world but a playground, workshop, or place of study that is in fact a generative space, one facilitative of the materialization of creatively grasped virtualities. It is place as process: or, in geographer Doreen Massey's words, place as a distinctive mixture, "gathering, and manifestation of local and global social, economic, and communications relations" that knot themselves up together for a length of time, and which become concretized in the objects that collectively constitute their place by assembling there.[7]

Jack Halberstam points out that Massey offers to queer theorists of embodiment, sexuality, and gender an alternative to the views of other postmodern geographers such as David Harvey and Edward Soja who privilege "the global" and distrust "the local" as place-bound, reactionary, and potentially fascist in its parochial distance from all things cosmopolitan.[8] No place can be more local than the body. Within systems of thought that have a vested interest in ignoring the inescapable fact that even the most global analysis is tied to the particular (raced, sexed, classed, educated) body of the analyst who conceives it (because not to do so would unmask its enabling privileges), no place is shunted to the periphery of consideration with greater alacrity than is the body. Reconceptualizing every place, including the lived space of the body, as a "glocal" hybrid opens an important line of critical inquiry. As sociologist Avery Gordon points out, "we have become adept at discovering the construction of social realities and deconstructing their architecture," but in telling the stories of these realities, we have not yet taken as seriously as we should the insight "that the intricate web of connections that characterize any event or problem *is* the story."[9]

Transsexual sadomasochism incarnates the processes within and through which the body materializes the specificity of its location, installing the body that practices it as a place—one as contingent, situated, and real as any armory or repurposed Victorian house. In offering this autoethnographic account of embodied knowledges (and knowledges of embodiment) produced in a particular dungeon space, neighborhood, and historic moment, through my own past practices of transsexual sadomasochism, my intent is not to attribute any particular importance to certain events simply because I, rather than someone else, participated in them. The goal, rather, is to open a critical space within which subjectively perceived phenomenological experiences can offer evidence for more widely applicable statements about the relationship between embodied subject and material environment. I offer these observations in the spirit of "pornosophy"—Shannon Bell's apt coinage for the militant insistence on an epistemic parity between the disparate knowledges of the scientist, the philosopher, and the whore—and as a refusal to discredit what our own carnality can teach us.[10]

Topoanalysis and Rhythmoanalysis

Transsexual sadomasochism in dungeon space enacts a poiesis (an act of artistic creation) that collapses the boundary between the embodied self, its world, and others, allowing one to interpenetrate the others and thereby constitute a specific place. It gestures toward the metaphysical counterscheme that haunts the margins of Western dualistic thought, wherein "the duality of subject and object," in the words of philosopher of science Gaston Bachelard, becomes "iridescent, shimmering, unceasingly active in its inversions."[11]

"We are the diagrams of the functions of inhabiting" the spaces where we have lived intimately, Bachelard writes in *The Poetics of Space*, his classic work on the experience of inhabiting the felicitous spaces we designate with concepts of "home." "The word habit is too worn a word to express this passionate liaison of our bodies, which do not forget," with these unforgettable spaces of our inhabitation.[12] Bachelard calls for a two-fold approach to spatial poetics: a "topoanalysis," conceived as an auxiliary to psychoanalysis, that offers "a systematic psychological study of the sites of our intimate lives."[13] Its complement, a "rhythmoanalysis" that accounts for the reiterative temporal practices— habitual movements—through which we inhabit those sites. He is particularly concerned with the fluctuating movement between the "real" and the "unreal" whose dynamic interlacings produce the shimmering iridescence of poetic reverie, or common daydreaming. Bachelard shares with his psychoanalytic contemporaries Laplanche and Pontalis a concept of fantasy as inhabited structure (and of structure as inhabited fantasy).[14] Space, as he conceives it, is simultaneously phantasmatic and material, furnishable with variable contents, both psychical and tangible, and within which it is possible to change positions as one would move about a house.

A hundred people or more might pack the Golden Bull for a well-attended LINKS party. One could not enter without an invitation. On party nights, one approached the grated street-level door, where a monitor checked the name you gave against the RSVP list. One then proceeded up a flight of stairs and through another door to an anteroom off the entrance hall, where one paid the cover charge, checked one's coat and, if need be, changed one's clothes. One then passed through a kitchen and living room out to the deck, where one set of stairs led up to the owner's private floor and another set led down to the labyrinthine dungeon. One room held a waterbed, another a jail cell, and yet other mattresses, racks, crosses, ropeworks and suspension hooks, with conveniently situated hardware screwed into the walls and ceilings. A bathroom was reserved for piss play, scat, and blood sports. Sharps containers emblazoned with biohazard warning labels were placed in visible locations in every room, as were copious amounts of condoms and lube. Safety monitors kept an eye out for trouble, and medical care providers were on-site in case of emergency. Drugs and alcohol were not allowed. Mirrors and Day-Glo graffiti covered the unfinished drywalls. It was there in the dungeon that I first met Ian, sometime around 1991.

Coupling, though tolerated with a certain libertarian aplomb, was not the dominant mode of interpersonal relationship in the dungeon. The general ethos of the space favored a respectful openness to spontaneous liaisons, improvised orchestrations, and serendipitous multiplicities—like a cocktail party without drinks where the conversations were pantomimed in leather, or a jam session around the edges of which a solo jazz musician might hover before joining in. This made the dungeon a welcoming and convivial place, where one was encouraged to encounter fellow creatures with a sense of wonder and curiosity, with patience rather than judgment. Every person became for others a unique opportunity for the universe to reveal itself from a slightly different perspective—and some of the views were stunning.

The carefully curated guest list favored those unlikely to fit into other, more rule-bound and identity-defined, dungeon spaces—it was neither gender-segregated nor compulsorily heterosexual; it honored those who abided by the customs of "old leather" and carried its inherited wisdom, while celebrating freeform experimentation that broke with traditional subcultural knowledge and practice. LINKS, as its name suggested, forged connections where they otherwise might not have existed. I first encountered there the word queer, as it since has come to be used in academic and community discourse, in chill-out conversations after dungeon sessions in the summer of 1990. We used it to name the previously unnamed social formation taking shape at our parties, which we saw as part of a larger political and conceptual shift in identity-based social movements related to the AIDS crisis and, a few months later, to anti–Gulf War activism. "Transgender" was a word I first encountered on a flyer advertising a LINKS "Gender Play Party," early in 1991. For most of us there, gender was something we explored, analyzed, and experimented with in the context of a broader engagement with bodily practices and power; people came at questions of gender from many different angles and emotional investments, with no one right way to proceed. Since the 1990s, considerable ink has been spilled about the relationship between queer and transgender, transgender and transsexual, transgender, and genderqueer. For me, these things were linked at the outset.

I wander one night into the dungeon's back room to find a writhing young body upright and spread-eagled, lashed naked to an X-shaped Saint Andrew's Cross, its head shaved, its scalp encircled with a garland of temporary hypodermic-needle piercings through which a fine steel wire had been woven and tightened into a "crown of thorns." Blood trickled down its face in an art-historical tableau vivant of martyrdom and plicked arrhythmically onto a plastic drop-cloth. A woman faced the young body, checking its pulse and respiration with a latex-gloved hand, wiping the proverbial blood, sweat and tears from its eyes and giving it occasional sips of water. Two others, whom I happened to know, were administering a thorough flogging. One was visibly tired—it had apparently been a long night. She gestured for me to take her place, and I stepped into the structure of the scene, surrendering myself to its established cadences.

Something serene and paradoxically solitary can be found in the experience of giving oneself over to the inhabitation and enactment of a shared pattern of motion—a contemplative solitude born of one's ecstatic displacement into a space where the body actively receives and transmits the movements of others, allowing awareness to flit and alight throughout the transsubjective ensemble. A whip strikes flesh with sufficient force to blossom the creature's skin red and welt it back toward the leather. The young thing moans a low moan, transforming the kinetic energy of the blow into an audible frequency by passing breath over slack vocal cords, and my attention is drawn toward the physicality of the assemblage we cohabit. "A child is being beaten," no doubt, but my sense in the moment is that the Freudians, so invested in textual analyses and narrative outcomes, fail to grasp the philosophical-critical dimension of sadomasochistic practice when they approach it through the lens of oedipal sexuality.[15] This is not, for me, primarily a sexual experience, and it is Freud's contemporary Bergson, rather than Freud himself, who comes to mind.

In a passage of *Matter and Memory*, Bergson discusses the structure of the nervous system in the "animal series" that extends (in his teleological schema) from the Monera to *Homo sapiens*, in which he observes that even as a simple mass of protoplasm, living matter is irritable and contractile, "open to the influence of external stimulation," to which it reacts physically, chemically, and mechanically. Stimulus/response is not an event structured by the boundary between inside and outside, between interior "self" and external "other," but is rather a continuous movement in which a force's vector is prolonged and deflected into the movements of living matter; it is a wave transmitting itself through various media. As organisms become more complexly organized, specialized parts—nerve cells, sense organs, the musculo-skeletal system—divide physiological labor in ways that permit more varied response. At some point, a neural organ—the brain—introduces the possibility of voluntary movement rather than automatic organic responses.

Bergson understands the brain to introduce a difference of degree rather than kind. In a simple reflex action, a "peripheral excitation" transmits a centripetal movement along an "afferent" nerve toward the central neural processing organ, before transmitting itself centrifugally back along an "efferent" nerve to "motor cells" that direct the energy of the stimulus back into the environment and thus continue its movement in a new direction. It is the complex branching of neurons in the brain that allows for voluntary responses; quite physically, Bergson suggests, the possibility of choice of movements is at root the lived awareness of stimuli circulating with electrochemical speed through multiple possible neural pathways in the brain, each of which can descend into a specific pattern of motor response. The brain, rather than having some "miraculous power" to change sensory input into a "representation of things" that can be symbolically manipulated, functions simply by introducing into the circulation of energetic flows through the body a duration, a time-lag (that is to say, more space) between the stimulus and response. Our consciousness of choice of movements in response to stimuli is nothing other than our inhabitation of a brainspace that holds the simultaneous presence of multiple potentials, each made possible by the physical complexity and carrying capacity of the neural network, only one of which will be actualized, in a quantum-like leap to a particular one of many virtualities, through the material actions of our body.[16]

Whether Bergson's story can be recognized as true by today's cognitive scientists is beside the point: reflecting on Bergson brings me to the place of poiesis. I envision my body as a meeting point, a node, where external lines of force and social determination thicken into meat and circulate as movement back into the world. So much that constitutes me I did not choose; but, now constituted, I feel myself to be in a place of agency. I occupy a critical space, a distance between stimulus and response created by the complex social pathways converging in the dungeon, in which through my presence I gain the capacity to choose which patterns I will repeat, or which new patterns I might envision and enact. I invent new choreographies of space and time as I dance my whip across the creature's ass. It is not that I somehow internalize as my own the structure or content of the scene in which I participate, receiving its impression the way clay would receive a sculptor's mark. It is rather a proprioceptive awareness, as I flog, of the role of my body as medium in the circuit of transmissions, and of the material efficacy I possess in my subjective ability to choose one thing rather than another, or to poetically imagine the shape of a new pattern. The imagination, Bachelard says, takes up its place here, "exactly where the function of unreality comes to charm or to disturb—always to awaken—the sleeping being lost in its automatisms."[17]

Gender is a percussive symphony of automatisms, reverberating through the space of our bodies before there is an awareness of awareness itself. Who can say why I heard its music the way I did? All I know is that from earliest memory I disliked being called "he" and longed to be addressed as "she." I wanted to look like what I considered myself to be and perceived that I was profoundly misplaced—all of which evoked in me the utter sadness of feeling irremediably lost and alone in a situation impossible to rectify. I was not where others looked for me, and I was where they saw me not. Lacan says that "the real" is the place that is always returned to; these feelings were real. I am agnostic as to their origin. I did not choose them. I chose only how I would inhabit the architecture of their affect.

For a long time, the little perceiving one who had been surprised to find, while still so very young, that it related to its place of habitation in a manner quite different from others whom it knew, remained quietly observant. It first encountered another to dwell with it in the awareness of its difference in the nineteenth year of its body's extrauterine life. My girlfriend and I had just finished fucking, and I was stretching next to our bed like a well-fed cat when I felt a pinch on my left buttock. Without turning around or looking down, I swatted vigorously at what I thought were my girlfriend's fingers. As it turned out, she had leaned over to bite me playfully on my ass-cheek; my slap caught her perfectly on the side of the face and sent her reeling across the room. She was sobbing, and I was mortified that I had hurt her. But what eventually became clear, through her tears and my guilty self-recriminations, was that she had found it terribly exciting that I had hit her, and a secret history of desire began spilling forth. She wondered if I might not do it again. In all honesty I had never even dreamed of doing such things to another person—but just as honestly, I also have to say that something previously unnamed and unrecognized in me did not hesitate to answer, "Yes." And so it was that I felt obliged to offer her the gift of a reciprocal vulnerability and invited her into a realm of feelings I had always occupied without companionship. After a pregnant pause she replied, "'The hardest thing about asking you to hit me was overcoming the fear of being hit by a man.'"

Cut to 1991, a decade later, and s/m had become for me what it was for many of the people who shared dungeon space at LINKS parties—a technology for the production of (trans)gendered embodiment, a mechanism for dismembering and disarticulating received patterns of identification, affect, sensation, and appearance and for reconfiguring, coordinating, and remapping them in bodily space. I could hear people use names and pronouns in reference to me that I could agree to answer to. I could feel the touch upon my body of clothes that encouraged certain modes of comportment or stylized manners of moving, clothing that gendered me in the act of wearing them. In dungeon space I could see a woman in the mirror, and step into the place of woman in the structure of another's desire, to witness those bodily signs—the heaves and shudders and seeping fluids—that attested to my viable occupation of that fantasized place for them.

There are those who say that magic is the art and science of creating change in accordance with the will. Transsexual body modification is one such practice.[18] It became the means through which I grasped a virtuality manifested in dungeon space and gave it a materiality capable of extending its effects beyond the dungeon walls. It is in such moments of magical transformation that, according to Bachelard, "the commitment of the imagining being is such that it no longer functions as the subject of the verb 'to adapt oneself.'" This is the moment of poeisis, when that which has been grasped extends itself into the world, thereby transforming not only "the imagining being," but others and the environment that holds them.

My arm tires and I take my turn supporting the young creature's head, holding its eyes with mine, cradling it, and attending to its bodily needs. Such are the intimate sites of queer reproduction. This moment of dungeon intimacy is but one of many over the years that collectively will conjure a new social reality. Deleuze is right to say that sadomasochism deromanticizes love and eroticizes the world.[19] Later, hanging out in the kitchen, I learn that my playmate calls himself Ian and lives in the world as a woman. He was just beginning a PhD program in US history, at another campus of the same university where I was in the final stages of finishing mine. We ran around together for a while, whenever he was in town, until he moved to New York. Sometimes, in the years ahead, we would happen upon one another at academic conferences. Small world.

Reprise

From Bernal Heights, the city of San Francisco spreads over the land to the north and west, a slow-moving accretion in steel and glass, brick, and concrete, of the human desire unleashed and focused upon this terrain by the famous gold rush of 1848—an alchemical transformation of precious metal into philosopher's stone that thinks through me on it.

This landscape is made of memories. Much of what I knew from the early '90s is now gone. That community dispersed for all the usual reasons: death, whimsy, jobs, familial obligations. The dot-com boom came in on top of that, property values rising like a tsunami that washed people away, across the Bay toward Oakland, or to the Sierra foothills, or over the mountains entirely and far away. It was a force of nature, and the space filled back in different from how it had been before. I see the armory, enormous Gay Pride rainbow flags flying from its turrets. It was purchased late in 2006 by Kink.com, an s/m internet porn site that had started shooting its own movies, needed more studio space, and loved the building's faux-Moorish interior stonework and soundstage-sized troop assembly rooms. Kink.com is a quintessentially San Franciscan kind of porn business—it provides safe working conditions, pays its workers well, and generously gives back to the neighborhood and the s/m community. And yet as it streams its dematerialized digital media images onto the World Wide Web, it supplies an image of the new relations between space and life now being materialized in the fabric of the city and enacts the relentless commodification and privatization of all we know.[20]

I wonder aloud about the space of my own body and the practices that have installed it here. I want to claim that transsexual sadomasochism affords me a glimpse of non-unique revolutionary potentials—exemplifying the materially productive effects of extending and prolonging into the world poetically generated patterns of response to external conditions, demonstrating how body modification can become a site of social transformation, proving that the real can be materialized differently than it now is or once was. Ian points toward the armory and reminds me that all present materializations become relics, and that nothing prevents their capture by normativizing processes or their absorption into the stream of commodities. He wonders if perhaps I am being sentimental, or nostalgic. Perhaps, but that's not how it feels.

A work by the avant-garde genderqueer performance group Antony and the Johnsons comes to mind, "The Cripple and the Starfish."[21] I have it on my iPod, and Ian and I share an earbud apiece to listen to ANOHNI, in the role of the titular cripple, sing of a sadomasochistic love:

> It's true I always wanted love to be hurtful
> And it's true I always wanted love to be filled with pain and bruises . . .
> And there's no rhyme or reason I'm changing like the seasons Watch!
>   I'll even cut off my finger
> It will grow back like a Starfish!
> I am very happy So please hit me
> I am very very happy So come on hurt me
> I'll grow back like a Starfish

I am moved, from my postoperative transsexual perspective, by the singer's plaintive association of amputation with the yearning for a transformation of affect. In the song, the (fantasy of the) self-inflicted bodily wound functions to create a space of subjective fulfillment. The empty space of the missing digit is produced, through an act of evacuation, as a space of regeneration. That space, being void and not filled, allows for the movement of desire into it. It is thus not memberlessness itself that is desired, but the subjective experience of transformative growth in which absence becomes the space of possibility.

In that the amputation of the member produces a space of actualization, it functions as *chora*—an ancient Greek concept with the double meaning of both an enclosed space and the act of enclosing, which figured prominently in Plato's cosmogony and which has become a contested site in feminist poststructuralist reworkings of the Western philosophical tradition. In Plato's *Timaeus*, the *chora* is as his phallocentric philosophy imagines the womb to be, a passive vessel for the active male elements from which the world is formed. Luce Irigaray, Julia Kristeva, Elizabeth Grosz, and others have emphasized the active function of enclosing, holding, and containing to assert the positive contribution of the *chora* in the process of generation as a space generative of movement that spills forth from containment.[22]

From my forward-facing perspective, I look back on my body as a psychically bounded space or container that becomes energetically open through the break of its surface—a rupture experienced as interior movement, a movement that becomes generative as it encloses and invests in a new space, through a perpetually reiterative process of growing new boundaries and shedding abandoned materialities: a mobile, membranous, temporally fleeting and provisional sense of enfolding and enclosure. This is the utopian space of my ongoing poeisis.

The August sun is farther west in the sky. Ian removes my iPod earbud and decides he needs to leave for home immediately to beat the traffic back across the bridge. We amble downhill toward house and car, chattering about the mundane details of the remainder of our respective days. He has to cook dinner and stay home with her kid while her partner goes to an art class, but that's all right because he's chairing his department this year and has a lot of administrative crap to catch up on. I'm meeting my son and his girlfriend in Oakland for anime and sushi, then coming home for a late night hot-tub-and-cocktails date with my partner before heading off to bed. I've accepted a visiting professorship in Vancouver this coming academic year and find my moments with him already suffused with a longing that extended absence shortly will bring. Tomorrow I really need to finish an overdue article, because the editor is breathing down my neck. Ian and I hug our fond goodbyes and kiss with a dungeon intimacy.[23]

Our bodies are spaces set in motion; motions set in space: what trace of their generative locations do these mobile architectures make as they extend into the world?

Notes

First published in *Parallax* 14, no. 1 (2008): 36–47. Thanks to Julian Carter for our renewed friendship, permission to speak freely, and comments on the text. Thanks as well to Rita Alfonso for critical input, and to Gretchen Till for conversations on architecture.

1   Volcano and Halberstam, *The Drag King Book*.
2   Treut, *Gendernauts*.
3   On the armory, see Till, "Space of Reception"; and Shermatta, "Mission Armory."
4   On the framing and inflection of architectural space, see Cache, *Earth Moves*.
5   Charting the queer geography of San Francisco is a work in progress; much of this commentary is drawn from personal knowledge, and from unpublished data in the "Sites Database," at the GLBT Historical Society, https://www.glbthistory .org/. See also Califia, "San Francisco: Revisiting the City of Desire"; G. Rubin, "The Valley of the Kings"; and Stryker, "How the Castro Became San Francisco's Gay Neighborhood."
6   Foucault, "Sexual Choice, Sexual Act," 19–20; Davis, "History and the Laboratory of Sexuality."

7   Massey, "A Global Sense of Place," 240.

8   Halberstam, *In a Queer Time and Place*, 12.

9   Gordon, *Ghostly Matters*, 20 (emphasis in original), as cited in Rocque Ramirez, "A Living Archive of Desire," 117.

10 Bell, "Fast Feminism."

11 Bachelard, *The Poetics of Space*, xxxv.

12 Bachelard, *The Poetics of Space*, 15.

13 Bachelard, *The Poetics of Space*, 8.

14 Jean Laplanche and Jean-Bertrand Pontalis, "Fantasme originaire, fantasme des origines, origine du fantasme" [Fantasy and the origins of sexuality], *Les Temps Modernes* 215 (1964): 1833–68, as reprinted in Burgin, Donald, and Kaplan, *Formations of Fantasy*.

15 Freud, "'A Child Is Being Beaten.'"

16 Bergson, *Matter and Memory*.

17 Bachelard, *The Poetics of Space*, xxxv.

18 Cameron, *Body Alchemy*.

19 Deleuze, "Coldness and Cruelty."

20 Robin Rinaldi, "The New Pornographers," *San Francisco 7 × 7*, August 1, 2006.

21 Antony and the Johnsons, "The Cripple and the Starfish," *Antony and the Johnsons* (Duturo, 2000), CD.

22 Grosz, "Women, Chora, Dwelling"; Butler, "Irigaray/Plato," in *Bodies That Matter*, 36–49; Sophia, "Container Technologies."

23 I am reminded of an article by Carolyn Dinshaw, who, in commenting on the queerness of the kiss between Gawain and Bertilak in *Sir Gawain and the Green Knight*, noted how the heteronormative text is "preoccupied with keeping the depths and fissures" of queerness "from bursting forth" from the men's kiss, as its words labor "to limit the significance of its signs, the nature of its characters, [and] the meanings of their actions," in order to reduce a "polyvalent sign" to "monovalent meaning." It is precisely the queer work of producing polyvalent meanings from "dungeon intimacies" that I hope my actions may accomplish. Dinshaw, "A Kiss Is Just a Kiss," 205.

PERFECT DAY

I still think of it as my perfect day; a day whose date I can't remember now, in June 1980. I was a few weeks shy of my nineteenth birthday and had blown every last cent of my savings to get myself to Europe, to spend the summer backpacking around to "find myself." For the first time in my life, I was entirely outside the context of family and friends, away from everybody who had any expectations of who I was or what I was supposed to be.

I'd made it across Germany and France to the UK and had worked my way north from London to the Lake District when my perfect day arrived. I was staying at a hostel in Ambleside and had planned a day of ridge walking—just me in my woolly gray sweater, low stone walls, contented sheep, and stunning views. I had been unwinding for weeks, visiting places I remembered from my army-brat childhood in Bavaria, getting my first taste of Paris hauteur, thrashing in the mosh pit at Hammersmith Palais when Burning Spear opened for The Clash. I had been to Stonehenge and Stratford-on-Avon, and now I was setting off to commune with the souls of romantic poets, a slim volume of Coleridge tucked in my daypack. I look back fondly, with some bemusement, on how sincere and naive I was then.

My thoughts were drifting, as teenage thoughts are wont to do, and turned to the question of love. I had been dissatisfied, I had to admit, but I myself was largely to blame. I had not been honest with my girlfriends—all four of them at that point—about what I was really looking for in a relationship. It was impossible to separate what I wanted from them, from what I wanted for myself. I can't honestly say that I considered myself a lesbian at that point in my life. I was born male but had puzzled over gender as long as I could remember. Gender had never been an assumption for me; had always been a question.

When I was very little, I remember nonchalantly thinking that I would grow up to be a woman. I'm agnostic about where these thoughts and feelings came from, but they were phenomenologically persistent and undeniably real. When I realized, around age five, the normative relationship between genital difference and social gender, it surprised and shocked me. This presented a *huge* problem. Were my self-perceptions wrong? Had I made a mistake? Or was everybody else wrong about me? What was real, and what wasn't? Who got to say who was a boy and who was a girl? Why, I wondered, did the pronoun "she" feel like the one I wanted to name me? Why, when somebody said "he," in reference to me, did I shrug inwardly, with the unvoiced qualifier, "Well, I understand why you might think so, but that's not really what I am"? These early conundrums became the bedrock of my later intellectual life as I pursued an unlikely career as a transgender theorist, historian, and filmmaker.

Living as a boy was nonconsensual. I had been plopped, never asked, into a gender I would not have chosen. I accepted my status only provisionally, pending further assessment of my situation. I didn't know if it would be possible for me to leave, any more than if it would be possible for me to stay. I started dreaming of bodily transformations as a potential escape route. I dreamed of machines that changed the shape of my genitals, gave me breasts, made my hair long. I dreamed the emotional logic of coercive normalization within consumer capitalism: some adult would recognize my girlish proclivities, take me out to buy girl things, but then laugh at me—as if they had successfully pulled a prank—when I admitted that I really thought of myself as a girl. I would always awaken feeling furious and betrayed.

I turned bookish, always looking from the corner of my eye for answers to the gender questions, and became precociously erudite in the process. My mind was often elsewhere than my body; still, I didn't let the unresolved status of my gender identity paralyze me. I tried to get on with things and make the best of it. I didn't needlessly resist my socialization, picked my battles, bided my time. I watched war movies, played football, swam competitively, learned to swear like a motherfucker and get stupid in public with alcohol. Like everybody else, I learned where the boundaries were drawn between masculinity and femininity and knew where I was situated. I learned that voicing questions about gender did not elicit helpful answers and sometimes created problems for oneself. Truth be told, I always felt like being a guy was a perfectly fine way of being in the world. I was just never convinced it was my way. I wondered why it mattered what gender you happened to be, but still couldn't shake my sense of preference.

I dreamed about girls, starting around age six. It usually went something like this. A classmate or neighbor-girl I thought was really funny or smart or cute or nice would confess she had a secret crush on me. (A black-haired, dark-eyed tomboy beauty in my first-grade class, who showed up at school every so often looking uncomfortable in a pink Jackie-O skirt and suit jacket was my first such inamorata.) My family, however, would be on the verge of moving away (which we did with some regularity in real life). The girl would want me to stay with her, and her parents would agree to take me in.

All of my clothes and toys would accidentally be sent away with my own family, and then, due to some emergency like falling in a mud puddle or being attacked by a stray dog, my only remaining set of boy's things would be ruined. Of course, my girlfriend would lend me some of her clothes until mine could be replaced, whereupon she would then discover, much to her surprise and delight, what a nice little girl I made. Her parents would be accommodating; they'd always wanted to raise another girl, and my own parents miraculously agreed to let me stay.

She and I would be *friends*—not boyfriend and girlfriend—just friends, practically sisters. We would do all sorts of things together because we really liked being with each other and would be best friends forever. Somewhere around puberty, these dreams became sexual. What could possibly be sweeter than discovering that your best friend, with whom you shared so many special things, loved you in a special sort of way?

So I wasn't quite a transsexual lesbian on that perfect day in the Lake District, a few weeks shy of my nineteenth birthday in the summer of 1980, but I was pretty darn close. I just didn't know what to call myself yet.

Somewhere between the ages of ten and thirteen (based on where I remember living at the time), I read a *Dear Abby* advice column in the newspaper. A woman wrote to say that she had discovered her husband had been sneaking into her closet and trying on her clothes; she wondered if her husband was secretly homosexual. Abby told her that homosexuals were people who loved people of their own sex and that it didn't have anything to do with cross-dressing. She said the woman's husband could possibly be a transsexual, who was a person who considered himself or herself a member of the opposite sex, but that most likely her husband was a transvestite, who was somebody who had no desire to change sex but enjoyed wearing the clothing of the opposite sex.

Eureka! Language is truly a gift from the gods. Not only did I now have definitive proof that I was not the only person to have ever questioned their own gender, I also had a vocabulary to help me frame my thoughts. And off to the public library I rode, unconsciously fey, on my purple Schwinn Sting-Ray with the banana seat and sissy bar, handle-bar streamers flying furiously in the wind.

The library was hugely disappointing. "Transsexualism" was indeed listed in the subject classifications of the card catalog, but the only books treating the topic were textbooks of abnormal psychology. I read that transsexuals were deeply disturbed people who feared being homosexual, or who felt guilty about being homosexual, and who wanted to be members of the other sex so that their sexual feelings would appear normal. Sadly, I concluded that I was not a transsexual after all, because not only did I not consider myself abnormal, I also did not consider homosexuality repulsive. In fact, I thought it sounded pretty cool.

My own budding desires revolved around what the porn magazines stashed under the mattresses in friends' bedrooms called "girl-on-girl action." I knew that if I was one of those women in the magazines, I wouldn't gingerly touch the tip of my tongue to the tip of hers, or place one long painted nail against her nipple—I'd crush her lips to mine and fondle her breast voraciously as she fondled mine. What I didn't know was how to put my body into the stories I saw in those pictures or into the fantasies of transformation I dreamed of at night.

I decided that, since I obviously wasn't transsexual, I must be some heretofore unnamed kind of creature. In retrospect, it seems like it would have been so easy to put two of those terms I found together—to name my emerging sense of self as both transsexual and homosexual—but at the time the categories seemed mutually exclusive, so round and round I went: I feel like I'm really a girl so I could be transsexual, but if I'm transsexual I'm supposed to want to be with guys, but if I'm transsexual in order to be with guys then that means I'm repulsed by homosexuality, but I'm actually attracted to homosexuality, especially homosexuality in women, but a homosexual woman wouldn't like me because I have a guy body, but I could be homosexually involved with women if I were a woman, and I could be a woman if I was transsexual, but I can't be transsexual because that means I'm attracted to guys and repulsed by homosexuality . . . and in the end, teenage passions being what teenage passions are, it was easier to just keep my mouth shut and date the women who wanted to date me, all of whom happened to be straight.

And that's what I was thinking about as I walked along the ridge lines of the Lakeland Fells on my perfect day. I was wondering who I would love, and who would love me, and how we would love, given the complexities of my gender. My girlfriends had all been nice people, and I still carry happy thoughts of good times with them all. One was a fiery-tempered cheerleader running away from an abusive father and living with an older brother. Another was a sweet, pot-smoking rock-and-roll groupie who was one of the most relaxed, fun-loving people I've ever yet encountered. The third was a high-strung, mixed-up daughter of nouveau riche parents; she had—I kid you not—two uteri. For the fourth, I was a way of rebelling against a controlling and over-protective mother. I enjoyed sex with them all. It actually felt fantastic to penetrate their vaginas with my penis, because it felt like my penis had gone away. It wasn't dangling about and poking around but was put away someplace nice that let me push the little spot at the base of my shaft that I always thought of as my clit right up against my girlfriend's bush, and grind against her until we both came. While fucking, my penis—superfluous—disappeared.

All my girlfriends thought I was such a sweet boy, said I wasn't like the other guys, said they could talk to me, said they liked the way I listened to them, said they appreciated that I liked to do things with them besides fuck and seemed to enjoy my just hanging out with them. Then something would happen, some slip, some antigay slur, perhaps. Maybe they would laugh the wrong way when television comedian Flip Wilson did his "Geraldine" character, or make gagging noises when talking about transsexual tennis player Renée Richards, whose story was then much covered in the daily papers. It was always something, some little pin to burst the bubble of what she and I could, in my dreams, be to each other. I would know then that she was not the one for me. Not that I ever let on, until the usual vagaries of time drifted us apart.

It wasn't much of a climax, my little epiphany, that afternoon on the ridge. It was more like something dropped away. I had been shedding bits of my familiar self for weeks, all across Europe, when another little piece of scale fell from my inner eye, and I found myself alone at last in a quiet moment of clarity and insight. It simply became obvious to me that I would never have a meaningful relationship with a woman unless I told her how I really felt about myself, which was that I loved women, had a male body, had never thought of myself as a man, didn't seem to qualify as a transsexual, and had never been turned on by anything other than the thought of being in a lesbian relationship.

The question of whether or not I would ever try to change my body, if that was somehow possible for a normal nontranssexual like me, or what kind of body I would have, or how I would live in public, had to be an open-ended question within the relationship. I didn't know yet what kind of flaming creature I was, but I wanted companionship while I tried to figure it out. I wanted to find somebody who was interested in the process. I decided that, upon returning home, I would make a point of dating bisexual women—women who knew how to eroticize a relationship with a woman but could enjoy making love with a male body. I would come out to my lovers about my sense of self early in the relationship, because if they couldn't hang with the situation, it was all for the best that things end quickly. And that, a few weeks later, is precisely what I did.

She was in my fencing class. There was something about the way she sat cross-legged, her unapologetic armpit hair, her awkward brashness, that big sexy Jewish nose that tipped me off. Dyke. Probably a hardcore feminist. I was smitten. Not being properly socialized into the subtleties of womyn-loving-womyn courtship, I tried to engage her with some stupid conversational gambit, and if she hadn't noticed that I was left-handed, she probably would have blown me off and life would have been very different. But left-handers have a slight advantage in fencing—our attacks always come from the off-side in relation to most everybody else's—and she wanted to practice against me. We spent the next decade fencing with each other, and we both drew blood in the end.

I loved that she would engage with me, fight with me, play with me, argue with me, take me as seriously as I took her. I loved that she spoke German. I loved that she loved movies and would talk about them and not just watch them and eat her popcorn and be done with it. We would disagree passionately over why we both liked the same thing. Our first date was a triple feature of Bergman, Fassbinder, and Herzog. Our second date was the *Rocky Horror Picture Show*. By our third date, we'd come out to each other—she wasn't sure she liked guys, I wasn't sure I was one. It worked for both of us, more or less from the time I was nineteen until I was almost thirty. We got married, went off to graduate school together, made a home together, had a child together. I was so happy being seen through my lover's eyes. I thought I knew what the shape of my life would look like. But I was wrong.

There was that nagging little question about my embodiment. We circled around it. All of our sex fantasies and bedroom stories and erotica-reading were lesbocentric. All of our family life felt gender egalitarian—how we split up the chores, how we parented, how we took turns with work and school and supported each other. It felt like lesbian domesticity. I grew increasingly disenchanted with only my lover seeing me as I saw myself. The person I was to myself, the person I was with her, was not the person I was to everyone else who mattered in my life. She insisted that I keep the matter between us alone. I grew increasingly alienated from my genitals but was perfectly happy to fuck with fingers, tongues, toys, or anything else. By this time, I'd come around to the conclusion that, regardless of what some old textbooks had said, one could in fact be a transsexual lesbian, that one had the power to name oneself. It was just a matter of persuading others to go along with you. I started describing myself to my partner as a preoperative transsexual lesbian who was still living as a man but no longer wanted to do so.

She did not want me to change. She feared what her family would think. We had both read feminist and lesbian literature and knew the feminist party line on transsexual lesbianism—no fake females allowed in the club. She feared we would be ostracized, would have no community, wouldn't find work, wouldn't have a place to live, would be poor and marginalized, our parents would disown us, and our child would be scarred for life by the stigma. These were not unrealistic fears, and she wanted to be safe. She wanted to retain heterosexual privilege, even if she felt she was queer. My body was her closet, and she didn't want me to come out.

Things turned ugly in all the ways that divorce is usually ugly. One afternoon, after a sleepless night filled with bitter grief and mutual recriminations, I was lying, dazed and spent, in the grass beside our apartment building. I felt as if my entire life was being ripped away and the void was staring into me. My thoughts spun back to that perfect day, a decade earlier, when familiar life had been stripped away in a more pleasant fashion, and I consciously stepped onto the path that led me here. I found again, unbidden as before, that same sense of inner clarity that welled within me then. The path went forward. I took my step, she and I parted ways, and I started my transition.

Regrets, I've had a few, but not about transitioning. Regardless of how it might have affected my relationships with other people, it's what was right for me. Nobody else can live my life for me, so how I live in my body for myself is the necessary basis for every other relationship I have with anyone else. I'm completely clear about that now. Fortunately, all of the people who really mattered in my life, except my ex, stayed with me through my transition, and I found wonderful new people along the way to share life's adventures.

I started living as a woman in the early 1990s in San Francisco, just as "queer" (as opposed to old-school baby-boomer gay and lesbian) was coming into currency. I'd never seen a good place for myself in the old economy of sexual identities anyway, and felt very comfortable calling myself queer. I was gender queer. I also liked a new word that started getting tossed around about this time, "transgender." I felt it fit me and created a bit of distance between the old medical mindset associated with "transsexual" and the bohemian life I was living. I cared nothing about passing, everything about being seen for what I was: a queer woman in the process of leaving a male body behind. I didn't care, if my girlfriend didn't, that I still sported nonstandard equipment. I was saving my pennies to replace the factory-installed model with something custom-built anyway, and just wanted her to love me and have crazy, sexy fun while I scraped my surgery money together. I wanted her to look forward to the prospect of eating me out as much as I looked forward to spreading my legs for her.

Life, in many respects, became a dream come true. My body, and the life I lived through it, was finally aligned with the structure of my deepest desires and identifications. I was happy. I had been prepared for a solitary existence post-transition but found that I was desirable to many women I desired. Lesbian transphobia, while real, turned out to be more monolithic in theory than in practice. I went wild for a few years, dated widely, played around casually, frequented orgies, slept my way across town. No names, but a few college professors, a couple of magazine editors, a stripper, a secretary, a dominatrix, a tattooist, a performance artist, a lawyer, a graphic designer, an abortion clinic manager, and two butch dykes in the process of transitioning female-to-male. (If I've forgotten anyone, forgive me.) I learned to see myself in relation to a lot of different women (and a few men), and I came into my own.

I would have been content to live my life with three of those people. One was dating someone else at the same time she was dating me, and ultimately chose to be with the other woman. I was sad, but these things happen, and I got over it. She and I run into each other now and then at professional meetings, and sometimes we get together for a drink when we happen to be in the same city. I always think it's nice to see her. Another I would have shacked up with quite happily had she felt able to leave a long-term nonmonogamous relationship. We had horrible timing with each other for years, one of us was involved in a primary relationship with somebody else when the other was free, and vice versa. After a while, we reconciled to the fact that for each of us the other was "the one that got away," and we settled down into a really warm, close, and ongoing friendship. The third became my life partner throughout my thirties.

She was younger than me by eight years, punky butch-of-center in appearance but an outdoorsy granola dyke just beneath the skin, same shoe size as me and almost my height, with hazel eyes like my father. We lived a life we considered self-consciously radical: polyamorous, collectivist, anarchist, activist, artistic, intellectual. I didn't have a regular job and made my living teaching around as adjunct faculty, writing books and magazine pieces, picking up speaking gigs, doing odd jobs and piecework, while doing my part to turn transgender studies into a recognized academic field. I told people I was just a girl who lived by her wits, and it was true. It was hard economically, but it was also utterly, romantically, wonderfully, free—just another word for nothin' left to lose.

We felt like we were reinventing the world, reinventing family, reinventing love, reinventing ourselves. She had a child we co-parented, along with my son, and we lived with people who felt more like kin than roommates. We all somehow managed to buy a house together before the dot-com boom drove real estate prices through the roof. It was a big place, and we turned it into a commune. We had the best dinner parties and the most interesting houseguests in the world. Somewhere along the way I finally had my surgery. We thought we were the revolution. And in a way, we were.

Revolutions have a way of turning out other than you expect, and this one was no exception. Our former housemates partnered up and moved away, and we started renting out rooms. My partner started her own business, started writing books of her own, and that took up a lot of her time. I landed a postdoctoral fellowship and then accepted a job as the executive director of a nonprofit organization. I worked a lot. The kids were getting older, and just schlepping them to school and karate and playdates with friends took a big chunk out of the daily schedule. Life wasn't quite as wild as it once was, but I felt fine. I felt like I was turning into the woman I'd once imagined I'd grow up to be.

Maybe it was lesbian bed-death. Maybe it was, truth be told, that she was freaked out by my genital surgery, and it triggered her survivor-of-sexual assault issues. Maybe she had been too young when we got together, and she had the best of intentions but just grew in a different direction. Maybe she never loved me the way that I loved her. Maybe it's that she secretly wanted to be monogamous. Maybe it's just that she fell in love with somebody else. Maybe it was that I'd gotten fat, or liked to drink more than she did, or would sometimes self-medicate my stress with nicotine. It was probably all of the above. After ten years that felt to me like our relationship was getting steadily better, she suddenly bugged out and left me for one of my former students, a trans guy I'd tried to mentor, somebody as much younger than her as she was to me. It blindsided and shattered me. For the second time in my life, I felt like my world had crashed, but this time there was no salving memory of a quiet inner place, unexpectedly encountered on a perfect summer day. There was only pain.

That was five years ago, but what they say is true—time is a healer. I'm in a new relationship now and so far, so good. My current partner is somebody I had dated during my polyamorous days with my second long-term lover, so she'd already been in my life for some time. After my unexpected breakup, we saw no reason to stop seeing each other, and we moved cautiously ahead. A year or so of inconsolable grieving on my part, tentative steps toward new couplehood, weekly relationship counseling (we are, after all, middle-aged, middle-class lesbians, for whom psychotherapy is a subcultural norm), and finally moving in together about a year ago. It feels solid. It feels like we've both been around the block a time or two now and know how to do relationships right this time. We take nothing for granted.

It's not always easy between us, but it's mostly the routine kind of not easy. We both have kids from previous relationships with us part-time, and blending families is sometimes a challenge. There are some unresolved in-law issues. We're from different class backgrounds. She's detail-oriented and I'm a big-picture gal who's fuzzy on the small stuff, which sometimes creates tension. She pouts when I travel, and I get annoyed when she kvetches. We both like to get our way and usually think we're right about everything. Some nights, one of us winds up sleeping alone in a huff. She'd been a lesbian for twenty years before she met me, but now that we're together, some of her old friends have distanced themselves. I'm sorry that she's suffered a loss for loving me. We've made new friends together, though, and kept the best of her old bunch as well as mine. My crowd thinks she's swell.

So, where does that leave us? We love each other and try to be nice to each other, because life's too short for unnecessary unpleasantness. We like traveling together and watching movies at home. We've established a good domestic rhythm. We find each other sexy. She often laughs at my jokes, and I think her smile is exquisitely beautiful every time I see it. We take pleasure in our work, and our material needs are abundantly met. We enjoy our hot tub and a cold cosmopolitan cocktail on chilly San Francisco nights. Sometimes when I'm soaking, watching the low clouds scuttle in from the sea, I think back to that perfect day, the summer I turned nineteen. I came down from the ridge in the evening, and walked back into town, where I picked up some lamb meat, rosemary, and potatoes to make myself a stew. After dinner I drew a hot bath and threw open the big, leaded glass bathroom window to look up at the hills I'd climbed earlier in the day. The steam rose and the water cooled as I lay in the tub, and the dusk turned darker, and the nighttime fell. I look at my partner and think: I have a lot of perfect days now.

Note

First published in *Trans People in Love*, edited by Tracie O'Keefe and Katrina Fox (New York: Routledge, 2008), 43–54.

KETAMINE JOURNAL

The closest I can come to describing today's experience in words is the *glocal hybridity* concept promulgated by feminist philosopher Doreen Massey. Basically, imagine any given point, including one's own body, as the intersection of a potentially infinite number of lines of influence or determination, some shorter (more local) and some longer (more global). These contingent, happenstance lines of different spatiotemporal lengths and durations are all knotted together, with no purely "local" place nor a strictly "global" one, just glocal hybridity, always and everywhere.

I visualize my body lying on a couch in a Castro District psychotherapy office as the convergent point of innumerable brightly colored storylines, like yarn threaded through a hole where a nail once was: short lines of proximal narratives—how I knew the person who referred me to the clinic—and longer storylines like the ones that brought me to the Bay Area for grad school, the ones that raveled my sense of being trans, the ones of how the Castro became queer and San Francisco psychedelic, how certain people colonized North America to become white. I visualize my individual lineage back to the southern plains of Oklahoma, to the Ozarks in Arkansas, to the Chesapeake Bay Tidewater in the eighteenth and seventeenth centuries and to Scotland before that. On my father's side, the ancestors came to North America from

Aberdeenshire in the 1660s. If Ancestry.com is to be believed (I know, as a good queer, that all kinship is fictive) my mother's mother's line can be traced back to Gruoch ingen Boite, Lady MacBeth, and through her to the legendary kings of Dál Riata. For a flash today I was zooming through a long green tube that ran toward them, back to a landscape that my waking self first visited in the summer of its nineteenth year.

At home.

Had the weird experience yesterday, so fresh from visiting some memory-conjured version of Scotland down in the K-hole, of receiving an email inviting me to write a short text to accompany the Scottish artist Charlotte Prodger's contribution to the 2019 Venice Biennale. Never was attracted to ketamine as a party drug, am still in the early stages of using it therapeutically to work with the emotional investments bound up in my chronic shoulder pain (too much "carrying the weight of the world"). It's dissociative, used mostly as an anesthetic, can alter proprioceptive sense of time and space, produce visual hallucinations and out-of-body experiences.

I'm finding the visualizations to be the least interesting part of it (mushrooms and acid so much better IMO) but what I'm finding super useful is my awareness in a different way to my experientially available bio-materiality ("body" feels too organized and contained a word for what it feels like). I seem able to sense where traumatic energetic residues are held in the tissue, can make tiny little physical micro-adjustments, let that energy go. K is becoming for me a sort of "chemical *savasana*," a heavy-duty shortcut to the yogic "corpse-pose."

Last night, watched a lot of Prodger's single-channel video work on Vimeo. Was blown away by how much her work resonates with foci in my academic working life, particularly my involvement in the Somatechnics Research Network, a transnational group of interdisciplinary scholars whose shared point of intellectual departure is the proposition that technology isn't something added on prosthetically to a preexisting "natural" body; rather, all embodiment is "always already" technologized. Any given embodiment and the forms of consciousness and identities it manifests are co-constitutive and co-emergent with particular technés and milieus. Even the form of our tool-using hominid body, with its prehensile hands, upright posture, bipedal locomotion, binocular vision, and big brain, is the evolutionary result of a particular relationship between the ability of certain stones to flake easily and hold a sharp edge, the distance of one tree branch from another in the canopy, the flatness of the savannah, the other life-forms our ancestors could eat. There is never a "before" technology for any of us, only changing technological modalities that create different arrangements, with different capacities, between different parts of an environment, some of which we experience as "us," and some of which we don't. The boundary shifts.

Sunday, December 16, 2018, Oklahoma City

At Mark and Sonya's house.

A week into a long visit with the bio-family in Oklahoma, have had little time to write. The progress of Mom's Parkinson's-related dementia has been accelerating since April, more swiftly since early November, and the time has come for a different level of support. We're moving her from an assisted-living community into what's euphemistically called memory care. Right thing to do—she's started falling—but still hard.

Have been thinking about the Prodger essay in fits and starts. Googled "maned lioness," and one of the first things that popped up was a *National Geographic* story about a maned lioness in the Oklahoma City Zoo. Her name is Bridgit. I went to visit her at the zoo today with my nephew, Leo, who's trans like me. Queer- and bio-family are pretty entangled. Bridgit the maned lioness of Oklahoma City was old news to Leo and my brother's family; they have an annual membership at the zoo and go there all the time. "Probably polycystic ovarian syndrome," says my brother, a nurse-practitioner. My niece Camber warned me not to expect too much. "Maned?" she shrugged. "More like Elvis mutton chops than bearded lady." True enough, I said after I'd seen Bridgit, but still, kinda cool? Camber shrugs again. "Sure, Bridgit's cool, but life's diverse, like us, right? No big deal? Just how it is." This is not the Oklahoma I ran to California from.

Tuesday, December 25, 2018, San Francisco

At home.

Good to be home. In spite of all the displacement wrought by tech-driven gentrification in San Francisco, I can still take a Christmas Day stroll up Bernal Hill to stretch my legs after a plane ride and run into fabulous people. Bumped into ecosexual post-porn art activists Annie Sprinkle and Beth Stevens, who live just over the hill from me, their buddy Joseph Kramer from the New School of Erotic Touch, and my colleague micha cárdenas, Annie and Beth's holiday house guest, a transmedia artist who was visiting from Santa Cruz.

It was wonderful/painful to be with Mom. I see time multiplying for her even as its content is being subtracted: every time she awakens from a little nap it's another new day. Every time she sees me sitting in the other chair, I've just arrived from California. Every time I kiss her goodbye, I'm on my way to the airport, several times a day, day after day, for two weeks. Location is indefinite for her, as are pronouns and person. She's back at her old job, in another town. I am my brother, sister, girlfriend, myself. Sometimes she speaks of herself in the third person; sometimes she addresses me as if I were she. Such an unexpected intimacy to be found in the collapse of the maternal boundary.

Kept using ketamine while there, 3 × 100 mg sublingual tablets every few days, to check out from the family drama for a couple of hours and work on my shoulder, but also as a touchstone for sharing Mom's intensifying experience of time and space, acquiring new dimensions, immersing myself in Prodger's video work at odd hours, suturing her eye, her voice, her ways of talking and seeing into the innermost crevices of my autobiographical experience at a profoundly melancholic moment in my family's history. She speaks in voiceover of her time working in an elder-care facility, of coming out to herself there, and I nod in recognition, seeing her hands move in the motion of those down-low gay men and women who, instead of me, have been touching my mother's body to minister to her most basic needs these past few years.

She speaks of going under anesthesia for surgery and the way this fucks with one's subjective experience of time, of gender trouble and public toilets, points her camera at hillsides rampant with bluebells and purple heather and the gray chop of the North Atlantic, and I nod at all of that, too. I've been there, done that, seen that, known that, but it's different now, transformed, seen through another eye, and I think: this is how worlds are formed, kinships forged, broken, remixed, ever old and new again.

Note

First published in *SaFo5*, edited by Charlotte Prodger (Argyll and Bute, Scotland: Cove Park, 2019), 19–26.

SEE BEAMS GLITTER

In one of the works collected in this gentle, fierce, and highly readable anthology of autobiographical writings, Cooper Lee Bombardier riffs on that famous line by Rutger Hauer as the android Roy Batty in Ridley Scott's dystopian sci-fi classic *Blade Runner*—a perennial touchstone for the trans perception of being uncannily different from our human cis-kin. As Batty's allotted span of life ebbs away, he yearns to convey what it means to have seen "attack ships on fire off the shoulder of Orion," and to have "watched C-beams glitter in the dark near the Tannhauser Gate." All those moments will be lost in time, he says, like tears in rain, when he dies. And then he dies.

Unlike the fictional Batty, the flesh-and-blood Bombardier has never been off-world, and the unbelievable things he says he's seen "are largely composed of small wonders, fleeting joys, and fragments of human behavior filtered through the lens of being seen as entirely one gender and then as another." "In the constellations of gender I've traversed, I've seen things that people who presume gender as fixed, innate, and unmoving would never conceive of as possible." Rather than evoking the grand pathos of dying, his words point us toward the humble grace to be found in the persistence of living. For now. Just for now.

I shared a gender constellation with Cooper a quarter-century ago in San Francisco. Those might not have been C-beams glittering in the darkness of dykey dive bars along a pregentrified Valencia Street, but something fabulous sure lit up the night down there, back then. Bombardier was one of the bright spots, in my opinion, pretty much from the moment he hit town in 1993. I'd see him hanging out at Red Dora's Bearded Lady Cafe, in the audience for a Harry Dodge and the Dodge Brothers set at Club Confidential, and interning at Black and Blue Tattoo, where I had some of my own inkwork done. I watched him perform his debut spoken-word piece "Lips like Elvis" for the TransCentral performance series at The Lab, an experimental art incubator in the Mission in 1997, and I remember thinking that this new crop of trans and genderqueer kids was gonna be alright.

Nostalgia is an easy trap to trip on. Whenever I think about "Trans San-Frisco" in the queer '90s, I constantly ask myself whether it could really have been as cool as I remember it feeling when I was living it. And I keep coming to the conclusion that, *yeah, I think it really was*. I'd spent my teens and twenties mournful that I'd missed out on the psychedelic '60s and was still a little too young and definitely too far away from New York's Downtown to have been part of the punk scene in its heyday. For those of us who had genders that were not made for the world we grew up in, being in San Francisco in the early '90s felt like stepping through a rip in the fabric of space-time into some new dimension of possibility. *And we had torn it open ourselves.* For the first time in my life, it felt like I was where something was *happening*. That I was part of it. That we were alive, becoming free, re/making a world by how we moved through it.

I read Cooper's words in the pages of this book and take comfort in knowing that I am not alone in my sense of the consequence of that time and place. Trans SanFrisco in the '90s was a thing. Its history has yet to be written, but the essays in this book are a great place to start. They document something that was not always pretty. It was before the antiretrovirals cocktails made HIV infection something other than a near-term death sentence; friends and lovers left those of us who survived far too soon.

For the first time since Vietnam, we were in a hot war, and clearly saw the connections between the overseas violence of the American Empire and that same Empire's domestic violence toward us as queer and trans people, who were still explicitly criminalized and excluded from large swaths of life. When the Cold War ended in the collapse of the Soviet Union, an unfettered global capitalism—embodied in the tech boom—exulted in a newfound fantasy of limitlessness that started lifting real estate San Francisco toward the stratosphere; it brought the increasing unlivability of the New World Order home, one increasingly insufficient paycheck at a time. People had to leave. Cooper did.

What I see most in these pages is not what Cooper left behind but what he took with him from those halcyon days when, as he puts it, "our permutations variegated faster than any taxonomy could pace." A quarter-century later, I see in his mature writing a confidence that comes from knowing early in life that what is possible can sometimes become real through our actions. I see intensity, invention, playfulness, persistence, openness. I see a sense of calm. Those are powerful attributes to cultivate and share in a world in which what gender means and does still needs to change, along with so much else that needs to change and that must be survived in the meantime.

I read Cooper Lee Bombardier's words, and I see the beams in them. Beams of a beautiful inner light. Beams of inner steel. An ineffable beaming without ground that is, for me, the essence of our shared trans-ness—not our flesh, which is but a means to life, but rather the force of the life that shines through it. I have no idea what the Tannhauser Gate might look like, but it can't be any grander than what being trans has already shown me. I glimpse those same visions of transcendence glittering in the pages of this book.

Note

First published in *Pass with Care: Memoirs*, by Cooper Lee Bombardier (New York City: Dottir Press, 2020), ix–xiii.

TRANS THEORY AS GENDER THEORY

II.

THE TIME HAS COME TO THINK
ABOUT GAYLE RUBIN

Most readers of these pages are long familiar with Gayle Rubin's fierce intel-lect, passion, and astounding depth and range of knowledge. Those as yet unfamiliar with her work and influence should prepare for a memorable encounter with a woman branded by the conservative cultural critic David Horowitz as one of the "101 most dangerous academics in America."[1]

When Heather Love invited me to introduce Rubin's keynote address at Rethinking Sex, a state-of-the-field conference on sexuality studies held at the University of Pennsylvania, March 4, 2009, in honor of Rubin's founda-tional contributions, I thought it would be prudent to refresh my memory of her two landmark articles: "The Traffic in Women" and "Thinking Sex," nei-ther of which I had read recently. In "The Traffic in Women," Rubin begins to develop her thoughts on the processes through which female humans are transformed into oppressed women by citing Karl Marx's observation that a cotton-spinning jenny is merely a machine for spinning cotton that "be-comes capital only in certain relations. Torn from these relationships it is no more capital than gold is itself money or sugar is the price of sugar." Likewise, Rubin contends, substituting "woman" for "spinning jenny," a woman "only becomes a domestic, a wife, a chattel, a playboy bunny, a prostitute, or a hu-man Dictaphone in certain relations. Torn from these relationships she is no more the helpmate of man than gold in itself is money...etc."[2] On turning my attention to "Thinking Sex," it struck me that there could be no more fitting words of tribute—no better way to demonstrate the extent to which Rubin's name has become synonymous with a certain kind of critically engaged, politically radical analysis of sexuality—than to imitate her own rhetorical strategy in "The Traffic in Women" by substituting her name, Gayle Rubin, for the words sex or sexuality in the opening paragraph of "Thinking Sex." And so, if I may, here I present that first paragraph with its metonymic substitution, as I delivered it at "Rethinking Sex":

> The time has come to think about Gayle Rubin. To some, Gayle Rubin may seem to be an unimportant topic, a frivolous diversion from more critical problems of poverty, war, disease, racism, famine, or nuclear annihilation. But it is precisely at times such as these, when people live with the possibility of unthinkable destruction, that people are likely to become dangerously crazy about Gayle Rubin. Contemporary conflicts over Gayle Rubin's values and erotic conduct have much in common with the religious disputes of earlier centuries. They acquire immense symbolic weight. Disputes over Gayle Rubin's behavior often become the vehicles for displacing social anxieties and discharging their attendant emotional intensity. Consequently, Gayle Rubin should be treated with special respect in times of great social stress.[3]

It was my great honor that night to treat Gayle Rubin with the special respect she so richly deserves. I first met Gayle more than twenty years ago, in 1989, on the back patio at the Eagle, a gay leather bar in San Francisco, at an event she had helped organize—The Beat Jesse Helms Flog-A-Thon—which was a fundraiser for the Democratic politician Harvey Gantt's sadly unsuccessful bid to unseat North Carolina's infamously racist and homophobic senior senator. I was a green little newcomer to the radical sexuality scene—a twenty-something grad student who, rather precariously, had one foot in the ivory tower at the University of California, Berkeley, and the other foot in the dungeons and drag bars of San Francisco.

I was happy as a pig in a poke that night at the Eagle, wallowing in what was for me at the time a truly revelatory excess of politically progressive pervert power, when I found myself in an animated conversation with some leatherdyke who seemed about ten years my senior, who had the charming remnants of a Carolinian accent, and who really seemed to know a lot about industrial and goth music. When it slowly dawned on me that I was talking to the Flog-A-Thon co-organizer, *the* Gayle Rubin, famous sex radical, founding figure of San Francisco's women's BDSM community, who had known Michel Foucault personally, I was more than a little starstruck.

Two decades later, I'm still a little starstruck and consider Gayle the most important role model for my own career, which, like Gayle's, has skirted the margins of academe before ultimately finding a place within it. I came out as transgender in 1991, just as I was finishing up my dissertation on the history of religion in antebellum New England. Actually, to be more precise, I came out as a lesbian-identified transsexual sadomasochist who was working on the history of the Mormons—and (surprise!) immediately felt the doors of academic employment quickly closing before me as I started my social transition from man to woman.

I know—what was I thinking? Honestly, I was thinking this: "If Gayle Rubin can produce a substantive body of critical and intellectual work, one that's explicitly grounded in her own bodily acts, desires, and identifications, and if she can do that while working on the edgy fringes of the academy where theory and practice meet, rather than producing safer and more palatable forms of disciplinary knowledge, if she can take precisely those ways of being in the world that marginalize her and instructively and productively dismantle them, and if she can do that and eventually land a job without apologizing for who she is and what she does—if Gayle can do all of that for kinky sex— then maybe, just maybe, I might be able to follow her example and do something similar for transgender people." That's what I set out to do in 1991, largely because Gayle's pioneering example made it seem possible to attempt such a thing.

I know that personally I owe Gayle Rubin a large measure of credit for whatever success I have had over the years in moving toward the goal of establishing transgender studies as a recognized academic specialization. Gayle has been a mentor and an inspiration, as I know she has been for so many other people. She first steered me toward the GLBT Historical Society in San Francisco, which was my intellectual home for many years and where I found a community of independent scholars such as herself, Allan Bérubé, and Willie Walker. She invited me to join reading groups that helped shape my thinking. She wrote the letters of recommendation that eventually landed me postdoctoral positions and professorships, and she's shown me innumerable other kindnesses—so I was pleased to be able to express my gratitude in such a public forum as the 2009 conference in her honor at the University of Pennsylvania, and I am pleased to offer them again, here in the pages of GLQ.

But I would be remiss if I did not also acknowledge Rubin's formative intellectual influence in helping to sharpen the critique transgender studies would make of existing scholarship, quite apart from her significance for me personally. At the 1982 Barnard Sex Conference, Rubin and the other "sex-positive" feminists ably demonstrated that feminism was too large a mantle to be claimed exclusively by any one faction of feminist thought. In arguing that consensual sadomasochism, pornography, and sex work could be framed as feminist practices, they forged the main lines of argument against a moralistic feminist orthodoxy that transgender scholars would continue to advance in the 1990s. Since trannies were lumped in with all the other perverts and outcasts from a good-girl feminism that considered trans folks to be either bad, sick, or wrong in our self-knowledges, it only behooved us to follow in the path of the powerful sisters who were talking back with such sass and eloquence in the face of feminist censure.

While it is certainly true that transgender scholarship in the early 1990s was necessarily on one side of the "sex wars" and not the other, just because we who were beginning to articulate that scholarship knew who our friends were, didn't mean we always agreed with their assessment of us. Sex-positive, protoqueer feminism sometimes made the mistake of regarding transgender merely as an erotic practice rather than as something potentially more expansive, as an expression of self or a mode of embodiment that could not be reduced simply to sexuality any more than woman could. Rubin herself, for example, in charting what she called a "moral sex hierarchy" in her article "Thinking Sex," listed transsexuality and cross-dressing as examples of sexuality clearly labeled as "bad" within dominant discourse, without seeming to recognize that this was a reductive sexualization of entire genres of personhood.

One main goal of Rubin's article, of course, was to challenge the way that some schools of feminism established hierarchies that placed their own perspective above all others and claimed the power to judge and condemn everything else as morally suspect. She went on to note how early second-wave feminism floundered when it tried to apply the concept of class to the category woman and succeeded only when it developed an analytic specific to gender-based oppression.

It followed, then, that feminism, as the study of gender, was likewise an insufficient frame of reference for nonnormative sexuality and that a new "sexuality studies" was called for that needn't abandon feminism any more than feminism needed to abandon political economy. Enacting those same discursive maneuvers to "rethink sex," transgender studies argued in turn that it addressed problematics of embodiment, identity, and desire not readily reducible to sexuality, problematics that eluded full capture by the concept of queerness. Rubin did not resist this miming of the movement of her thought; she was, rather, an enthusiastic participant in the conversations that reframed influential elements of her own earlier work.

For that generosity of mind and spirit, I am personally grateful, and I know the same is true for countless others in myriad ways. If I may be so bold as to use these pages on behalf of all of us whom Gayle Rubin has helped, in one way or another, I would like to express our collective gratitude. Rubin shaped the field of sexuality studies and planted seeds for future developments not only through her keen scholarship but also through the many scholars she has nurtured, encouraged, and cheered on. Simply put, she's a mensch—thank you, Gayle.

Notes

First published in GLQ: *A Journal of Lesbian and Gay Studies* 17, no. 1 (2011): 79–84. Copyright 2011, Duke University Press. All rights reserved. Reprinted by permission of the copyright holder.

1 Horowitz, *The Professors*, 307–11.
2 G. Rubin, "Traffic in Women," 158. The quotation from Marx is from *Wage-Labor and Capital*, 28.
3 Cf. G. Rubin, "Thinking Sex," 3–4.

TRANSGENDER FEMINISM
Queering the Woman Question

Many years ago, I paid a visit to my son's kindergarten room for parent-teacher night. Among the treats in store for us parents that evening was a chance to look at the My Favorite Things book that each child had prepared over the first few weeks of classes. Each page was blank except for a pre-printed line that said, "My favorite color is (blank)" or "My favorite food is (blank)," or "My favorite story is (blank)." Students were supposed to fill in the blanks with their favorite things and draw an accompanying picture.

My son had filled the blanks and empty spaces of his book with many such things as "green," "pizza," and "Goodnight Moon," but I was unprepared for his response to "My favorite animal is (blank)." His favorite animal was "yeast." I looked up at the teacher, who had been watching me in anticipation of this moment. "Yeast?" I said, and she, barely suppressing her glee, said, "Yeah. And when I asked why yeast was his favorite animal, he said, 'It just makes the category animal seem more interesting.'"

At the risk of suggesting that the category "woman" is somehow not interesting enough without a transgender supplement, which is certainly not my intent, I have to confess that there is a sense in which "woman," as a category of human personhood, is indeed, for me, more interesting when we include transgender phenomena within its rubric. The work required to encompass transgender within the bounds of womanhood takes women's studies and queer feminist theorizing in important and necessary directions. It takes us directly into the basic questions of the sex/gender distinction and of the concept of a sex/gender system that lie at the heart of Anglophone feminism. Once there, transgender phenomena ask us to follow basic feminist insights to their logical conclusions (biology is not destiny, and one is not born a woman, right?). And yet, transgender phenomena simultaneously threaten to refigure the basic conceptual and representational frameworks within which the category "woman" has been conventionally understood, deployed, embraced, and resisted.

Perhaps "gender," transgender tells us, is not related to "sex" in quite the same way that an apple is related to the reflection of a red fruit in the mirror; it is not a mimetic relationship. Perhaps "sex" is a category that, like citizenship, can be attained by the nonnative residents of a particular location by following certain procedures. Perhaps gender has a more complex genealogy, at the levels of individual psychobiography as well as collective sociohistorical process, than can be grasped or accounted for by the currently dominant binary sex/gender model of Eurocentric modernity. And perhaps what is to be learned by grappling with transgender concerns is relevant to a great many people, including nontransgendered women and men. Perhaps transgender discourses help us think in terms of embodied specificities, as women's studies has traditionally tried to do, while also giving us a way to think about gender as a system with multiple nodes and positions, as gender studies increasingly requires us to do.

Perhaps transgender studies, which emerged in the academy at the intersection of feminism and queer theory over the course of the last decade or so, can be thought of as one productive way to "queer the woman question."[1] If we define "transgender phenomena" broadly as anything that disrupts or denaturalizes normative gender and calls our attention to the processes through which normativity is produced and atypicality achieves visibility, "transgender" becomes an incredibly useful analytical concept. What might "transgender feminism"—a feminism that focuses on marginalized gender expressions as well as on normative ones—look like?

As a historian of the United States, my training encourages me to approach currently salient questions by looking at the past through new eyes. Questions that matter now, historians are taught to think, are always framed by enabling conditions that precede them. Thus, when I want to know what transgender feminism might be, I try to learn what it has already been. When I learned, for example, that the first publication of the post–World War II transgender movement, a short-lived early 1950s magazine called *Transves-*

tia, was produced by a group calling itself The Society for Equality in Dress,[2] I not only saw that a group of male transvestites in Southern California had embraced the rhetoric of first wave feminism and applied the concept of gender equality to the marginalized topic of cross-dressing; I also came to think differently about Amelia Bloomer and the antebellum clothing reform movement. To the extent that breaking out of the conventional constrictions of womanhood is both a feminist and transgender practice, what we might conceivably call transgender feminism arguably has been around since the first half of the nineteenth century.

Looking back, it is increasingly obvious that transgender phenomena are not limited to individuals who have "transgendered" personal identities. Rather, they are signposts that point to many different kinds of bodies and subjects, and they can help us see how gender can function as part of a more extensive apparatus of social domination and control. Gender as a form of social control is not limited to the control of bodies defined as "women's bodies," nor to the control of female reproductive capacities. Because genders are categories through which we recognize the personhood of others (as well as ourselves), because they are categories without which we have great difficulty in recognizing personhood at all, gender also functions as a mechanism of control when some loss of gender status is threatened or when claims of membership in a gender are denied.

Why is it considered a heterosexist put-down to call some lesbians mannish? Why, if a working-class woman does certain kinds of physically demanding labor, or if a middle-class woman surpasses a certain level of professional accomplishment, is their feminine respectability called into question? Stripping away gender and misattributing gender are practices of social domination, regulation, and control that threaten social abjection; they operate by attaching transgender stigma to various unruly bodies and subject positions, not just to "transgendered" ones.[3]

There is also, however, a lost history of feminist activism by self-identified transgender people waiting to be recovered. My own historical research into twentieth-century transgender communities and identities teaches me that activists on transgender issues were involved in multi-issue political movements in the 1960s and 1970s, including radical feminism. The ascendancy of cultural feminism and lesbian separatism by the mid-1970s—both of which cast transgender practices, particularly transsexuality, as reactionary patriarchal anachronisms—largely erased knowledge of this early transgender activism from feminist consciousness. Janice Raymond, in her outrageously transphobic book, *The Transsexual Empire* (1979), went so far as to suggest that "the problem of transsexualism would best be served by morally mandating it out of existence" (178).[4]

Even in this period, however, when identity politics effectively disconnected transgender feminism from the broader women's movement and before the queer cultural politics of the 1990s revitalized and expanded the transgender movement, it is possible to find startling historical episodes that compel us to re-examine what we think we know about the feminist history of the recent past. The Radical Queens drag collective in Philadelphia, for example, had a "sister house" relationship with a lesbian separatist commune during the early 1970s, and participated in mainstream feminist activism through involvement with the local chapter of NOW. In the later 1970s in Washington, DC, secretive clubs for married heterosexual male crossdressers began holding consciousness-raising sessions; they argued that to identify as feminine meant they were politically obligated to come out as feminists, speak out as transvestites, and work publicly for passage of the Equal Rights Amendment.[5]

In addition to offering a revisionist history of feminist activism, transgender issues also engage many of the foundational questions in the social sciences and life sciences as they pertain to feminist inquiry. The biological body, which is typically assumed to be a single organically unified natural object characterized by one, and only one, of two available sex statuses, is demonstrably no such thing. The so-called "sex of the body" is an interpretive fiction that narrates a complex amalgamation of gland secretions and reproductive organs, chromosomes and genes, morphological characteristics and physiognomic features. There are far more than two viable aggregations of sexed bodily being.

At what cost, for what purposes, and through what means do we collapse this diversity of embodiment into the social categories "woman" and "man"? How does the psychical subject who forms in this material context become aware of itself, of its embodied situation, of its position in language, family, or society? How does it learn to answer to one or the other of the two personal pronouns "he" or "she," and to recognize "it" as a disavowed option that forecloses personhood? How do these processes vary from individual to individual, from place to place, and from time to time? These are questions of importance to feminism, usually relegated to the domains of biology and psychology, that transgender phenomena can help us think through. Transgender feminism gives us another axis, along with critical race studies or disability studies, to learn more about the ways in which bodily difference becomes the basis for socially constructed hierarchies, and helps us see in new ways how we are all inextricably situated, through the inescapable necessity of our own bodies, in terms of race, sex, gender, or ability.

When we look cross-culturally and transhistorically at societies, as anthropologists and sociologists tend to do, we readily see patterns of variations in the social organization of biological reproduction, labor, economic exchange, and kinship; we see a variety of culturally specific configurations of embodiment, identity, desire, social status, and social role. Which of these patterns do we call "gender," and which do we call "transgender"? The question makes sense only in reference to an unstated norm that allows us to distinguish between the two. To examine "transgender" cross-culturally and transhistorically is to articulate the masked assumptions that produce gender normativity in any given (time-bound and geographically constrained) context. To examine "transgender" is thus to risk decentering the privileged standpoint of white Eurocentric modernity. It is to denaturize and de-reify the terms through which we ground our own genders in order to confront the possibility of radically different ways of being in the world. This, too, is a feminist project.[6]

A third set of concerns that make transgender feminism interesting for women's studies is the extent to which "transgender," for more than a decade now, has served as a laboratory and proving ground for the various postmodern and poststructuralist critical theories that have transformed humanities scholarship in general over the past half century, and have played a role in structuring the generational debates about "second wave" and "third wave" feminism. This is a debate in which I take an explicitly partisan position, largely in response to the utterly inexcusable level of overt transphobia in second wave feminism. The second wave feminist turn to an untheorized female body as the ultimate ground for feminist practice has to be understood historically in the context of reactionary political pressures that fragmented all sorts of movements posing radical threats to the established order and required them to find new, often ontological, bases for political resistance. An unfortunate consequence was that it steered feminist analysis in directions ill equipped it to engage theoretically with the emerging material conditions of social life within advanced capitalism that collectively have come to be called, more or less usefully, "postmodernity."

The overarching tendency of second wave feminism to couch its political analyses within moral narratives that link "woman" with "natural," "natural" with "good," "good" with "true," and "true" with "right" has been predicated on an increasingly nonutilitarian modernist epistemology. Within the representational framework of Eurocentric modernity, which posits gender as the superstructural sign of the material referent of sex, transgender practices have been morally condemned as unnatural, bad, false, and wrong, in that they fundamentally misalign the proper relationship between sex and gender. The people who engage in such misrepresentations can be understood only as duped or duplicitous, fools or enemies to be pitied or scorned. The failure of second wave feminism to do justice to transgender issues in the 1970s, '80s, and afterward is rooted in its more fundamental theoretical failure to recognize the conceptual limits of modernist epistemology.[7]

Transgender theorizing in third wave feminism begins from a different—postmodern—epistemological standpoint that imagines new ways for sexed bodies to signify gender. Within the feminist third wave, and within humanities scholarship in general, transgender phenomena have come to constitute important evidence in recent arguments about essentialism and social construction, performativity and citationality, hybridity and fluidity, antifoundationalist ontologies and nonreferential epistemologies, the proliferation of perversities, the collapse of difference, the triumph of technology, the advent of posthumanism, and the end of the world as we know it. While it is easy to parody the specialized and sometimes alienating jargon of these debates, the issues at stake are quite large, involving as they do the actual as well as theoretical dismantling of power relations that sustain various privileges associated with normativity and injustices directed at minorities. Because these debates are irreducibly political, because they constitute an ideological landscape upon which material struggles are waged within the academy for research funds and promotions, for tenure and teaching loads, transgender phenomena have come to occupy a curiously strategic location in the working lives of humanities professionals, whether they like it or not. This brings me at last to the crux of my remarks.

For all the reasons I have suggested, transgender phenomena are interesting for feminism, women's studies, gender studies, sexuality studies, and so forth. But interesting, by itself, is not enough, when hard decisions about budgets and staffing have to be made in academic departments, when priorities and commitments have to be actualized through classroom allocations and affirmative action hiring. Interesting also has to be important, and transgender is rarely considered important. All too often, transgender is thought to name only a largely irrelevant class of phenomena on the marginal fringe of the hegemonic gender categories man and woman, or else it is seen as one of the later, minor accretions to the gay and lesbian movement, along with bisexual and intersexed. At best, transgender is considered a portent of a future that seems to await us, for good or ill. But it remains a canary in the cultural coal mine, not an analytical workhorse for pulling down the patriarchy and other associated social ills.

As long as transgender is conceived as the fraction of a fraction of a fraction of a movement, as long as it is thought to represent only some inconsequential outliers in a bigger and more important set of data, there is very little reason to support transgender concerns at the institutional level. Transgender will always lose by the numbers. The transgender community is tiny. In (so-called) liberal democracies that measure political strength by the number of votes or the number of dollars, transgender does not count for much or add up to a lot. But there is another way to think about the importance of transgender concerns at this moment in our history.

One measure of an issue's potential is not how many people directly identify with it but, rather, how many other issues it can be linked with in a productive fashion. How can an issue be articulated, in the double sense of "articulation," meaning both "to bring into language," and "the act of flexibly conjoining."[8] Articulating a transgender politics is part of the specialized work that I do as an activist transgender intellectual. How many issues can I link together through my experience of the category transgender?

To the extent that I am perceived as a woman (which is most of the time), I experience the same misogyny as other women; and to the extent that I am perceived as a man (which happens every now and then), I experience the homophobia directed toward gay men—both forms of oppression, in my experience, being rooted in a cultural devaluation of the feminine. My transgender status, to the extent that it is apparent to others, manifests itself through the appearance of my bodily surface and my shape, in much the same way that race is constructed, in part, through visuality and skin, and in much the same way that the beauty system operates by privileging certain modes of appearance. My transsexual body is different from most other bodies, and while this difference does not impair me, it has been medicalized, and I am sometimes disabled by the social oppression that takes aim at the specific form of my difference.

Because I am formally classified as a person with a psychopathology known as Gender Identity Disorder, I am subject to the social stigma attached to mental illness, and I am more vulnerable to unwanted medical-psychiatric interventions. Because changing personal identification documents is an expensive and drawn-out affair, I have spent part of my life as an undocumented worker. Because identification documents such as driver's licenses and passports are coded with multiple levels of information, including previous names and "AKAS," my privacy, and perhaps my personal safety, is at risk every time I drive too fast or cross a border. When I travel, I always have to ask myself whether some aspect of my appearance, some bit of data buried in the magnetic strip on some piece of plastic with my picture on it, will create suspicion and result in my detention?

In this era of terror and security, we are all surveyed, we are all profiled, but some of us have more to fear from the state than others. Staying home, however, does not make me safer. If I risk arrest by engaging in nonviolent demonstrations, or violent political protest, the incarceration complex would not readily accommodate my needs. Even though I am a postoperative male-to-female transsexual, I could wind up in a men's prison where I would be at extreme risk of rape and sexual assault. Because I am transgendered, I am more likely to experience discrimination in housing, employment, and access to health care, and I am more likely to experience violence. These are not abstract issues: I have lost jobs and not been offered jobs because I am transgendered. I have had doctors walk out of exam rooms in disgust; I have had more trouble finding and retaining housing because I am transgendered; I have had my home burglarized and my property vandalized, and I have been assaulted because I am transgendered.

Let me recapitulate what I can personally articulate through transgender: misogyny, homophobia, racism, looksism, disability, medical colonization, coercive psychiatrization, undocumented labor, border control, state surveillance, population profiling, the prison-industrial complex, employment discrimination, housing discrimination, lack of health care, denial of access to social services, and violent hate crimes. These issues are my issues not because I think it is chic to be politically progressive. These issues are my issues not because I feel guilty about being white, highly educated, or a citizen of the United States. These issues are my issues because my bodily being lives the space where these issues intersect. I articulate these issues when my mouth speaks the words that my mind puts together from what my body knows. It is by winning the struggles over these issues that my body as it is lived for me survives—or by losing them, that it will die. If these issues are your issues as well, then transgender needs to be part of your intellectual and political agenda. It is one of your issues.

I conclude now with some thoughts on yet another aspect of transgender articulation, the one mentioned in my title, which is how transgender issues articulate, or join together, feminist and queer projects. "Trans-" is troublesome for both LGBT communities and feminism; but the kind of knowledge that emerges from this linkage is precisely the kind of knowledge that we desperately need in the larger social arena. Trans is not a "sexual identity" and therefore fits awkwardly in the LGBT rubric. That is, "transgender" does not describe a sexual orientation (like homosexual, bisexual, heterosexual, or asexual), nor are transgender people typically attracted to other transgender people in the same way that lesbians are attracted to other lesbians, or gay men to other gay men. Transgender status is more like race or class, in that it cuts across the categories of sexual identity.[9]

Neither is transgender (at least currently, in Eurocentric modernity) an identity term like "woman" or "man" that names a gender category within a social system. It is a way of being a man or a woman, or a way of marking resistance to those terms. Transgender analyses of gender oppression and hierarchy, unlike more normative feminist analyses, are not primarily concerned with the differential operations of power upon particular identity categories that create inequalities within gender systems; rather they are concerned with how the system itself produces a multitude of possible positions that it then works to center or to marginalize.

Transgender practices and identities are a form of gender trouble, in that they call attention to contradictions in how we tend to think about gender, sex, and sexuality. But the transgender knowledges that emerge from these troubling contradictions can yoke together queer and feminist projects in a way that helps break the impasse of identity politics that has so crippled progressive movements in the United States. Since the early 1970s, progressive politics have fragmented along identity lines practically to the point of absurdity. While it undoubtedly has been vital over the past few decades of movement history to enunciate the particularities of all our manifold forms of bodily being in the world, it is equally important that we now find new ways of articulating our commonalities without falling into the equally dead-end logic of totalizing philosophies and programs.

Transgender studies offers us one critical methodology for thinking through the diverse particularities of our embodied lives, and for thinking through the commonalities we share through our mutual enmeshment in more global systems. Reactionary political movements have been very effective in telling stories about shared values—family, religion, tradition. We who work at the intersection of queer and feminist movements, we who have a different vision of our collective future, need to become equally adept in telling stories that link us in ways that advance the cause of justice and that hold forth the promise of happy endings for all our strivings. Bringing transgender issues into women's studies, and into feminist movement building, is one concrete way to be engaged in that important work.

While it is politically necessary to include transgender issues in feminist theorizing and organizing, it is not intellectually responsible nor ethically defensible to teach transgender studies in academic women's studies without being engaged in peer-to-peer conversations with various sorts of trans and genderqueer people. Something crucial is lost when academically based feminists fail to support transgender inclusion in the academic workplace.

Genderqueer youth who have come of age after the "queer" nineties are now passing through the higher education system, and they increasingly fail to recognize the applicability of prevailing modes of feminist discourse for their own lives and experiences. How we each live our bodies in the world is a vital source of knowledge for us all, and to teach trans studies without being in dialogue with trans people is akin to teaching race studies only from a position of whiteness, or teaching gender studies only from a position of masculinity. Why is transgender not a category targeted for affirmative action in hiring and valued the same way that racial diversity is valued? It is past time for feminists who have imagined that transgender issues have not been part of their own concerns to take a long, hard look in the mirror. What in their own constructions of self, their own experiences of gender, prevents their recognition of transgender people as being somehow like themselves—as people engaged in parallel, intersecting, and overlapping struggles, who are not fundamentally Other?

Transgender phenomena now present queer figures on the horizon of feminist visibility. Their calls for attention are too often received, however, as an uncomfortable solicitation from an alien and unthinkable monstrosity best left somewhere outside the village gates. But justice, when we first feel its claims upon us, typically points us toward a future we can scarcely imagine. At the historic moment when racial slavery in the United States at long last became morally indefensible and the nation plunged into civil war, what did the future of the nation look like? When greenhouse gas emissions finally become equally morally indefensible, what shape will a post-oil world take? Transgender issues make similar claims of justice upon us all and promise equally unthinkable transformations.[10] Recognizing the legitimacy of these claims will change the world, and feminism along with it, in ways we can now hardly fathom. It is about time.

Notes

First published in *Third Wave Feminism: A Critical Exploration*, edited by Stacy
Gillis, Gillian Howie, and Rebecca Munford (London: Palgrave, 2007), 59–70.

1   This essay was first delivered as a keynote address at the Third Wave Feminism
conference at the University of Exeter, UK, July 25, 2002; and it was presented
in revised form at the Presidential Session plenary on Transgender Theory at
the National Women's Studies Association annual meeting, Oakland, California,
June 17, 2006. Many of the ideas I present here have been worked out in greater
detail elsewhere in my work (see Stryker, "My Words to Victor Frankenstein";
Stryker, "The Transgender Issue"; Stryker, "Transgender Studies: Queer Theory's Evil Twin"; and Stryker, "(De)subjugated Knowledges"); see also Zalewski,
"A Conversation with Susan Stryker." For another account of the relationship between recent feminist scholarship and transgender issues, see Heyes, "Feminist
Solidarity after Queer Theory."

2   Meyerowitz, "A New History of Gender," 179.

3   My thoughts on the role of transgender phenomena for understanding US
history in general are significantly indebted to Meyerowitz, "A New History of
Gender."

4   See also Hausman, *Changing Sex*, 9–14, for an overview of cultural feminist critiques of transsexuality; and see Billings and Urban, "The Sociomedical Construction of Transsexualism," for a particularly cogent exposition and application
of this approach.

5   See also Victor Silverman and Members of the Gay and Lesbian Historical Society for transgender involvement in progressive grassroots political activism in
the San Francisco Bay Area in the 1960s.

6   On cross-cultural studies of transgender phenomena, see Blackwood and Wieringa, *Female Desires*; and Morgan and Towle, "Romancing the Transgender
Native."

7   For a poststructuralist, antifoundationalist critique of second wave feminism, see
Butler, "Contingent Foundations."

8   The concept of *articulation* is taken from Laclau and Mouffe, *Hegemony and Socialist Strategy*, 93–194.

9   On the trouble transgender presents to identity movements, see Gamson, "Must
Identity Movements Self-Destruct?"

10 On monstrosity and justice, see N. Sullivan, "Transmogrification."

TRANSGENDER HISTORY, HOMONORMATIVITY, AND DISCIPLINARITY

The current attention to homonormativity has tended to focus on gay and lesbian social, political, and cultural formations and their relationship to a neoliberal politics of multicultural diversity that meshes with the assimilative strategies of transnational capital. Lisa Duggan's *The Twilight of Equality? Neoliberalism, Cultural Politics, and the Attack on Democracy* (2003), which describes a "new homonormativity that does not challenge heterosexist institutions and values, but rather upholds, sustains, and seeks inclusion within them," is generally acknowledged as the text through which this term has come into wider currency.[1]

There is, however, an older formulation of homonormativity that nevertheless merits retention, one closer in meaning to the "homo-normative" social codes described in 1998 by Jack Halberstam in *Female Masculinity*, in accordance with which expressions of masculinity in women are as readily disparaged within gender-normative gay and lesbian contexts as within heteronormative ones.[2] It is this earlier sense of homonormativity that is most pertinent to the thoughts I offer here on homonormativity and transgender history, both as an object of scholarly inquiry and as a professional disciplinary practice.

Terminological History

Homonormativity, as I first heard and used the term in the early 1990s, was an attempt to articulate the double sense of marginalization and displacement experienced within transgender political and cultural activism. Like other queer militants, transgender activists sought to make common cause with any groups—including nontransgender gays, lesbians, and bisexuals—who contested heterosexist privilege. However, we also needed to name the ways that homosexuality, as a sexual orientation category based on constructions of gender it shared with the dominant culture, sometimes had more in common with the straight world than it did with us.[3]

The grassroots conversations in which I participated in San Francisco in the first half of the 1990s used the term homonormative when discussing the relationship of transgender to queer, and queer to gay and lesbian. Transgender itself was a term then undergoing a significant shift in meaning. Robert Hill, who has been researching the history of heterosexual male cross-dressing communities, found instances in community-based publications of words like *transgenderal, transgenderist,* and *transgenderism* dating back to the late 1960s.[4] The logic of those terms, used to describe individuals who lived in one social gender but had a bodily sex conventionally associated with the other, aimed for a conceptual middle ground between transvestism (merely changing one's clothing) and transsexualism (changing one's sex). By the early 1990s, primarily through the influence of Leslie Feinberg's 1992 pamphlet *Transgender Liberation: A Movement Whose Time Has Come,* transgender was beginning to refer to something else—an imagined political alliance of all possible forms of gender antinormativity. It was in this latter sense that transgender became articulated with queer.[5]

This "new transgender" marked both a political and generational distinction between older transvestite/transsexual/drag terminologies and an emerging gender politics that was explicitly and self-consciously queer. It began for me in 1992, when the San Francisco chapter of Queer Nation distributed one of its trademark DayGlo crack-and-peel stickers that read "Trans Power/Bi Power/Queer Nation." The transsexual activist Anne Ogborn encountered someone on the street wearing one of those stickers, but with the words "Trans Power" torn off. When Ogborn asked if there was any significance to the omission, she was told that the wearer did not consider trans people to be part of the queer movement.[6]

Ogborn attended the next Queer Nation general meeting to protest transphobia within the group, whereupon she was invited, in high Queer Nation style, to organize a transgender caucus.[7] As a result, Transgender Nation, of which I was a founding member, came into being as the first explicitly queer transgender social change group in the United States. The group survived the soon-to-be-defunct Queer Nation and became, in its own brief existence from 1992 to 1994, a touchstone in the transgender inclusion debates then raging in San Francisco's emerging lesbian, gay, bisexual, and transgender (LGBT) community.

In a contradictory environment simultaneously welcoming and hostile, transgender activists staked their own claims to queer politics. We argued that sexual orientation was not the only significant way to differ from heteronormativity—that homo, hetero, and bi, in fact, all depended on similar understandings of "man" and "woman," which trans problematized. People with trans identities could describe themselves as men and women—or resist binary categorization altogether—but in doing either, they queered the dominant relationship of sexed body and gendered subject. We drew a distinction between *orientation queers* and *gender queers*. Tellingly, gender queer, necessary for naming the minoritized/marginalized position of difference within queer cultural formations more generally, has stuck around as a useful term; orientation queer, naming queer's unstated norm, has seemed redundant in most contexts and has not survived to the same extent.

When San Francisco gays and lesbians who were active in queer politics in the first half of the 1990s were antagonistic to transgender concerns, we accused them of being anti-heteronormative in a homonormative fashion. The term was an intuitive, almost self-evident, back-formation from the ubiquitous heteronormative, suitable for use where homosexual community norms marginalized other kinds of sex/gender/sexuality difference. Although I do not recall specific instances where the term *homonormative* was used, or who used it, the general discussions in which the term would have been deployed were playing themselves out in any number of places in which transgender inclusion was being contested: within Queer Nation and ACT-UP and AIDS agencies; at community meetings to organize for the March on Washington in 1993 and the twenty-fifth anniversary of the Stonewall uprising in 1994; at town-hall meetings about gays in the military and about domestic partnerships during the hopeful early days of the first Clinton administration; during policy discussions about including gender identity in the proposed federal Employment Nondiscrimination Act; in catfights over who could attend the Michigan Womyn's Music Festival; at meetings of the Harvey Milk and Alice B. Toklas Democratic Clubs; at Pride Parade meetings; at membership meetings and board meetings of practically every lesbian and gay nonprofit organization in the city; at the San Francisco Human Rights Commission committee on lesbian and gay issues; in flame wars in the letters-to-the-editors columns of the *Bay Times* and the BAR (*Bay Area Reporter*); and in coffee shops, bars, dance clubs, dungeon spaces, and bedrooms throughout the city.

The homonormative accusation tended to be leveled against a handful of favorite targets: gays and lesbians who saw transgender issues as entirely distinct from their own and who resisted any sort of transgender participation in queer politics and culture; lesbians who excluded male-to-female transgender people but nervously engaged with female-to-male people, on the grounds that the former were really men and the latter were really women; and, putting a somewhat finer point on the matter, those who conceptualized "T" as an identity category analogous to "GLB" and who advocated for a GLBT community on that basis. In the first instance, homonormativity was a threat to a broadly conceived politics of alliance and affinity, regardless of identity; it aimed at securing privilege for gender-normative gays and lesbians based on adherence to dominant cultural constructions of gender, and it diminished the scope of potential resistance to oppression. In the second instance, homonormativity took the shape of lesbian subcultural norms that perversely grounded themselves in reactionary notions of biological determinism as the only legitimate basis of gender identity and paradoxically resisted feminist arguments that "woman" and "lesbian" were political rather than ontological categories. The third instance requires a more subtle and expansive explication.

In this case, homonormativity lies in misconstruing trans as either a gender or a sexual orientation. Misconstrued as a distinct gender, trans people are simply considered another kind or type of human than either men or women, which leads to such homonormative attempts at "transgender inclusion" as questionnaires and survey instruments within GLBT contexts that offer respondents opportunities for self-identification structured along the lines of

—Man
—Woman
—Transgender (check one)

Misconstrued as a sexual orientation category, trans appears as a desire, akin to kink and fetish desire, for cross-dressing or (more extremely) genital modification. The "T" in this version of the LGBT community becomes a group of people who are attracted to one another on the basis of enjoying certain sexual practices—in the same way that gay men are attracted to gay men, and lesbians are attracted to lesbians, on the basis of a shared desire for particular sexual practices. "T" is thus homonormatively constructed as a properly distinct group of people with a different orientation than gays, lesbians, and bisexuals (or, for that matter, straights). In this model of GLBT intracommunity relations, each identity is happily attracted to its own kind and leaves the other groups to their own devices except in ceremonial circumstances (like pride parades and other public celebrations of diversity), or whenever political expediency calls for coalitional action of some sort.

In either homonormative deformation, "T" becomes a separate category to be appended, through a liberal politics of minority assimilation, to gay, lesbian, and bisexual community formations. Trans thus conceived does not trouble the basis of the other categories—indeed, it becomes a containment mechanism for "gender trouble" of various sorts that works in tandem with assimilative gender-normative tendencies within the sexual identities.[8]

Transgender activism and theory, on the other hand, tend to treat trans as a modality rather than a category. Trans segments the sexual orientations and gender identities in much the same manner as race and class—in other words, a transsexual woman (someone with a transsexual mode of embodiment who lives in the social category woman) can be a lesbian (someone who lives in the social category woman and is sexually oriented toward women), just as a black man could be gay, or a bisexual person could be poor. In doing so, transgender theory and activism call attention to the operations of normativity within and between gender/sexual identity categories, raise questions about the structuration of power along axes other than the homo/hetero and man/woman binaries, and identify productive points of attachment for linking sexual orientation and gender identity activism to other social justice struggles.

A decade before homonormative became a critically chic term elsewhere, I thus suggest, transgender praxis and critique required an articulation of the concept of homonormativity. The border wars that transgender activists fought within queer communities of the 1990s had important consequences for shaping contemporary transgender politics and theorizing, and for charting a future path toward radical activism. Transgender relations to gay and lesbian community formations necessarily became strategic—sometimes oppositional, sometimes aligned, sometimes fighting rearguard actions for inclusion, sometimes branching out in entirely different and unrelated directions. Central issues for transgender activism—such as gender-appropriate state-issued identification documents that allow trans people to work, cross borders, and access social services without exposing themselves to potential discrimination—suggest useful forms of alliance politics, in this instance, with migrant workers and diasporic communities, that are not organized around sexual identity. One operation of homonormativity exposed by transgender activism is that homo is not always the most relevant norm against which trans needs to define itself.

Antihomonormative Transgender History

As important as queer identitarian disputes have been for present and future transgender politics, they have been equally important for reinterpreting the queer past. I first started researching the transgender history of San Francisco, particularly in relation to the city's gay and lesbian community, while participating in the Bay Area's broader queer culture during the early 1990s. In 1991, during my final year as a PhD student in US history at the University of California at Berkeley, the same year I began transitioning from male to female, I became deeply involved with an organization then known as the Gay and Lesbian Historical Society of Northern California. That organization, now the GLBT Historical Society, houses the preeminent collection of primary source materials on San Francisco Bay Area gay, lesbian, bisexual, and transgender communities, and is one of the best collections of sexuality-related materials anywhere in the world. I started there as a volunteer in the archives, joined the board of directors in 1992, and later became the first executive director of the organization, from 1999 to 2003.

Through my long and intimate association with the GLBT Historical Society as well as through two years of postdoctoral funding from the Sexuality Research Fellowship Program of the Social Science Research Council, I had ample opportunity to exhaustively research the status of transgender issues within gay and lesbian organizations and communities in post–World War II San Francisco. I was able to scan all the periodical literature, community newspapers, collections of personal papers, organizational records, ephemera, and visual materials—tens of thousands of items—for transgender-related content. This research was motivated by several competing agendas. It was first and foremost a critically queer project, one informed by theory, guided by practice, and framed by my historical training at Berkeley in the decade between Michel Foucault's death and Judith Butler's arrival; I wanted training to account for the precipitation of new categories of personal and collective identity from the matrix of possible configurations of sex, gender, identity, and desire; trace their genealogies and modes of discourse; and ana-lyze the cultural politics of their interactions with each other and society at large. It was also a project to recover the history of transgender experience specifically, in a way that resisted essentializing transgender identities, and to make that knowledge available as content for transgender-related social jus-tice work. Only those who are "crushed by a present concern," and who want to "throw off their burden at any cost," Friedrich Nietzsche wrote in "On the Use and Abuse of History for Life," have "a need for a critical . . . historiography."[9]

And finally, I was motivated by polemical and partisan considerations; I wanted to offer an empirically grounded account of transgender history that recontextualized its relation to gay and lesbian normativity and countered the pathologizing, moralizing, condescending, dismissive, and generally wrong-headed treatment of transgender issues so often found in gay and lesbian dis-courses of that time.

Over the course of my research, gender-policing practices came into fo-cus as an important mechanism for shaping the landscape of sexual identity community formations described in the major historiographical accounts.[10] As homosexual communities in mid-twentieth-century San Francisco re-defined themselves as political minorities, they distanced themselves from older notions of "inversion" that collapsed gender transposition and homo-sexual desire into one another; they simultaneously drew their boundaries at least partly in relation to new and rapidly evolving scientific discourses on transgender phenomena and related medico-legal techniques for changing sex. Homophile groups such as the Mattachine Society and the Daughters of Bilitis were not initially antagonistic to transgender issues; they sometimes fielded queries from people questioning their gender or seeking a community in which to express a transgender identity, but they tended to redirect such queries elsewhere.[11] Transgender issues tended to be seen within the homo-phile movement as parallel rather than intersecting, at least partially due to the central role that gender normativity played in the homophile movement's public politics of respectability in the 1950s and early 1960s.

In lesbian contexts this took the form of class-based criticisms of butch-femme roles, while in the gay male world it expressed itself through the con-demnation of the hypermasculine styles found in the leather, motorcycle, and cowboy subcultures, as well as of the femininity of "swish" styles and public female impersonation. Drag remained an important subcultural id-iom, especially for gay men and working-class lesbians, but one typically con-fined to clubs, bars, and private parties. Street drag was almost universally condemned and largely relegated to territories coextensive with prostitution, hustling, and other economically marginalized activities. Thus, from the outset of the post–World War II gay rights movement, transgender practices and identities marked communal boundaries between the normative and the transgressive.

One particular archival discovery seemed so perfectly attuned to all my research motivations, however, and so seemingly significant yet almost entirely unknown, that I initially questioned whether it could possibly be true. In the centerfold of the program for the first Gay Pride Parade in San Francisco, held in 1972, I found a description of a 1966 riot in San Francisco's Tenderloin District, in which drag queens and gay hustlers banded together at a popular late-night hangout called Gene Compton's Cafeteria to fight back against police harassment and social oppression. The key text reads as follows:

> In the streets of the Tenderloin, at Turk and Taylor on a hot August night in 1966, Gays rose up angry at the constant police harassment of the drag queens by the police. It had to be the first ever recorded violence by Gays against police anywhere. For on that evening when the sfpd paddy wagon drove up to make their "usual" sweeps of the streets, Gays this time did not go willingly. It began when the police came into a cafeteria, still located there at Turk and Taylor, Compton's, to do their usual job of hassling the drag-queens and hair-fairies and hustlers setting at the table. This was with the permission of management, of course. But when the police grabbed the arm of one of the transvestites, he threw his cup of coffee in the cop's face, and with that, cups, saucers, and trays began flying around the place, and all directed at the police. They retreated outside until reinforcements arrived, and the Compton's management ordered the place closed, and with that, the Gays began breaking out every window in the place, and as they ran outside to escape the breaking glass, the police tried to grab them and throw them into the paddy wagon, but they found this no easy task for Gays began hitting them "below the belt" and drag-queens smashing them in the face with their extremely heavy purses. A police car had every window broken, a newspaper shack outside the cafeteria was burned to the ground, and general havoc was raised that night in the Tenderloin. The next night drag-queens, hair-fairies, conservative Gays, and hustlers joined in a picket of the cafeteria, which would not allow drags back in again. It ended'with the newly installed plate glass windows once more being smashed. The Police Community Relations Unit began mediating the conflict, which was never fully re-

solved, which ended in a group called VANGUARD being formed of the
street peoples and a lesbian group of street people being formed called
the STREET ORPHANS, both of which later became the old GAY LIB-
ERATION FRONT in San Francisco, and is today called the GAY ACTIV-
ISTS ALLIANCE.[12]

The story seemed important in several respects. First, what reportedly
happened at Compton's Cafeteria bore obvious similarities to the famous
Stonewall uprising in New York in 1969, where the militant phase of gay liberation is commonly supposed to have begun, but reputedly preceded it by
three years. How the San Francisco gay activist community positioned the
Compton's story vis-à-vis Stonewall in their first commemorative Gay Pride
Parade was clearly intended as an early revisionist account of gay liberation
history. Furthermore, the inciting incident of the riot was described as an
act of antitransgender discrimination, rather than an act of discrimination
against sexual orientation.

At the time I came across this source in 1995, the role of drag queens in
the Stonewall riots had become a site of conflict between transgender and
normative gay/lesbian histories—transgender activists pointed to the act of
mythologizing Stonewall as the "birth" of gay liberation as a homonormative
co-optation of gender queer resistance, while homonormative gay and lesbian commentators tended to downplay the significance of antidrag oppression at Stonewall—and whatever I could learn about the Compton's incident
would certainly inform that debate. The 1972 document also related a genealogy of gay liberation activism at odds with the normative accounts—one
rooted in the socioeconomics of the multiethnic Tenderloin sex-work ghetto
rather than in campus-based activism oriented toward countercultural white
youth of middle-class origin. For all these reasons, the Compton's Cafeteria
riot became a central focus of my research into San Francisco's transgender
history and its intersectional relationship to the history of gay and lesbian
communities.

Although the 1972 document proved factually inaccurate in several particulars (the picketing happened before the riot, for example), I was ultimately able to verify its basic account of the Compton's Cafeteria riot and to
situate that event in a history of transgender community formation and po-
liticization that both complemented and contested homonormative gay and
lesbian history. Most important, I was able to connect the location and timing of the riot to social, political, geographical, and historical circumstances
in San Francisco in ways that the Stonewall story had never connected gay

liberation discourse to similar circumstances in New York—thereby opening up new ways to think about the relationship between identity politics and broader material conditions. The 1966 riot at Compton's Cafeteria took place at the intersection of several broad social issues that continue to be of concern today, such as discriminatory policing practices in minority communities, the lack of minority access to appropriate health care, elitist urban land-use policies, the unsettling domestic consequences of foreign wars, and civil rights campaigns that aim to expand individual liberties and social tolerance on matters of sexuality and gender.[13]

Homonormative Disciplinarity

Although the history of the Compton's Cafeteria riot provides a productive point of critique and revision for homonormative accounts of the recent history of sexual identity communities and movements, most knowledge of this event has circulated through works of public history (most notably the 2005 public television documentary *Screaming Queens: The Riot at Compton's Cafeteria*), work by nonacademic writers, and in community-based publications, rather than through professional academic channels.[14] In those few instances in which this history has been examined in peer reviewed journals, the articles have been placed, as this one has been, in sections of the journals set aside for uses other than feature articles. In the one instance where this has not been the case, the article was written by another (nontransgendered) scholar who interviewed me and made use of primary source documents I directed her to, in order to relate the Compton's Cafeteria riot to her own research interest in the sociology of historical memory.[15]

I point this out not as a complaint—it was my own decision to pursue the public history dissemination of my research findings; I actually guest-edited a journal issue that put my own research into the back matter and anonymized my authorship, and I have eagerly collaborated with other scholars who have never failed to accurately and appropriately cite the use of my research in their own projects. My aim, rather, is to call needed attention to the micropolitical practices through which the radical implications of transgender knowledges can become marginalized. Even in contexts such as this special homonormativities issue of *Radical History Review*, which explicitly called for transgender scholarship that could generate "new analytical frameworks for talking about lesbian, gay, bisexual, transgender, and queer history that expand and challenge current models of identity and community formation as well as models of political and cultural resistance," transgender knowledges are far too easily subjugated to what Michel Foucault once called "the hierarchies of erudition."[16]

In my original abstract for this issue, I proposed not only to recount the little-known history of the Compton's Cafeteria riot but also to call attention to the multiple normativizing frames of reference that kept the Compton's story "hidden in plain sight" for so long—the confluence of class, race, and gender considerations, as well as the homonormative gaze that did not construct transgender subjects, actions, embodiments, or intentions as the objects of its desire. I wanted, too, to make methodologically explicit the critical role of embodied difference in the practice of archival research.

As a range of new scholarship on the recent so-called archival turn in the humanities begins to make evident, embodiment—that contingent accomplishment through which the histories of our identities become invested in our corporeal space—not only animates the research query but modulates access to the archive in both its physical and its intellectual arrangement. Discussing how my transsexual embodiment figured into reading a gay and lesbian archive against the grain served the larger purpose of calling critical attention to homonormative constructions of knowledge embedded in the content and organization of the archive itself. My goal was to offer a radical critique not just of historiography but of the political epistemology of historical knowledge production.

Because the tone of what I proposed was deemed "personal," due to how I situated my own research activities as part of the narrative, and because, I suspect, I tend to work outside the academy, I was invited to contribute an essay to either the "Reflections" or "Public History" section of *Radical History Review*, rather than a feature article. I felt some reservations in doing so because my intent had been to do something else. "Reflections" are not as intellectually rigorous as the documented arguments expected in feature articles, and "Public History," as distinguished from what academic historians do, can come off as a form of popularization in which knowledge produced by specialists is transmitted to the consuming masses through less intellectually accomplished intermediaries. The journal's own division of knowledge into "less formal" and "more formal" categories, and the positioning of my work within this two-tiered economy, would replicate the very hierarchies I had set out to critique by containing what I had to say within a structurally less legitimated space.

The most basic act of normativizing disciplinarity at work here is not directly related to the increasingly comfortable fit between gender-normative homosexuality and neoliberal policy. It is rooted in a more fundamental and culturally pervasive disavowal of intrinsically diverse modes of bodily being as the lived ground of all knowing and of all knowledge production. In an epistemological regime structured by the subject-object split, the bodily situatedness of knowing becomes divorced from the status of formally legitimated objective knowledge; experiential knowledge of the material effects of one's own antinormative bodily difference on the production and reception of what one knows consequently becomes delegitimated as merely subjective. This in turn circumscribes the radical potential of that knowledge to critique other knowledge produced from other bodily locations, equally partial and contingent, which have been vested with the prerogatives of a normativity variously figured as white, masculinist, heterosexist, or Eurocentric—as feminism, communities of color, and third world voices have long maintained, and as the disabled, intersexed, and transgendered increasingly contend.

The peculiar excitement of academic humanities work at this moment in time lies, in my estimation, in the potential of interdisciplinary critical work to produce new strategies through which disruptive knowledges can dislodge the privileges of normativity. Breaking "personal voice" away from the taint of "mere" subjective reflection and recuperating embodied knowing as a formally legitimated basis of knowledge production is one such disruptive strategy. Deploying disciplinary distinctions that foreclose this possibility is not. But that is precisely why the opportunity provided by the editors of this volume for my words to occupy these pages under the heading of an "Intervention" was ultimately such a welcome one. In the end, it has enabled the critique I intended to offer all along, albeit not in the form or manner I initially proposed, while opening up the space to push the argument one turn further.

Homonormativity, I conclude, is more than an accommodation to neoliberalism in its macropolitical manifestations. It is also an operation at the micropolitical level, one that aligns gay interests with dominant constructions of knowledge and power that disqualify the very modes of knowing threatening to disrupt the smooth functioning of normative space and that displace modes of embodiment calling into question the basis of authority from which normative voices speak. Because transgender phenomena unsettle the categories on which the normative sexualities depend, their articulation can offer compelling opportunities for contesting the expansion of neoliberalism's purview through homonormative strategies of minority assimilation.

And yet, even well-intentioned antihomonormative critical practices that take aim at neoliberalism can fall short of their goal when they fail to adequately account for the destabilizing, crosscutting differences within sexual categories that transgender issues represent. Such critical practices can function in unintentionally homonormative ways that circumvent and circumscribe, rather than amplify, the radical potential of transgender phenomena to profoundly disturb the normative—even in so seemingly small a thing as where an article gets placed in a journal. Creating a proper space for radical transgender scholarship, in the double sense of scholarship on transgender issues and of work by transgender scholars, should be a vital part of any radically antinormative intellectual and political agenda.

Notes

1   Duggan, *The Twilight of Equality?*, 50.
2   Halberstam, *Female Masculinity*, 9.
3   I posted an earlier version of these observations on the genealogy of homonormative on qstudy-lL@listserv.buffalo.edu, November 7, 2006.
4   Robert Hill, personal communication, October 6, 2005; see also Hill, "A Social History of Heterosexual Transvestism."
5   I have made this argument elsewhere; see Stryker, "The Transgender Issue"; Stryker, "Transgender Studies: Queer Theory's Evil Twin"; and Stryker, "(De)subjugated Knowledges." On Feinberg's use of "transgender," see Feinberg, *Transgender Liberation*, reprinted in Stryker and Whittle, *Transgender Studies Reader*, 205–20. On page 206, Feinberg, after listing a variety of what s/he terms "gender outlaws," that is, "transvestites, transsexuals, drag queens and drag kings, cross-dressers, bull-daggers, stone butches, androgynes, diesel dykes," notes that "we didn't choose these words" and that "they don't fit all of us." Because "it's hard to fight an oppression without a name connoting pride," s/he proposes "transgender" to name "a diverse group of people who define ourselves in many different ways." While acknowledging that this term itself may prove inadequate or short-lived, s/he intends for it to be "a tool to battle bigotry and brutality" and hopes that "it can connect us, that it can capture what is similar about the oppressions that we endure."
6   Ann Ogborn, interview by the author, July 5, 1998, Oakland, CA.
7   Gerard Koskovich, an early member of Queer Nation–San Francisco, recalls "lively critiques regarding the group's awareness and inclusiveness regarding transgender and bisexual issues." He writes: "I recall a telling incident at one of the earliest QN meetings that I attended: A lesbian in her early 30s made comments to the general meeting to the effect that she didn't appreciate gay men wearing drag, an act that she portrayed as an expression of misogyny—in short, she offered an old-school lesbian-feminist reading. This led to a group discussion

of the uses of drag as a critique of gender norms—a discussion that ultimately changed the woman's mind. That early anti-drag moment quickly gave way to Queer Nation celebrating personal styles that transgressed gender norms in various ways—a phenomenon that fit well with the in-your-face politics of representation that drove many QN actions." Personal communication, December 8, 2006.

8   Valentine, "I Went to Bed with My Own Kind Once"; Valentine, "The Categories Themselves."

9   Nietzsche, "On the Use and Abuse of History for Life," in *Untimely Mediations*.

10 D'Emilio, *Sexual Politics, Sexual Communities*; Armstrong, *Forging Gay Identity*; Boyd, *Wide Open Town*; Meeker, *Contacts Desired*; Gallo, *Different Daughters*.

11 Meyerowitz, *How Sex Changed*.

12 Broshears, "History of Christopher Street West—SF," 8.

13 A fuller treatment of this material exceeds the space limitations of this essay, but it can be found elsewhere in Susan Stryker, "At the Crossroads of Turk and Taylor," 2020 (MW).

14 Silverman and Stryker, *Screaming Queens*; Stryker, "The Compton's Cafeteria Riot of 1966," 5, 19; Stryker, "The Riot at Compton's Cafeteria"; Friedman, *Strapped for Cash*, 129–33; Carter, *Stonewall*, 109–10.

15 Members of the Gay and Lesbian Historical Society, "MTF Transgender Activism in San Francisco's Tenderloin"; Armstrong and Crage, "Movements and Memory"; see also Meyerowitz, *How Sex Changed*, 229.

16 Foucault, *Society Must Be Defended*, 7–8.

LESBIAN GENERATIONS
Transsexual . . . Lesbian . . . Feminist

I interpreted, quite literally, perhaps *too* literally, Leila Rupp's kind invitation to "speak informally for about ten minutes" in the roundtable on lesbian generations by putting the emphasis on "informally" and extemporizing some rather haphazardly organized thoughts on what generation of lesbian I considered myself to be. The venue being the Big Berks and the personal, of course, still being political, I assumed in framing my remarks that an ample amount of autobiographical reflection would be, if not original in its methodological implications, then intelligible or at least excusable under the circumstances.

When my turn came to speak, I offered an impromptu performance in which I sought to cite generational, ethnic, national, and class-based competencies of lesbian identity, while simultaneously ironically distancing myself from those very norms through a calculated and strategic cultivation of affect. By which I mean to say: I tried to make people laugh, and I was pleased to have succeeded through a variety of techniques (gesture, expression, phrasing, timing, embodied context) that don't render well on the printed page. You had to be there. What follows is a loose rendition of that performance into text.

I tried to be funny (1) to demonstrate that lesbian feminists can, in fact, have a sense of humor, and (2) because ironic distancing—a self-protective critique from within of something I actually care about being part of—has been a mode of survival for me as the particular sexual and gendered subject that I am. As decades of feminist injunctions to be mindful of intersectionality have taught us, all identities are complicated; none can be articulated in monolithic purity and isolation, nor can the messily lived complexity of identity's intermingled attributes be disarticulated and hierarchically arranged other than by conceptual and narrative operations that are always political and often violent.

While I don't deny that my whiteness, upward economic mobility, level of educational and professional attainment, or coastal cultural mores inform my lesbian identity, these intersections have not been particularly difficult to occupy; they are, after all, forms of privilege. Being transsexual—well, that presented more of a challenge. Being transsexual *and* lesbian, with one identity being no more or less ontologized than the other and no more or less constructed, has been a fraught identitarian intersection indeed. Hence, as Donald O'Conner put it so eloquently in *Singin' in the Rain*, "make 'em laugh." Contemplating other approaches to this conversation just makes my stomach churn.

Taking things too literally, by the way, such as the way I took Leila Rupp's invitation to participate on the lesbian generations' roundtable, is something transsexuals are often accused of doing—literalizing that which is properly metaphorical. For example, I might, when called upon to do so, defend my practices of embodiment or stake my claim to gender authenticity by protesting that Simone de Beauvoir herself said, "One is not born a woman, but rather becomes one," to which a critic would reply, "But she didn't mean it like *that*. Why do you always have to be so *literal*?"

I was born in 1961, which means I'm turning fifty the summer that I'm writing this. I graduated from high school and started college in 1979. The words feminist, lesbian, and transsexual were the labels available to me in my native English at the time when I was doing my formative identity work, and they all stuck. Eventually. Transsexual was the one I consciously wrestled with from the earliest age. I came across the term in a *Dear Abby* advice column published in my hometown newspaper in southwestern Oklahoma in the early 1970s when I was about eleven.

I had always felt transgendered but had never before that moment seen reflected back to me from the world one scrap of evidence that such feelings might map onto an objective reality shared by others, rather than being just a subjective perception of my own. I immediately rushed down to my public library to find out more about this potentially life-changing bit of information but was disappointed to learn, from the textbooks on abnormal psychology that were the only source of information available to me, that transsexuals were profoundly psychopathological people with a deep aversion to homosexuality who mutilated their bodies in order to appear straight.

Damn. I wasn't a transsexual after all, I thought to my little eleven-year-old self, because I was pretty sure I wasn't crazy, and I actually thought homosexuality sounded kind of cool. I have no more insight into the origins of my sexual orientation than into the origins of my gender identification, just an awareness of the lifelong presence and persistence of both. Go figure—you could get a PhD in trying to sort out how such things can be possible and still not have a good answer. But as far back as I can recall, I always thought of myself, to myself, as a girl who liked girls, and who wanted to be liked as a girl by girls who liked girls. That has been the inalterable transhomosexual structure of my desire and bodily sense.

"The Girl from Ipanema" was a big hit on the radio when I was about five, and I remember projecting myself into it as a proto-femme-lesbian fantasy: I was the tall and tan and young and lovely one, who walked just like a samba that swung so cool and swayed so gentle. As Astrud Gilberto rhymed it in slightly mangled syntax, "Each day as she walks to the sea, she looks straight ahead not at he." That was the me I wanted to be: femininely desirable, oblivious to the male gaze, heading toward something powerful and dynamic and as big as an ocean that could engulf and sweep over me like a lover.

The feminist part came later, but it seemed like a no-brainer. After my father died unexpectedly when I was thirteen, my brother and I were raised by our widowed single mother, and it didn't take a rocket scientist to see that "equal pay for equal work" was simply fair or that the government assistance programs we lived on after my mother decided to go to college to become a social worker helped keep our family together. I earned a reputation as a wild-eyed liberal among my high school friends because I supported the Equal Rights Amendment—although raised a boy, I'd been putting myself in the other guy's shoes, so to speak, my whole life and knew that I wouldn't want anybody discriminating against *me* just because of my gender.

I knew "nice" girls who needed abortions and "bad" girls who hated their horrible pimps; I heard unfiltered misogynistic and sexist locker-room talk from guys who took me for one of their own; I knew from firsthand experience the kinds of psychic woundedness from histories of sexual violence that can echo down through the generations of a family. Feminism, once I was exposed to the concept of it during my undergraduate honors seminar in US history (we read and discussed *The Feminine Mystique*), simply made a lot of sense to me as a political framework and fit with my perceptions of what a just world should look like. I came to consciousness as a "second waver."

So, there I was, at age nineteen, a transsexual-lesbian-feminist-wannabe, trying to figure out how to put my life together, with all relevant authorities telling me that the pieces couldn't possibly fit. Gender identity disorder officially entered the *Diagnostic and Statistical Manual* of the American Psychiatric Association in 1980, and for people like me, who were assigned "male" at birth, being attracted to people assigned "female" at birth was a contraindication for diagnosis, and pathologization offered the only access route to the medically controlled techniques of body modification that promised any sense of sustainable embodiment. Janice Raymond's paranoiac *The Transsexual Empire* was published a year earlier (it and the psychiatrist Robert Stoller's *Perversion: The Erotic Form of Hatred* were the only two books on transsexuality I could find in my college library). Raymond specifically attacked as "rapists" people who wanted to become "Sappho by surgery," alleging that they—that is to say, me—were symbolically inserting a male presence into a feminine space where it was unwelcome and, hence, were anathema to feminism and lesbianism.

Raymond's book taught me the valuable lesson that there was more than one kind of feminism. At the very least there was the feminism that held that social structures, gendering practices, government policies, economic disparities, and media representations needed to be changed through political action in order to end gender-based oppression; then there was the feminism that one might want to have vulnerable conversations with (and within) about sexuality and gender, provided there was some mutual respect and reciprocity involved; and then there was the aggressive crazy-talk kind that spewed venom every bit as toxic as that served up by the fundamentalist Right, the kind that would lash out to hurt you if you threatened it. That's the part that still makes my stomach churn, waiting for it to pop up when least expected, the part that makes irony and humor feel safe.

One question roundtable participants were asked to consider was: What makes someone part of "lesbian history"? I feel very much a part of that history in the 1970s and 1980s, although not in a way most people would readily recognize—I was neither a subject nor an object of that history, but rather an *abject* of it, relegated to the negative space that circumscribed and defined its positivity. I was no less generationally marked by that historically contingent experience of lesbian feminism for being excluded from its field of intelligibility. This makes me curious, in turn, about the subjectivities of those women able to appear positively as lesbian feminists who were likewise shaped by a tacit transphobia that, however palpable to me, remained largely invisible to them. Negative affect, it would seem, is a technology that operates on all bodies, centering some and displacing others.

Between the Scylla of a preemptive categorical exclusion and the Charybdis of compulsory psychopathologization, I kept my head down for a decade and deferred gender transitioning. I got through the 1980s with the help of graduate school, Michel Foucault, poststructuralism, and Gayle Rubin, sublimating my various dysphorias into a dissertation on the cultural politics of emergent forms of personal and collective identity, and by knocking around in radical sexuality subcultures in the San Francisco Bay Area. The queer movement that erupted around 1990 felt like what I had been waiting for all along, and I threw myself into it without hesitation. New groups such as the Lesbian Avengers, the post-identity politics of Queer Nation, and the eruption onto the scene of this new term, *transgender*, opened up a vital space of possibility. I felt at last that I had someplace to transition *into*: a place for coming out as a transsexual lesbian feminist.

Some of the lines of research I've pursued as a scholar for the past twenty years, as well as my efforts to help establish transgender studies as a recognized academic field, have been motivated to a significant degree by the lesbian feminist identity politics I lived through, albeit in a queer sort of isolation, during the late 1970s and 1980s—a coda, or perhaps a second act, to the "sex wars" that aim to reframe what can be properly considered feminist positions on embodiment, identity, desire, and gender. Looking forward now to future developments in the fields of gender and women's history and its intersection with transgender studies, there are a few emerging matters coming into focus that merit brief mention before winding these remarks to a close.

Another question roundtable participants were asked to consider was: How do we address the contentious borders between lesbian and transgender identities, between passing women and transmen, between gender identity and sexual identity? It seems both obvious yet necessary to point out that the transgender border question cannot be reduced to one between "passing women" and "transmen." This border has indeed been a hot-button issue for some time now, and has received high-profile scholarly treatment in works like Jack Halberstam's *Female Masculinity*. But there is another border. Trans-women are like Canadians in contemporary US discourse on border surveillance and immigration; we're not on the border that gets most of the attention these days, and yet there is a history there, too, of boundaries marked through wars, of cultural conflict, of tropes of nation and citizenship being deployed, of access barriers thrown up to the restricted country of feminist womanhood—all of which is overripe for rigorous historical appraisal.

I know of only one scholar thus far, Finn Enke at the University of Wisconsin, Madison, who is doing academic work on transgender women and transgender issues in US feminism in the 1970s.[1] There are rich veins of historical material yet to be mined there. Check out the *Alternative Press Index* headings for "transsexual" and "transvestite" and you will find tantalizing leads about transpeople doing political support work for prisoners convicted of sex crimes, participating in gay liberation, joining feminist collectives and establishing women's buildings, organizing rallies against the war in Vietnam, and speaking out about disability in lesbian feminist communities.

There is a new history yet to be written of this recent past, one that upends our received narratives about the 1970s. In Philadelphia, for example, a group called Radical Queens partnered with the separatist Dyke Tactics to push jointly for economic and political transformation. A group of formerly closeted heterosexual male cross-dressers in Washington, DC, came out to support the ERA, arguing that in good conscience they couldn't claim to be "woman identified" if they didn't participate in feminist causes. A dating service in California, the Salmacis Society (named for the typically unheralded female nymph in Greek mythology who fused her body with the demigod Hermaphroditus to become part of a doubly sexed being), promoted "femme-femme" relationships between all sexes and genders.

And there is still much work to do in documenting how transsexual and transgender issues became flashpoints and turning points in the histories of better-known social movements: the ejection of revolutionary street-queen Sylvia Rivera from the Christopher Street Liberation Day commemoration, for example; or Robin Morgan's verbal attack on transsexual lesbian feminist Beth Elliot at the West Coast Lesbian Conference; or Janice Raymond's campaign to have Sandy Stone fired by the Olivia Records women's music collective. Investigating these and similar acts of transgender exclusion from broader movements shines a light on the otherwise invisible operations of the unacknowledged normativities through which social change often moves forward.

Trying to speak intelligibly from a trans-lesbian-feminist sensibility has required developing critiques of dominant forms of womanhood and lesbianism as well as of queerness, critiques that in retrospect look a lot like the emerging critiques of neoliberal homonationalism. To wit: the kind of female homosexual or homonormative male that is increasingly recognized as a legitimate version of the subject-citizen within Eurocentric modernity secures her or his relationship to state and market precisely by not troubling the regulative framework known as *gender*—a biopolitical technique of bodily administration that transgender embodiment can profoundly problematize.

In hindsight, a lot of the trash talk about transfolks since the rise of gay liberation and second wave feminism sounds like a subspecies of modernization discourse. Some (homo)normative, nontransgendered gays, lesbians, and feminists frequently posit themselves (as in recent debates about trans inclusion in the proposed Employment Nondiscrimination Act) as more progressive, more modern, more liberated, more politically advanced, more befitting of rights than those backward trans people who are either sick, bad, or wrong, who need to be saved from themselves, who need to be educated and have their consciousnesses raised by their more enlightened leaders so that they will become fit bearers of rights at some unspecified point in the future—after real women and men, both queer and straight, get theirs.

But a queer, feminist, transgender analysis of contemporary society, one that can expose and articulate from the inside the relations of power that cast aside all things transgender as inconsequential, marginal phenomena can actually function as a potent site from which to launch a radical, antireactionary, future-oriented, countermodern critique of modernity itself. Hopefully, this sense of the critical potential of a queer feminist transgender studies resonates with other, more familiar, discursive maneuvers within feminism.

Writers such as Gayatri Spivak and Chandra Mohanty have helped teach people to see that Western feminism risks repeating the colonizing gesture of "white men saving brown women from brown men" to the extent that it simply puts white womanhood in the geopolitical place of the white man. A new wave of feminist transgender scholarship, such as Afsaneh Najmabadi's meticulous work on the state funding of transsexual surgeries in the Islamic Republic of Iran,[2] highlights the extent to which transsexuals can now be held up as evidence to support contemporary kinds of neocolonial intervention through a structurally identical conceptual operation—namely, Western activists waving the bloody shirt of human rights to save disempowered, queer subjects in distant lands from the backward Islamists who want to transsexualize their bodies to fit them into an oppressive, fundamentalist heteropatriarchy rather than allowing them to become the liberated modern gays they rightfully should be in a free world.

So what is one to make of the fact that in 1979 (during the Iranian Revolution and the hostage crisis at the US Embassy in Tehran, one might note), Janice Raymond published her fantasy of a "transsexual empire" in which "she-male" infiltrators of women's space subvert feminism from within and become, like the "eunuchs" of old (this is her language, not my gloss), guardians of the harem in service to their patriarch masters? Laughter would be an entirely sufficient response, were it not for the pernicious persistence of the "paranoid style" in US politics and cultural life—certain strands of feminism not excepted—and for the seeming effortlessness with which transsexual women can be slotted into a phantasmatic structure that imagines a stealthy enemy at once foreign, internal, and (as is increasingly the case) Orientalized and Islamized.

When transsexual women are not rendered objects of fear (think here of how the guy-in-a-dress-rapist-in-the-women's-room caricature is deployed to defeat antidiscrimination legislation), they're made into objects of fun (think here of every cross-dressing shtick you've ever seen in a so-called comedy). This is really no laughing matter. (See me perform my righteous feminist anger?) It's not just that transphobic violence can kill and that trans women need to take back a night of their own. It's also that, if we take seriously the discursive maneuvers that foist upon transwomen the most outrageous of constructs, and if we collectively hold space for conversation in a manner that allows transwomen to speak of their subjection to those constructs and of their evasions of those constructs, then transwomen will at last be in a position to report on the state-sanctioned violence of coercive gender-normativization in a voice every bit as powerful as the ones Audre Lorde used to talk about Black and Gloria Anzaldúa used to talk about borders.

So: How many transsexual lesbian feminists does it take to change a light bulb? That's *really* not funny—because we're not trying to change light bulbs; we're trying to change the world.

Notes

First published in *Feminist Studies* 39, no. 2 (Summer 2013): 375–83.

1 Subsequently published as Enke, *Finding the Movement.* (MW)
2 Najmabadi, *Professing Selves.*

WHEN MONSTERS SPEAK

III.

MY WORDS TO VICTOR FRANKENSTEIN ABOVE THE VILLAGE OF CHAMOUNIX

Performing Transgender Rage

Introductory Notes

The following work is a textual adaptation of a performance piece originally presented at Rage across the Disciplines, an arts, humanities, and social sciences conference held June 10–12, 1993, at California State University, San Marcos. The interdisciplinary nature of the conference, its theme, and the organizers' call for both performances and academic papers inspired me to be creative in my mode of presenting a topic then much on my mind. As a member of Transgender Nation—a militantly queer, direct-action transsexual advocacy group—I was at the time involved in organizing a disruption and protest at the American Psychiatric Association's 1993 annual meeting in San Francisco. A good deal of the discussion at our planning meetings concerned how to harness the intense emotions emanating from transsexual experience—especially rage—and mobilize them into effective political actions.

I was intrigued by the prospect of critically examining this rage in a more academic setting through an idiosyncratic application of the concept of gender performativity. My idea was to perform, self-consciously, a queer gender rather than simply talk about it, thus embodying and enacting the concept simultaneously under discussion. I wanted the formal structure of the work to express a transgender aesthetic by replicating our abrupt, often jarring transitions between genders—challenging generic classification with the forms of my words just as my transsexuality challenges the conventions of legitimate gender and my performance in the conference room challenged the boundaries of acceptable academic discourse.

During the performance, I stood at the podium wearing genderfuck drag—combat boots, threadbare Levi 501s over a black lace body suit, a shredded Transgender Nation T-shirt with the neck and sleeves cut out, a pink triangle, quartz crystal pendant, grunge metal jewelry, and a six-inch long marlin hook dangling around my neck on a length of heavy stainless-steel chain. I decorated the set by draping my black leather biker jacket over my chair at the panelists' table. The jacket had handcuffs on the left shoulder, rainbow freedom rings on the right-side lacings, and Queer Nation–style stickers reading SEX CHANGE, DYKE, and FUCK YOUR TRANSPHOBIA plastered on the back.

Monologue

The transsexual body is an unnatural body. It is the product of medical science. It is a technological construction. It is flesh torn apart and sewn together again in a shape other than that in which it was born. In these circumstances, I find a deep affinity between myself as a transsexual woman and the monster in Mary Shelley's *Frankenstein*. Like the monster, I am too often perceived as less than fully human due to the means of my embodiment; like the monster's, as well, my exclusion from human community fuels a deep and abiding rage in me that I, like the monster, direct against the conditions in which I must struggle to exist.

I am not the first to link Frankenstein's monster and the transsexual body. Mary Daly makes the connection explicit by discussing transsexuality in "Boundary Violation and the Frankenstein Phenomenon," in which she characterizes transsexuals as the agents of a "necrophilic invasion" of female space (69–72). Janice Raymond, who acknowledges Daly as a formative influence, is less direct when she says that "the problem of transsexuality would best be served by morally mandating it out of existence"; but in this statement she nevertheless echoes Victor Frankenstein's feelings toward the monster: "Begone, vile insect, or rather, stay, that I may trample you to dust. You reproach me with your creation."[1] It is a commonplace of literary criticism to note that Frankenstein's monster is his own dark, romantic double, the alien Other he constructs and upon which he projects all he cannot accept in himself; indeed, Frankenstein calls the monster "my own vampire, my own spirit set loose from the grave."[2] Might I suggest that Daly, Raymond, and others of their ilk similarly construct the transsexual as their own particular golem?[3]

The attribution of monstrosity remains a palpable characteristic of most lesbian and gay representations of transsexuality, displaying in unnerving detail the anxious, fearful underside of the current cultural fascination with transgenderism.[4] Because transsexuality more than any other transgender practice or identity represents the prospect of destabilizing the foundational presupposition of fixed genders upon which a politics of personal identity depends, people who have invested their aspirations for social justice in identitarian movements say things about us out of sheer panic that, if said of other minorities, would see print only in the most hate-riddled, white supremacist, Christian fascist rags.

To quote extensively from one letter to the editor of a popular San Francisco gay/lesbian periodical:

> I consider transsexualism to be a fraud, and the participants in it . . . perverted. The transsexual [claims] he/she needs to change his/her body in order to be his/her "true self." Because this "true self" requires another physical form in which to manifest itself, it must therefore war with nature. One cannot change one's gender. What occurs is a cleverly manipulated exterior: what has been done is mutation. What exists beneath the deformed surface is the same person who was there prior to the deformity. People who break or deform their bodies [act] out the sick farce of a deluded, patriarchal approach to nature, alienated from true being.

Referring by name to one particular person, self-identified as a transsexual lesbian, whom she had heard speak in a public forum at the San Francisco Women's Building, the letter-writer went on to say: "When an estrogenated man with breasts loves a woman, that is not lesbianism, that is mutilated perversion. [This individual] is not a threat to the lesbian community, he is an outrage to us. He is not a lesbian, he is a mutant man, a self-made freak, a deformity, an insult. He deserves a slap in the face. After that, he deserves to have his body and mind made well again."[5]

When such beings as these tell me I war with nature, I find no more reason to mourn my opposition to them—or to the order they claim to represent—than Frankenstein's monster felt in its enmity to the human race. I do not fall from the grace of their company—I roar gleefully away from it like a Harley-straddling, dildo-packing leatherdyke from hell.

The stigmatization fostered by this sort of pejorative labelling is not without consequence. Such words have the power to destroy transsexual lives. On January 5, 1993, a twenty-two-year-old preoperative transsexual woman from Seattle, Filisa Vistima, wrote in her journal, "I wish I was anatomically 'normal' so I could go swimming. . . . But no, I'm a mutant, Frankenstein's monster." Two months later Filisa Vistima committed suicide. What drove her to such despair was the exclusion she experienced in Seattle's queer community, some members of which opposed Filisa's participation because of her transsexuality—even though she identified as and lived as a bisexual woman.

The Lesbian Resource Center where she served as a volunteer conducted a survey of its constituency to determine whether it should stop offering services to male-to-female transsexuals. Filisa did the data entry for tabulating the survey results; she didn't have to imagine how people felt about her kind. The Seattle Bisexual Women's Network announced that if it admitted transsexuals, the SBWN would no longer be a women's organization. "I'm sure," one member said in reference to the inclusion of bisexual transsexual women, "the boys can take care of themselves."

Filisa Vistima was not a boy, and she found it impossible to take care of herself. Even in death she found no support from the community in which she claimed membership. "Why didn't Filisa commit herself for psychiatric care?" asked a columnist in the *Seattle Gay News*. "Why didn't Filisa demand her civil rights?" In this case, not only did the angry villagers hound their monster to the edge of town, they reproached her for being vulnerable to the torches. Did Filisa Vistima commit suicide, or did the queer community of Seattle kill her?[6]

I want to lay claim to the dark power of my monstrous identity without using it as a weapon against others or being wounded by it myself. I will say this as bluntly as I know how: I am a transsexual, and therefore I am a monster. Just as the words "dyke," "fag," "queer," "slut," and "whore" have been reclaimed, respectively, by lesbians and gay men, by anti-assimilationist sexual minorities, by women who pursue erotic pleasure, and by sex industry workers, words like "creature," "monster," and "unnatural" need to be reclaimed by the transgendered. By embracing and accepting them, even piling one on top of another, we may dispel their ability to harm us. A creature, after all, in the dominant tradition of Western European culture, is nothing other than a created being, a made thing. The affront you humans take at being called a "creature" results from the threat the term poses to your status as "lords of creation," beings elevated above mere material existence. As in the case of being called "it," being called a "creature" suggests the lack or loss of a superior personhood.

I find no shame, however, in acknowledging my egalitarian relationship with nonhuman material Being; everything emerges from the same matrix of possibilities. "Monster" is derived from the Latin noun *monstrum*, "divine portent," itself formed on the root of the verb *monere*, "to warn." It came to refer to living things of anomalous shape or structure, or to fabulous creatures like the sphinx who were composed of strikingly incongruous parts, because the ancients considered the appearance of such beings to be a sign of some impending supernatural event. Monsters, like angels, functioned as messengers and heralds of the extraordinary. They served to announce impending revelation, saying, in effect, "Pay attention; something of profound importance is happening."

Hearken unto me, fellow creatures. I who have dwelt in a form unmatched with my desire, I whose flesh has become an assemblage of incongruous anatomical parts, I who achieve the similitude of a natural body only through an unnatural process, I offer you this warning: the Nature you bedevil me with is a lie. Do not trust it to protect you from what I represent, for it is a fabrication that cloaks the groundlessness of the privilege you seek to maintain for yourself at my expense. You are as constructed as me; the same anarchic Womb has birthed us both. I call upon you to investigate your nature as I have been compelled to confront mine. I challenge you to risk abjection and flourish as well as have I. Heed my words, and you may well discover the seams and sutures in yourself.

Criticism

In answer to the question he poses in the title of his recent essay, "What Is a Monster? (According to *Frankenstein*)," Peter Brooks suggests that whatever else a monster might be, it "may also be that which eludes gender definition" (219). Brooks reads Mary Shelley's story of an overreaching scientist and his troublesome creation as an early dissent from the nineteenth-century realist literary tradition, which had not yet attained dominance as a narrative form. He understands Frankenstein to unfold textually through a narrative strategy generated by tension between a visually oriented epistemology, on the one hand, and another approach to knowing the truth of bodies that privileges verbal linguisticality, on the other (199–200). Knowing by seeing and knowing by speaking/hearing are gendered, respectively, as masculine and feminine in the critical framework within which Brooks operates.

Considered in this context, Shelley's text is informed by—and critiques from a woman's point of view—the contemporary reordering of knowledge brought about by the increasingly compelling truth claims of Enlightenment science.[7] The monster problematizes gender partly through its failure as a viable subject in the visual field; though referred to as "he," it thus offers a feminine, and potentially feminist, resistance to definition by a phallicized scopophilia. The monster accomplishes this resistance by mastering language in order to claim a position as a speaking subject and enact verbally the very subjectivity denied it in the specular realm.

Transsexual monstrosity, however, along with its affect, transgender rage, can never claim quite so secure a means of resistance because of the inability of language to represent the transgendered subject's movement over time between stably gendered positions in a linguistic structure. Our situation effectively reverses the one encountered by Frankenstein's monster. Unlike the monster, we often successfully cite the culture's visual norms of gendered embodiment. This citation becomes a subversive resistance when, through a provisional use of language, we verbally declare the unnaturalness of our claim to the subject positions we nevertheless occupy.[8]

The prospect of a monster with a life and will of its own is a principal source of horror for Frankenstein. The scientist has taken up his project with a specific goal in mind—nothing less than the intent to subject nature completely to his power. He finds a means to accomplish his desires through modern science, whose devotees, it seems to him, "have acquired new and almost unlimited powers; they can command the thunders of heaven, mimic the earthquake, and even mock the invisible world with its shadows. . . . More, far more, will I achieve," thought Frankenstein. "I will pioneer a new way, explore unknown powers, and unfold to the world the deepest mysteries of creation."[9] The fruit of his efforts is not, however, what Frankenstein anticipated. The rapture he expected to experience at the awakening of his creature turned immediately to dread. "I saw the dull yellow eyes of the creature open. His jaws opened, and he muttered some inarticulate sounds, while a grin wrinkled his cheeks. He might have spoken, but I did not hear; one hand was stretched out, seemingly to detain me, but I escaped" (56, 57).

The monster escapes, too, and parts company with its maker for a number of years. In the interim, it learns something of its situation in the world, and rather than bless its creator, the monster curses him. The very success of Mary Shelley's scientist in his self-appointed task thus paradoxically proves its futility: rather than demonstrate Frankenstein's power over materiality, the newly enlivened body of the creature attests to its maker's failure to attain the mastery he sought. Frankenstein cannot control the mind and feelings of the monster he makes. It exceeds and refutes his purposes.

My own experience as a transsexual parallels the monster's in this regard. The consciousness shaped by the transsexual body is no more the creation of the science that refigures its flesh than the monster's mind is the creation of Frankenstein. The agenda that produced hormonal and surgical sex reassignment techniques is no less pretentious, and no more noble, than Frankenstein's. Heroic doctors still endeavor to triumph over nature. The scientific discourse that produced sex reassignment techniques is inseparable from the pursuit of immortality through the perfection of the body, the fantasy of total mastery through the transcendence of an absolute limit, and the hubristic desire to create life itself.[10] Its genealogy emerges from a metaphysical quest older than modern science, and its cultural politics are aligned with a deeply conservative attempt to stabilize gendered identity in service of the naturalized heterosexual order.

None of this, however, precludes medically constructed transsexual bodies from being viable sites of subjectivity. Nor does it guarantee the compliance of subjects thus embodied with the agenda that resulted in a transsexual means of embodiment. As we rise up from the operating tables of our rebirth, we transsexuals are something more, and something other, than the creatures our makers intended us to be. Though medical techniques for sex reassignment are capable of crafting bodies that satisfy the visual and morphological criteria that generate naturalness as their effect, engaging with those very techniques produces a subjective experience that belies the naturalistic effect biomedical technology can achieve. Transsexual embodiment, like the embodiment of the monster, places its subject in an unassimilable, antagonistic, queer relationship to a Nature in which it must nevertheless exist.

Frankenstein's monster articulates its unnatural situation within the natural world with far more sophistication in Shelley's novel than might be expected by those familiar only with the version played by Boris Karloff in James Whale's classic films from the 1930s. Film critic Vito Russo suggests that Whale's interpretation of the monster was influenced by the fact that the director was a closeted gay man at the time he made his *Frankenstein* films. The pathos he imparted to his monster derived from the experience of his own hidden sexual identity.[11] Monstrous and unnatural in the eyes of the world but seeking only the love of his own kind and the acceptance of human society, Whale's creature externalizes and renders visible the nightmarish loneliness and alienation that the closet can breed. But this is not the monster who speaks to me so potently of my own situation as an openly transsexual being. I emulate instead Mary Shelley's literary monster, who is quick-witted, agile, strong, and eloquent.

In the novel, the creature flees Frankenstein's laboratory and hides in the solitude of the Alps, where, by stealthy observation of the people it happens to meet, it gradually acquires a knowledge of language, literature, and the conventions of European society. At first it knows little of its own condition. "I had never yet seen a being resembling me, or who claimed any intercourse with me," the monster notes. "What did this mean? Who was I? What was I? Whence did I come? What was my destination? These questions continually recurred, but I was unable to solve them."[12] Then, in the pocket of the jacket it took as it fled the laboratory, the monster finds Victor Frankenstein's journal, and learns the particulars of its creation. "I sickened as I read," the monster says. "Increase of knowledge only discovered to me what a wretched outcast I was" (124, 125).

Upon learning its history and experiencing the rejection of all to whom it reached out for companionship, the creature's life takes a dark turn. "My feelings were those of rage and revenge," the monster declares. "I, like the archfiend, bore a hell within me" (130). It would have been happy to destroy all of Nature, but it settles, finally, on a more expedient plan to murder systematically all those whom Victor Frankenstein loves. Once Frankenstein realizes that his own abandoned creation is responsible for the deaths of those most dear to him, he retreats in remorse to a mountain village above his native Geneva to ponder his complicity in the crimes the monster has committed. While hiking on the glaciers in the shadow of Mont Blanc, above the village of Chamounix, Frankenstein spies a familiar figure approaching him across the ice. Of course, it is the monster who demands an audience with its maker. Frankenstein agrees, and the two retire together to a mountaineer's cabin. There, in a monologue that occupies nearly a quarter of the novel, the monster tells Frankenstein the tale of its creation from its own point of view, explaining to him how it became so enraged.

These are my words to Victor Frankenstein, above the village of Chamounix. Like the monster, I could speak of my earliest memories, and how I became aware of my difference from everyone around me. I can describe how I acquired a monstrous identity by taking on the label "transsexual" to name parts of myself that I could not otherwise explain. I, too, have discovered the journals of the men who made my body, and who have made the bodies of creatures like me since the 1930s. I know in intimate detail the history of this recent medical intervention into the enactment of transgendered subjectivity; science seeks to contain and colonize the radical threat posed by a particular transgender strategy of resistance to the coerciveness of gender: physical alteration of the genitals.[13] I live daily with the consequences of medicine's definition of my identity as an emotional disorder. Through the filter of this official pathologization, the sounds that come out of my mouth can be summarily dismissed as the confused ranting of a diseased mind.

Like the monster, the longer I live in these conditions, the more rage I harbor. Rage colors me as it presses in through the pores of my skin, soaking in until it becomes the blood that courses through my beating heart. It is a rage bred by the necessity of existing in external circumstances that work against my survival. But there is yet another rage within.

Journal (February 18, 1983)

Kim sat between my spread legs, her back to me, her tailbone on the edge of the table. Her left hand gripped my thigh so hard the bruises are still there a week later. Sweating and bellowing, she pushed one last time and the baby finally came. Through my lover's back, against the skin of my own belly, I felt a child move out of another woman's body and into the world. Strangers' hands snatched it away to suction the sticky green meconium from its airways. "It's a girl," somebody said. Paul, I think. Why, just then, did a jumble of dark, unsolicited feelings emerge wordlessly from some quiet back corner of my mind? This moment of miracles was not the time to deal with them. I pushed them back, knowing they were too strong to avoid for long.

After three days, we were all exhausted, slightly disappointed that complications had forced us to go to Kaiser instead of having the birth at home. I wonder what the hospital staff thought of our little tribe swarming all over the delivery room: Stephanie, the midwife; Paul, the baby's father; Kim's sister Gwen; my son Wilson and me; and the two other women who make up our family, Anne and Heather. And of course, Kim and the baby. She named her Denali, after the mountain in Alaska. I don't think the medical folks had a clue as to how we all considered ourselves to be related to each other. When the labor first began, we all took turns shifting between various supporting roles, but as the ordeal progressed, we settled into a more stable pattern. I found myself acting as birth coach. Hour after hour, through dozens of sets of contractions, I focused everything on Kim, helping her stay in control of her emotions as she gave herself over to this inexorable process, holding on to her eyes with mine to keep the pain from throwing her out of her body, breathing every breath with her, being a companion.

I participated, step by increasingly intimate step, in the ritual transformation of consciousness surrounding her daughter's birth. Birth rituals work to prepare the self for a profound opening, an opening as psychic as it is corporeal. Kim's body brought this ritual process to a dramatic resolution for her, culminating in a visceral, cathartic experience. But my body left me hanging. I had gone on a journey up to the point at which my companion had to go on alone, and I needed to finish my trip for myself. To conclude the birth ritual I had participated in, I needed to move something in me as profound as a whole human life.

I floated home from the hospital, filled with a vital energy that wouldn't discharge. I puttered about until I was alone: my ex had come over for Wilson; Kim and Denali were still at the hospital with Paul; Stephanie had gone, and everyone else was out for a much-needed walk. Finally, in the solitude of my home, I burst apart like a wet paper bag and spilled the emotional contents of my life through the hands I cupped like a sieve over my face. For days, as I had accompanied my partner on her journey, I had been progressively opening myself and preparing to let go of whatever was deepest within. Now everything in me flowed out, moving up from inside and out through my throat, my mouth because these things could never pass between the lips of my cunt. I knew the darkness I had glimpsed earlier would reemerge, but I had vast oceans of feeling to experience before that came up again.

Simple joy in the presence of new life came bubbling out first, wave after wave of it. I was so incredibly happy. I was so in love with Kim, had so much admiration for her strength and courage. I felt pride and excitement about the queer family we were building with Wilson, Anne, Heather, Denali, and whatever babies would follow. We've all tasted an exhilarating possibility in communal living and these nurturing, bonded kinships for which we have no adequate names. We joke about pioneering on a reverse frontier: venturing into the heart of civilization itself to reclaim biological reproduction from heterosexism and free it for our own uses. We're fierce; in a world of "traditional family values," we need to be.

Sometimes, though, I still mourn the passing of old, more familiar ways. It wasn't too long ago that my ex and I were married, woman and man. That love had been genuine, and the grief over its loss real. I had always wanted intimacy with women more than intimacy with men, and that wanting had always felt queer to me. She needed it to appear straight. The shape of my flesh was a barrier that estranged me from my desire. Like a body without a mouth, I was starving in the midst of plenty. I would not let myself starve, even if what it took to open myself for a deep connectedness cut off the deepest connections I actually had. So, I abandoned one life and built this new one. The fact that she and I have begun getting along again, after so much strife between us, makes the bitterness of our separation somewhat sweet.

On the day of the birth, this past loss was present even in its partial recovery; held up beside the newfound fullness in my life, it evoked a poignant, hopeful sadness that inundated me.

Frustration and anger soon welled up in abundance. In spite of all I'd accomplished, my identity still felt so tenuous. Every circumstance of life seemed to conspire against me in one vast, composite act of invalidation and erasure. In the body I was born with, I had been invisible as the person I considered myself to be; I had been invisible as a queer while the form of my body made my desires look straight. Now, as a dyke, I am invisible among women; as a transsexual, I am invisible among dykes. As the partner of a new mother, I am often invisible as a transsexual, a woman, and a lesbian. I've lost track of the friends and acquaintances these past nine months who've asked me if I was the father. It shows so dramatically how much they simply don't get what I'm doing with my body. The high price of whatever visible, intelligible, self-representation I have achieved makes the continuing experience of invisibility maddeningly difficult to bear.

The collective assumptions of the naturalized order soon overwhelmed me. Nature exerts such a hegemonic oppression. Suddenly I felt lost and scared, lonely, and confused. How did that little Mormon boy from Oklahoma I used to be grow up to be a transsexual leatherdyke in San Francisco with a Berkeley PhD? Keeping my bearings on such a long and strange trip seemed a ludicrous proposition. Home was so far gone behind me it was gone forever, and there was no place to rest. Battered by heavy emotions, a little dazed, I felt the inner walls that protect me dissolve to leave me vulnerable to all that could harm me. I cried and abandoned myself to abject despair over what gender had done to me.

Everything's fucked up beyond all recognition. This hurts too much to go on. I came as close today as I'll ever come to giving birth—literally. My body can't do that; I can't even bleed without a wound, and yet I claim to be a woman. How? Why have I always felt that way? I'm such a goddamned freak. I can never be a woman like other women, but I could never be a man. Maybe there really is no place for me in all creation. I'm so tired of this ceaseless movement. I do war with nature. I am alienated from Being. I'm a self-mutilated deformity, a pervert, a mutant, trapped in monstrous flesh. God, I never wanted to be trapped again. I've destroyed myself. I'm falling into darkness I am falling apart.

I enter the realm of my dreams. I am underwater, swimming upward It is dark. I see a shimmering light above me. I break through the plane of the water's surface with my lungs bursting. I suck for air—and find only more water.

My lungs are full of water. Inside and out, I am surrounded by it. Why am I not dead if there is no difference between me and what I am in? There is another surface above me and I swim frantically towards it. I see a shimmering light. I break the plane of the water's surface over and over and over again. This water annihilates me. I cannot be, and yet—an excruciating impossibility—I am I will do anything not to be here.

    I will swim forever
    I will die for eternity.
    I will learn to breathe water.
    I will become the water.
    If I cannot change my situation I will change myself.

In this act of magical transformation
I recognize myself again.

I am groundless and boundless movement.
I am a furious flow.
I am one with the darkness and the wet.

And I am enraged.

Here at last is the chaos I held at bay.
Here at last is my strength.

I am not the water—
I am the wave,
and rage
is the force that moves me.

Rage
gives me back my body
as its own fluid medium.

Rage
punches a hole in water
around which I coalesce
to allow the flow to come through me.

Rage
constitutes me in my primal form.
It throws my head back
pulls my lips back over my teeth
opens my throat

and rears me up to howl: and no sound dilutes
the pure quality of my rage.

No sound
exists
in this place without language
my rage is a silent raving

Rage
throws me back at last
into this mundane reality
in this transfigured flesh
that aligns me with the power of my Being.

In birthing my rage,
my rage has rebirthed me.

Theory

A formal disjunction seems particularly appropriate at this moment because the affect I seek to examine critically, what I've termed "transgender rage," emerges from the interstices of discursive practices and at the collapse of generic categories. The rage itself is generated by the subject's situation in a field governed by the unstable but indissoluble relationship between language and materiality, a situation in which language organizes and brings into signification matter that simultaneously eludes definitive representation and demands its own perpetual rearticulation in symbolic terms.

Within this dynamic field, the subject must constantly police the boundary constructed by its own founding in order to maintain the fictions of "inside" and "outside" against a regime of signification/materialization whose intrinsic instability produces the rupture of subjective boundaries as one of its regular features. The affect of rage, as I seek to define it, is located at the margin of subjectivity and the limit of signification. It originates in recognition of the fact that the "outsideness" of a materiality that perpetually violates the foreclosure of subjective space within a symbolic order is also necessarily "inside" the subject as grounds for the materialization of its body and the formation of its bodily ego.

This primary rage becomes specifically transgender rage when the inability to foreclose the subject occurs through a failure to satisfy norms of gendered embodiment. Transgender rage is the subjective experience of being compelled to transgress what Judith Butler has referred to as the highly gendered regulatory schemata that determine the viability of bodies, of being compelled to enter a "domain of abjected bodies, a field of deformation" that in its unlivability encompasses and constitutes the realm of legitimate subjectivity.[14] Transgender rage is a queer fury, an emotional response to conditions in which it becomes imperative to take up, for the sake of one's own continued survival as a subject, a set of practices that precipitates one's exclusion from a naturalized order of existence that seeks to maintain itself as the only possible basis for being a subject.

However, by mobilizing gendered identities and rendering them provisional, open to strategic development and occupation, this rage enables the establishment of subjects in new modes, regulated by different codes of intelligibility. Transgender rage furnishes a means for disidentification with compulsorily assigned subject positions. It makes the transition from one gendered subject position to another possible by using the impossibility of complete subjective foreclosure to organize an outside force as an inside drive, and vice versa. Through the operation of rage, the stigma itself becomes the source of transformative power.[15]

I want to stop and theorize at this particular moment in the text because in the lived moment of being thrown back from a state of abjection in the aftermath of my lover's daughter's birth, I immediately began telling myself a story to explain my experience. I started theorizing, using all the conceptual tools my education had put at my disposal. Other true stories of those events could undoubtedly be told, but upon my return, I knew for a fact what lit the fuse to my rage in the hospital delivery room. It was the nonconsensuality of the baby's gendering. You see, I told myself, wiping snot off my face with a shirt sleeve, bodies are rendered meaningful only through some culturally and historically specific mode of grasping their physicality that transforms the flesh into a useful artifact.

Gendering is the initial step in this transformation, inseparable from the process of forming an identity by means of which we're fitted to a system of exchange in a heterosexual economy. Authority seizes upon specific material qualities of the flesh, particularly the genitals, as outward indication of future reproductive potential, constructs this flesh as a sign, and reads it to enculturate the body. Gender attribution is compulsory; it codes and deploys our bodies in ways that materially affect us, yet we choose neither our marks nor the meanings they carry.[16]

This was the act accomplished between the beginning and the end of that short sentence in the delivery room: "It's a girl." This was the act that recalled all the anguish of my own struggles with gender. But this was also the act that enjoined my complicity in the nonconsensual gendering of another. A gendering violence is the founding condition of human subjectivity; having a gender is the tribal tattoo that makes one's personhood cognizable. I stood for a moment between the pains of two violations, the mark of gender and the unlivability of its absence. Could I say which one was worse? Or could I only say which one I felt could best be survived?

How can finding one's self prostrate and powerless in the presence of the Law of the Father not produce an unutterable rage? What difference does it make if the father in this instance was a pierced, tattooed, purple-haired punk fag anarchist who helped his dyke friend get pregnant? Phallogocentric language, not its particular speaker, is the scalpel that defines our flesh. I defy that Law in my refusal to abide by its original decree of my gender. Though I cannot escape its power, I can move through its medium. Perhaps if I move furiously enough, I can deform it in my passing to leave a trace of my rage. I can embrace it with a vengeance to rename myself, declare my transsexuality, and gain access to the means of my legible reinscription. Though I may not hold the stylus myself, I can move beneath it for my own deep self-sustaining pleasures.

To encounter the transsexual body, to apprehend a transgendered consciousness articulating itself, is to risk a revelation of the constructedness of the natural order. Confronting the implications of this constructedness can summon up all the violation, loss, and separation inflicted by the gendering process that sustains the illusion of naturalness. My transsexual body literalizes this abstract violence. As the bearers of this disquieting news, we transsexuals often suffer for the pain of others, but we do not willingly abide the rage of others directed against us. And we do have something else to say, if you will but listen to the monsters: the possibility of meaningful agency and action exists, even within fields of domination that bring about the universal cultural rape of all flesh. Be forewarned, however, that taking up this task will remake you in the process.

By speaking as a monster in my personal voice, by using the dark, watery images of Romanticism and lapsing occasionally into its brooding cadences and grandiose postures, I employ the same literary techniques Mary Shelley used to elicit sympathy for her scientist's creation. Like that creature, I assert my worth as a monster in spite of the conditions my monstrosity requires me to face and redefine a life worth living. I have asked the Miltonic questions Shelley poses in the epigraph of her novel: "Did I request thee, Maker, from my clay to mould me man? Did I solicit thee from darkness to promote me?"

With one voice, her monster and I answer, "No," without debasing ourselves, for we have done the hard work of constituting ourselves, on our own terms, against the natural order. Though we forego the privilege of naturalness, we are not deterred, for we ally ourselves instead with the chaos and blackness from which Nature itself spills forth.[17]

If this is your path, as it is mine, let me offer whatever solace you may find in this monstrous benediction: May you discover the enlivening power of darkness within yourself. May it nourish your rage. May your rage inform your actions, and your actions transform you, as you struggle to transform your world.

Notes

First published in GLQ: *A Journal of Lesbian and Gay Studies* 1, no. 3 (1994): 237–54. Copyright 1994, Duke University Press. All rights reserved. Reprinted by permission of the copyright holder.

1 Raymond, *Transsexual Empire*, 178; Shelley, *Frankenstein*, 95.

2 Shelley, *Frankenstein*, 74.

3 While this comment is intended as a monster's disdainful dismissal, it nevertheless alludes to a substantial debate on the status of transgender practices and identities in lesbian feminism. H. S. Rubin, in a sociology dissertation in progress at Brandeis University, [H. Rubin, "Transformations"] argues that the pronounced demographic upsurge in the female-to-male transsexual population during the 1970s and 1980s is directly related to the ascendancy within lesbianism of a "cultural feminism" that disparaged and marginalized practices smacking of an unliberated "gender inversion" model of homosexuality—especially the butch-femme roles associated with working-class lesbian bar culture. Cultural feminism thus consolidated a lesbian feminist alliance with heterosexual feminism on a middle-class basis by capitulating to dominant ideologies of gender. The same suppression of transgender aspects of lesbian practice, I would add, simultaneously raised the specter of male-to-female transsexual lesbians as a particular threat to the stability and purity of nontranssexual lesbian-feminist identity. See Echols, *Daring to Be Bad*, for the broader context of this debate; and Raymond, *Transsexual Empire*, for the most vehement example of the antitransgender position.

4 The current meaning of the term *transgender* is a matter of some debate. The word was originally coined as a noun in the 1970s by people who resisted categorization as either transvestites or transsexuals and who used the term to describe their own identity. Unlike transsexuals but like transvestites, transgenders do not seek surgical alteration of their bodies but do habitually wear clothing that represents a gender other than the one to which they were assigned at birth. Unlike transvestites but like transsexuals, however, transgenders do not alter the vestimentary coding of their gender only episodically or primarily for sexual gratifi-

cation; rather, they consistently and publicly express an ongoing commitment to their claimed gender identities through the same visual representational strategies used by others to signify that gender. The logic underlying this terminology reflects the widespread tendency to construe "gender" as the sociocultural manifestation of a material "sex." Thus, while transsexuals express their identities through a physical change of embodiment, transgenders do so through a noncorporeal change in public gender expression that is nevertheless more complex than a simple change of clothes. This essay uses *transgender* in a more recent sense, however, than its original one. That is, I use it here as an umbrella term that refers to all identities or practices that cross over, cut across, move between, or otherwise queer socially constructed sex/gender boundaries. The term includes, but is not limited to, transsexuality, heterosexual transvestism, gay drag, butch lesbianism, and such non-European identities as the Native American berdache or the Indian Hijra. Like *queer*, *transgender* may also be used as a verb or an adjective. In this essay, transsexuality is considered to be a culturally and historically specific transgender practice/identity through which a transgendered subject enters into a relationship with medical, psychotherapeutic, and juridical institutions in order to gain access to certain hormonal and surgical technologies for enacting and embodying itself.

5   Mikuteit, letter, 3–4 (heavily edited for brevity and clarity).

6   The preceding paragraph draws extensively on, and sometimes paraphrases, O'Hartigan, "I Accuse," and Kahler, "Does Filisa Blame Seattle?"

7   See Laqueur, *Making Sex*, 1–7, for a brief discussion of the Enlightenment's effect on constructions of gender. Feminist interpretations of Frankenstein to which Brooks responds include Gilbert and Gubar, "Horror's Twin"; Jacobus, "Is There a Woman in This Text?"; and Homans, "Bearing Demons."

8   Openly transsexual speech similarly subverts the logic behind a remark by Bloom, that "a beautiful 'monster,' or even a passable one, would not have been a monster." Bloom, afterword, 618.

9   Shelley, *Frankenstein*, 47. Subsequent page references are given parenthetically.

10 Billings and Urban, in "The Sociomedical Construction of Transsexualism" (269), document especially well the medical attitude toward transsexual surgery as one of technical mastery of the body. Irvine, in *Disorders of Desire* (259), suggests how transsexuality fits into the development of scientific sexology, though caution is advised in uncritically accepting the interpretation of transsexual experience she presents in this chapter. In spite of some extremely transphobic concluding comments, Meyer, in "I Dream of Jeannie," offers a good account of the medicalization of transgender identities; for a transsexual perspective on the scientific agenda behind sex reassignment techniques. See also Stone, "The 'Empire' Strikes Back," especially the section entitled "All of reality in late capitalist culture lusts to become an image for its own security" (280–304).

11 Russo, *The Celluloid Closet*, 49–50: "Homosexual parallels in *Frankenstein* (1931) and *Bride of Frankenstein* (1935) arose from a vision both films had of the monster as an antisocial figure in the same way that gay people were 'things' that

should not have happened. In both films the homosexuality of director James Whale may have been a force in the vision."

12   Shelley, *Frankenstein*, 116, 130. Subsequent page references are given parenthetically.

13   In the absence of a reliable critical history of transsexuality, it is best to turn to the standard medical accounts themselves. See, especially, Benjamin, *Transsexual Phenomenon*; Green and Money, *Transsexualism and Sex Reassignment*; and Stoller, *Sex and Gender*. For overviews of cross-cultural variation in the institutionalization of sex/gender, see W. Williams, *Spirit and the Flesh*, 252–76; Shapiro, "Transsexualism," 262–68. For accounts of particular institutionalizations of transgender practices that employ surgical alteration of the genitals, see Nanda, *Neither Man nor Woman*; Roscoe, "Priests of the Goddess." Adventurous readers curious about contemporary nontranssexual genital alteration practices may contact E.N.I.G.M.A. (Erotic Neoprimitive International Genital Modification Association), SASE to LaFarge-werks, 2329 N. Leavitt, Chicago, IL 60647.

14   Butler, *Bodies That Matter*, 16.

15   See Butler, "Introduction," 4, and passim, *Bodies That Matter*.

16   A substantial body of scholarship informs these observations: H. Rubin, "Transformations" provides a productive starting point for developing not only a political economy of sex, but of gendered subjectivity; on gender recruitment and attribution, see Kessler and McKenna, *Gender*; on gender as a system of marks that naturalizes sociological groups based on supposedly shared material similarities, I have been influenced by some ideas on race in Guillaumin, "Race and Nature"; and by Wittig, "The Mark of Gender."

17   Although I mean "chaos" here in its general sense, it is interesting to speculate about the potential application of scientific chaos theory to model the emergence of stable structures of gendered identities out of the unstable matrix of material attributes, and on the production of proliferating gender identities from a relatively simple set of gendering procedures.

TRANSGENDER STUDIES
Queer Theory's Evil Twin

If queer theory was born of the union of sexuality studies and feminism, transgender studies can be considered queer theory's evil twin: it has the same parentage but willfully disrupts the privileged family narratives that favor sexual identity labels (like gay, lesbian, bisexual, and heterosexual) over the gender categories (like man and woman) that enable desire to take shape and find its aim.

In the first volume of GLQ, I published my first academic article, "My Words to Victor Frankenstein above the Village of Chamounix: Performing Transgender Rage," an autobiographically inflected performance piece drawn from my experiences of coming out as a transsexual. The article addressed four distinct theoretical moments. The first was Judith Butler's then recent, now paradigmatic, linkage of gender with the notion of trouble. Gender's absence renders sexuality largely incoherent, yet gender refuses to be the stable foundation on which a system of sexuality can be theorized.[1] A critical reappraisal of transsexuality, I felt, promised a timely and significant contribution to the analysis of the intersection of gender and sexuality.

The second moment was the appearance of Sandy Stone's "The 'Empire' Strikes Back: A Posttranssexual Manifesto," which pointedly criticized Janice G. Raymond's paranoiac *Transsexual Empire* and called on transsexual people to articulate new narratives of self that better expressed the authenticity of transgender experience. I considered my article on transgender rage an explicit answer to that call.

The third moment was Leslie Feinberg's little pamphlet, *Transgender Liberation*. Feinberg took a preexisting term, *transgender*, and invested it with new meaning, enabling it to become the name for Stone's theorized post-transsexualism. Feinberg linked the drive to inhabit this newly envisioned space to a broader struggle for social justice. I saw myself as a fellow traveler.

Finally, I perceived a tremendous utility, both political and theoretical, in the new concept of an anti-essentialist, postidentitarian, strategically fluid "queerness." It was through participation in Queer Nation—particularly its San Francisco–based spin-off, Transgender Nation—that I sharpened my theoretical teeth on the practice of transsexuality.

When I came out as transsexual in 1992, I was acutely conscious, both experientially and intellectually, that transsexuals were considered abject creatures in most feminist and gay or lesbian contexts; yet, I considered myself both feminist and lesbian. I saw GLQ as the leading vehicle for advancing the new queer theory, and I saw in queer theory a potential for attacking the antitranssexual moralism so unthinkingly embedded in most progressive analyses of gender and sexuality without resorting to a reactionary, homophobic, and misogynistic counteroffensive.

I sought instead to dissolve and recast the ground that identity genders in the process of staking its tent. By denaturalizing and thus depriviledging nontransgender practices of embodiment and identification, and by simultaneously enacting a new narrative of the wedding of self and flesh, I intended to create new territories, both analytic and material, for a critically refigured transsexual practice. Embracing and identifying with the figure of Frankenstein's monster, claiming the transformative power of a return from abjection, felt like the right way to go.

Looking back a decade later, I see that in having chosen to speak as a famous literary monster, I not only found a potent voice through which to offer an early formulation of transgender theory but also situated myself (again, like Frankenstein's monster) in a drama of familial abandonment, a fantasy of revenge against those who had cast me out, and a yearning for personal redemption. I wanted to help define *queer* as a family to which transsexuals belonged. The queer vision that animated my life, and the lives of so many others in the brief historic moment of the early 1990s, held out the dazzling prospect of a compensatory, utopian reconfiguration of community. It seemed an anti-oedipal, ecstatic leap into a postmodern space of possibility in which the foundational containers of desire could be ruptured to release a raw erotic power that could be harnessed to a radical social agenda. That vision still takes my breath away.

A decade later, with another Bush in the White House and another war in the Persian Gulf, it is painfully apparent that the queer revolution of the early 1990s yielded, at best, only fragile and tenuous forms of liberal progress in certain sectors and did not radically transform society—and as in the broader world, so too in the academy. Queer theory has become an entrenched, though generally progressive, presence in higher education, but it has not realized the (admittedly utopian) potential I (perhaps naively) sensed there for a radical restructuring of our understanding of gender, particularly of minoritized and marginalized manifestations of gender, such as transsexuality. While queer studies remains the most hospitable place to undertake transgender work, all too often queer remains a code word for "gay" or "lesbian," and all too often transgender phenomena are misapprehended through a lens that privileges sexual orientation and sexual identity as the primary means of differing from heteronormativity.

Most disturbingly, *transgender* increasingly functions as the site in which to contain all gender trouble, thereby helping secure both homosexuality and heterosexuality as stable and normative categories of personhood. This has damaging, isolative political corollaries. It is the same developmental logic that transformed an anti-assimilationist *queer* politics into a more palatable LGBT civil rights movement, with T reduced to merely another (easily detached) genre of sexual identity rather than perceived, like race or class, as something that cuts across existing sexualities, revealing in often unexpected ways the means through which all identities achieve their specificities.

The field of transgender studies has taken shape over the past decade in the shadow of queer theory. Sometimes it has claimed its place in the queer family and offered an in-house critique, and sometimes it has angrily spurned its lineage and set out to make a home of its own. Either way, transgender studies is following its own trajectory and has the potential to address emerging problems in the critical study of gender and sexuality, identity, embodiment, and desire in ways that gay, lesbian, and queer studies have not always successfully managed. This seems particularly true of the ways that transgender studies resonates with disability studies and intersex studies, two other critical enterprises that investigate atypical forms of embodiment and subjectivity that do not readily reduce to heteronormativity, yet that largely fall outside the analytic framework of sexual identity that so dominates queer theory.

As globalization becomes an ever more inescapable context in which all our lives transpire, it is increasingly important to be sensitive to the ways that identities invested with the power of Euro-American privilege interact with non-Western identities. If the history and anthropology of gender and sexuality teach us anything, it is that human culture has created many ways of putting together bodies, subjectivities, social roles, and kinship structures—that vast apparatus for producing intelligible personhood that we call "gender." It is appallingly easy to reproduce the power structures of colonialism by subsuming non-Western configurations of personhood into Western constructs of sexuality and gender.

It would be misguided to propose transgender studies as queer theory for the global marketplace—that is, as an intellectual framework that is less inclined to export Western notions of sexual selves, less inclined to expropriate indigenous non-Western configurations of personhood. Transgender studies, too, is marked by its First World point of origin. But the critique it has offered to queer theory is becoming a point of departure for a lively conversation, involving many speakers from many locations, about the mutability and specificity of human lives and loves. There remains in that emerging dialogue a radical queer potential to realize.

Notes

1   Butler, *Bodies That Matter*.

TRANSING THE QUEER (IN)HUMAN

My very first article, "My Words to Victor Frankenstein above the Village of Chamounix," published in *GLQ* twenty years ago, addressed questions of transgender embodiment and affect through the figuration of (in)human monstrosity. I have stayed close ever since to the themes and approaches laid out in that initial work and have noted with interest how current queer critical attention to the nonhuman world of objects, and to the weird potential becomings of vital materialities and matterings, resonate with the concerns I addressed back then.

At the time, my goal was to find some way to make the subaltern speak. Transsexuals such as myself were then still subordinated to a hegemonic interlocking of cis sexist feminist censure and homosexual superiority, psychomedical pathologization, legal proscription, mass media stereotyping, and public ridicule. The only option other than reactively saying "no we're not" to every negative assertion about us was to change the conversation, to inaugurate a new language game. My strategy for attempting that was to align my speaking position with everything by which "they" abjected us. It was to forgo the human, a set of criteria by which I could only fail as an embodied subject.

It was to allow myself to be moved by the centrifugal force pushing me away from the anthropocentric, to turn that expulsive energy into something else through affective labor, and to return it with a disruptive difference. I embraced "darkness" as a condition of interstitiality and unrepresentability beyond the positive registers of light and name and reason, as a state of transformable negativity, as a groundless primordial resource. As I said then, "I feel no shame in acknowledging my egalitarian relationship with nonhuman material being. Everything emerges from the same matrix of possibilities." Speaking as-if Frankenstein's monster—an articulate, surgically constructed (in)human biotechnological entity—felt like a clever, curiously cognizable strategy for speaking as a transsexual, for talking back to hegemonic forces and finding a way around.

I like to put parentheses around the "in" in (in)human because what appeals to me most about monstrosity as I have lived it is its intimate vacillation with human status, the simultaneously there-and-not-there nature of a relationship between the two. (In)human suggests the gravitational tug of the human for bodies proximate to it, as well as the human's magnetic repulsions of things aligned contrary to it. It speaks to the imperiousness of a human standard of value that would measure all things yet finds all things lacking and less-than in comparison to itself; at the same time, it speaks to the resistance of being enfolded into the human's inclusive exclusions, to fleeing the human's embrace. (In)human thus cuts both ways, toward remaking what human has meant and might yet come to be, as well as toward what should be turned away from, abandoned in the name of a better ethics.

Over two decades, I have worked to establish transgender studies as a recognized interdisciplinary academic field by editing journals and anthologies, organizing conferences, making films, conducting historical research, training students, hiring faculty, and building programs. My goal has been to create venues in which trans voices can be in productive dialogue with others in ways that reframe the conditions of life for those who—to critically trans (rather than critically queer) Ruth Gilmore's definition of racism—experience "the state-sanctioned or extralegal production and exploitation of group-differentiated vulnerability to premature death" because of their gender nonnormativity.[1]

This, for me, has been an "other conversation" that becomes possible when monsters speak. I consider working to enable more felicitous conditions of possibility for more powerful acts of transgender speech to be vital work that nevertheless carries many risks: it can bring too much that might better remain wild to the attention of normativizing forces, produce forms of gender intelligibility that foreclose alternatives and constrain freedom, consolidate identities in rigid and hierarchized forms, police discourses through institutionalization, and privilege some speakers over others.

Yet I still believe that advancing transgender studies within the academy is a risk worth taking if we bring our most radical visions of justice with us as we try to create something new, something better than the past has bequeathed us. I see the positive work of building transgender studies as one way to address half of the (in)human problematic: to abolish what "human" historically has meant, and to begin to make it mean otherwise through the inclusion of what it casts out (without, of course, abjecting something else in the process).

At the same time, in the (in)human problematic's other dimension, I am eager to make work with as much distance from the anthropic as possible. This is what I have tried to explore in the other half of my working life, through my involvement with the Somatechnics Research Network. Coined by a group of interdisciplinary critical and cultural studies scholars at Macquarie University in Sydney who were inspired by Nikki Sullivan's brilliant deconstructive work on body modification, *somatechnics* emerged as a shorthand label for a robust ontological account of embodiment as process.[2]

Its conversations draw on Maurice Merleau-Ponty's phenomenology of the body as sedimented habitual practices, as well as on rich Australian traditions of feminist philosophies of the body and critical studies of whiteness, race, and (post)coloniality.[3] Its ethical stance draws much from Jean-François Lyotard's *differend* and Emmanuel Levinas's stranger at the door, while its welcoming of strangeness owes much to queer and crip sensibilities.[4]

As a portmanteau word (soma, body, + technics, tools or techniques), somatechnics seeks to name the mutually constitutive and inextricably enmeshed nature of embodiment and technology, of being(s) and the means or modes of their (or its) becoming. Like Donna Haraway's *natureculture*, somatechnics dispenses with the additive logic of the "and" to signify the nonseparateness of phenomena that are misrepresented as the conjunction of separable parts.[5] It plays alongside the Derridean "always already" of embodiment's technologization as well as alongside Bernard Stiegler's notion of the body's "originary technicity."[6] At the same time, somatechnics provides a name for the "whole intermediary cluster of relations" that Michel Foucault tells us traverses the capillary spaces linking the anatamopolitical and biopolitical poles of biopower, that constitute a nexus of techniques of subjective individualization and techniques of totalizing control of populations.[7] It is the circuitry, and the pulse, through which materiality flexes itself into new arrangements.

Jami Weinstein is right to point out that somatechnics can carry forward a humanist remainder to whatever extent it concerns itself solely with people. But why must our interest in bodies be confined to human bodies alone? Following Giorgio Agamben, we can acknowledge that within the metaphysics of Western biopolitics, the human emerges precisely where bare biological life (zoe) is simultaneously captured by the political order (polis) to potentiate as the good life while also being excluded as mere life, the life shared with animals and other entities in the kingdom of the living.[8]

The threshold of biopolitical viability thus opens in two directions. Somatechnics, as a frame of reference in which body+milieu+means-of-becoming are constantly trading places and trying on each other's clothes, has the capacity to render the human nothing more than a local instantiation of more fundamental processes under special conditions. If transgender looks back to the human with the goal of making it something else, somatechnics faces a posthuman future.

In these repeated trans movements across the cut of (in)human difference, we find a potential for agential intra-action through which something truly new, something queer to what has come before, begins to materialize itself.

Notes

First published in GLQ: *A Journal of Lesbian and Gay Studies* 21, nos. 2–3 (2015): 227–30. Copyright 2015, Duke University Press. All rights reserved. Republished by permission of the copyright holder.

1 Gilmore, *Golden Gulag.*
2 N. Sullivan, "Transmogrification."
3 Merleau-Ponty, *Phenomenology of Perception.*
4 Lyotard, *The Differend*; Levinas, *Humanism of the Other.*
5 Haraway, *The Companion Species Manifesto.*
6 Stiegler, *Technics and Time.*
7 Foucault, *History of Sexuality*, vol. 1.
8 Agamben, *Homo Sacer*, 1–5.

MORE WORDS ABOUT "MY WORDS TO VICTOR FRANKENSTEIN"

This short essay marks the third time I've commented in GLQ on its publication of my 1994 article, "My Words to Victor Frankenstein above the Village of Chamounix," a performative text that riffs on a scene in Mary Shelley's novel, in which the creature talks back to its maker, to stage a transsexual retort to the devaluation of trans lives through attributions of unnaturalness and artificiality. As such, it helps map a particular dimension of queer theory's development over the last twenty-five years.

While it's difficult to assess the importance of one's own work, I can certainly say I'm happy that my Frankenstein article still has a life of its own, a quarter-century after I first let it loose in the world, and that it remains one of the most read works in GLQ's history (currently at number two, after Cathy Cohen's magnificent "Punks, Bulldaggers, and Welfare Queens"). I have a Google alert set for it and take great pleasure in seeing mentions of it pop up in my inbox from time to time, like postcards from the Travelocity gnome that keep me apprised of how and where it moves and of the company it keeps. It's gained a cult following, supplying pull-quotes for innumerable Tumblr and Twitter accounts, and it has contributed to wide-ranging scholarly conversations on embodiment, techno-cultural studies, gothic literature, and science fiction, affect theory, posthumanism, animal studies, radical veganism, philosophy of the body, and the relationship between queer and trans studies, to name but a few of the contexts in which it has circulated.[1]

Although I didn't conceptualize it this way at the time, my Frankenstein article offered an implicit critique of what, in today's lingo, could be called an unstated cisnormative bias in queer theory. As I was writing it, I was reading the pair of articles on the queer politics of gay shame by Judith Butler and Eve Sedgwick that opened the inaugural issue of GLQ and served as a point of departure for a new phase in queer studies' institutionalization; they supplied an unacknowledged background to my own thoughts on the affect of rage.[2]

Shame, as I understood it to be articulated in early queer theory, was predicated on the prior consolidation of a gendered subject and emanated from the subjective perception that one was a "bad" instantiation of something that one recognized and accepted oneself as being. But what if one balked at that gendering interpellation and was thus compelled to confront not bad feelings but the hegemonic materio-discursive practices that produce the meanings of our flesh to render us men or women in the first place? I was not ashamed that in the name of my own psychical life I needed to struggle against the dominant mode of gender's ontologization—I was enraged.

The first opportunity to reflect on "My Words to Victor Frankenstein" came in the tenth anniversary issue of GLQ (2004), to which I contributed an essay called "Transgender Studies: Queer Theory's Evil Twin," which made explicit what previously had been unstated in my earlier work. My own involvement in self-styled radical queer networks in the early 1990s had led me to assume that "queer" was a family to which I belonged as a trans person, and guest-editing "The Transgender Issue" of GLQ (1998) helped confirm me in that belief. But as the new millennium dawned, it felt increasingly necessary to flag the ways that cisnormative queer theory naturalized the binary gender categories of man and woman, as the enabling condition of queer sexuality's intelligibility, and relegated questions about the production of the categories themselves to a marginal status or treated those questions as altogether extraneous to queer theory. Trans studies, I suggested, like queer of color or queer crip critique, offered a different way to imagine how queerness could be constituted by attending to other registers of difference than sexuality.

By the time I revisited the article yet again, in 2015, for GLQ's special double issue "Queer Inhumanisms," the ground of queer theory had moved in directions that made my old article appear more prescient than marginal in its focus on a mode of embodiment excluded from the status of human and thereby deemed less worthy of life.[3] Reflecting a broader shift in the humanities and social sciences, queer theory increasingly linked a biopolitical framework, which analyzed the segmentation of populations and the hierarchizing of its groups, with assemblage theories that helped conceptualize connections across scales of existence from the subatomic to the cosmic, and an ontological perspective that emphasized the intrinsic fluidity and liveliness of materiality.

In this emerging paradigm, questions about the interrelatedness of such categorizations of life as species, race, or sex and of how those categories, materialized in ways that created greater or less capacities for living, came to the foreground. As queer theory turned toward establishing transversal connections between many varieties of life enfleshed in ways that subordinated them to the white heteromasculine able-bodied figure atop Eurocentric modernity's humanist hierarchy of values—Man—it could now look differently on the figure of transsexual monstrosity already nestled within its folds, waiting to be apprehended anew.

Karen Barad's "TransMaterialities: Trans*/Matter/Realities and Queer Political Imaginings," published in the "Queer Inhumanisms" issue of GLQ, articulated the affinities between my old Frankenstein article and the so-called new materialisms far more cogently than I ever have while deftly calling needed attention to the fraught relationship I suggested between processes of transsexuation and racialization. In the original 1994 article, I had written that my "rage colors me." I deliberately played on the polysemic shades of "color" to make space for holding a question that I did not then know how to properly frame, let alone answer, but which I would now pose as follows: To what extent might the affect that emanated from my own enmeshment as a white transgender person in what Alexander Weheliye has since termed "racializing biopolitical assemblages" share some kinship with affects emanating from others who have been differently racialized than I, differently subordinated in the hierarchies of life than I, yet with whom I could strive toward some commons that better sustains all of our differently enfleshed lives?[4]

Katrina Roen was the first scholar to comment on that phrase about transgender rage and color in her 2001 article "Transgender Theory and Embodiment: The Risk of Racial Marginalization" and to note, accurately, of me, "That she is colored by rage is explicit. How she is colored by race is not" (256). The unstated whiteness norm of academic transgender theorizing is something with which I have been deeply complicit, even in my best efforts to do otherwise.

One genealogy of transgender studies traces its root to Sandy Stone's "The 'Empire' Strikes Back: A Posttranssexual Manifesto," modeled, in part, on

Donna Haraway's "Cyborg Manifesto," and written during Stone's years as Haraway's student in the History of Consciousness program at the University of California, Santa Cruz, in the late 1980s and early 1990s. Haraway explicitly acknowledged that her figuration of the cyborg drew on queer of color feminisms; but Stone, crafting her own manifesto in the heady atmosphere where Gloria Anzaldúa published *Borderlands/La Frontera: The New Mestiza* and Chela Sandoval was writing the dissertation that became *Methodology of the Oppressed*, did not make the deeper lineage or broader context of her figuration of the post-transsexual similarly explicit as her mentor had done for the cyborg, and it's taken a generation of scholarship to recover the ancestors and kin of color invisibilized within the post-transsexual strand of thinking that I think of as my home.

In Barad's engagement with my Frankenstein article, which they approach from the vantage point of quantum field theory, they dwell on the theme I dwelled on, of being a becoming that emerges from a nothingness that nevertheless teems with lively potentials. I still think the greatest strength of my article is the way it affectively transforms the experience of being abjected from the human because of one's mode of embodiment into the joyously empowering experience of embodying a new modality of techno-cultural life, predicated on different premises than those that subtend Man. And yet I take to heart Barad's critique of the metaphorics I deployed in the representation of that insight, of being thrown into "darkness," and emerging from the "blackness" from which "Nature itself spills forth."[5]

As Barad notes, however much my language aims at voicing a condition of unrepresentability or interstitiality, however much it strives to communicate a sense of the void as "full and fecund, rich and productive, actively creative and alive," it recapitulates "the underlying metaphysics of colonialist claims such as terrae nullius—the alleged void that the white settler claims to encounter in 'discovering undeveloped lands,' that is, lands allegedly devoid of the marks of 'civilization'—a logic that associates the beginning of space and time, of place and history, with the arrival of the white man."[6]

In other words, I inadvertently perpetuate the racist trope of imagining blackness as the unmarked and unacknowledged condition on which the existence of whiteness depends. Marquis Bey, in a recent article, "The Trans*-ness of Blackness, the Blackness of Trans*-ness," does a much better job than I at expressing my ill-formed intent when he says that blackness and transness "are differently inflected names for an anoriginal lawlessness" that manifests "in the modern world differently as race and gender fugitivity" (275).

I have no idea where "My Words to Victor Frankenstein" will go from here, or what it might have to do with queer theory in the future, or if it and queer theory will go anywhere else at all from here; all things come to an end at some point. But as we celebrate the bicentennial of Mary Shelley's novel and come to an even greater appreciation of how that work has always posed a feminist and implicitly queer, posthuman critique of Eurocentric biopolitical modernity, I'd be delighted for my own words to share in some degree the longevity of the words that inspired them, as they tag along for the ride with that famous literary monster and, hopefully, find new ways to have something to say to whatever present moments yet may come.

Notes

First published in GLQ: *A Journal of Lesbian and Gay Studies* 25, no. 1 (2019): 39–44. Copyright 2019, Duke University Press. All rights reserved. Republished by permission of the copyright holder.

1   See Barad, "TransMaterialities'"; Galofre and Misse, *Politicas trans*; Liberazioni, "Monstri (e) Queer"; N. Sullivan, "Transmogrification"; Weaver, "Monster Trans"; Zigarovich, *The TransGothic in Literature and Culture.*
2   Butler, *Bodies That Matter*; Sedgwick, "Queer Performativity."
3   See Muñoz et al., "Dossier: Theorizing Queer Inhumanisms."
4   Weheliye, *Habeas Viscus.*
5   Stryker, "My Words to Victor Frankenstein," 251.
6   Barad, "TransMaterialities," 417.

CONCLUSION

Interview, McKenzie Wark and Susan Stryker

MCKENZIE WARK (MW): All right, we are recording. I want to go right back and ask you a little bit about your PhD. I'd love to know a little more about that.

SUSAN STRYKER (SS): First, my version of the origin story about you editing a collection of my work: I saw something on Twitter where I was, I'll just say, flattered to see you tweet something like "I really appreciate how Susan Stryker seems to always be on the edge of the conversation, wherever the conversation happens to be at a given moment." I appreciated that you had a historical perspective, being, like me, a trans of a certain age, who could offer some long takes on trans-ness both in and beyond the academy. And I thought: yeah, thank you. I do try to say what I feel needs to be said in the moment, and that of course changes over time.

I tweeted back something like: "I've been thinking about publishing an edited collection of my older writings, if anybody would like to do that." And then you tweeted: "That's a hard yes." I thought, "Oh great, McKenzie's gonna do this, check that off life's big to-do list." I really appreciate you taking the time to work with my words, offering your perspective on them, curating what is, after thirty years, a voluminous stream of occasional writings.

But, yeah, my PhD work. I wrote on history of religion, on early Mormon history. I joke about it and say it was a crypto-queer and trans dissertation. I'm an old enough trans that, back in the early '80s when I started graduate school, the idea of writing a dissertation on the history of sexuality was a radical idea. Trans history was not anything that was legible to the academy at that time. But I was able to write a dissertation on what I thought was an adjacent topic.

A little bit of background. I had trans feelings my whole life, even as a small child. Around five years old, I started paying attention to what Talia Bettcher calls the "WTF?" of trans experience; that is, I started asking questions about how I could be who I was, and what I might need to do to stay alive as me. By the time I was around ten or eleven, I knew the word *transsexual*; I knew about surgery and hormones and name changes. I knew that living your authentic life was an option if you could navigate the process. I wasn't sure how to access that, or if that was exactly what I needed to do.

That knowledge planted in my mind this historical question of whether somebody like me, but who lived before hormones and surgery, might be a thing. Like, what would you do? How would you live? Could you live? Would it be possible for somebody in an early historical moment to feel like I felt if they lived before some of the technical possibilities for changing embodiment existed? Because I certainly had those feelings before I knew about particular ways of being to act on them.

Or was it that even deeper metahistorical questions were at play? About how identification and desire take shape in the first place, so that one comes to want things or to be things in historically specific ways? So, there was always for me a question about what I would call the historicity of identity, about the contingency of oneself in the context within which one becomes a self. And so that question—"haunted" is maybe too melodramatic a word—but certainly that question was present in my thoughts from very early on.

That historicist bent eventually led me to a PhD program in US history, at Berkeley, in 1983. My dissertation was titled *Making Mormonism: A Case Study on the Formation of Marginal Cultural Identities*. The elevator speech version is basically this: In 1825 there's no such thing as a Mormon. The word doesn't exist. Twenty years later, there's a church, a body of scripture, innovative forms of kinship, a social movement, a political movement, an anti-Mormon backlash, a transcontinental migration; there are people making "I-statements" and "we-statements" about being a Mormon and belonging to a Mormon community, referencing an identity that simply didn't exist when most of the people identifying as such were born. There was a tremendous amount of cultural activity that took place around and through the emergence of a new category of personal and collective identity.

Those are exactly the kinds of questions that I was interested in, as a trans person, about trans-ness. I wrote my dissertation on Mormonism to explore those questions. And then, as I started transitioning late in grad school, it became really clear to me that being an out trans lesbian was not exactly the easiest way to get a job as a professor of early national period US history, specializing in the cultural history of religion, focusing specifically on Mormons.

MW: Or anything, really.

SS: Right. One of my other bitter jokes is that most trans women are allowed to have only one job, which is figuring out how to get other people to pay them for being a trans woman. I put aside for many years the idea that I would ever have an academic career, and just got busy trying to figure out how to make money as a trans woman using whatever skills I could muster, through whatever opportunities I could create for myself. I thought, well, okay, I know how to think historically, I can do archival research, I know how to write and talk. I'm just gonna start doing work in trans history, culture, politics, art, whatever, and figure out how to get paid for it. I never published my dissertation, but I gutted its theoretical and methodological apparatus to inform the work that I started doing on trans history in the early '90s. It absolutely shaped how I think.

MW: The first section of your writing that I put together is mostly set in "Trans SanFrisco," in the Bay Area in the early '90s. What is your impression, looking back now, on what that context was like? I'm interested in what was enabling and what was not for a kind of a trans person at that time.

SS: I started at Berkeley in 1983 and finished in '91, although the degree was not awarded until '92. I've quipped that my academic training at Berkeley took place between the time Foucault left (I overlapped with him by a semester) and the time Judith Butler arrived. There was an intellectual conversation happening at Berkeley in the wake of Foucault that was trending in the direction of Butler. Tom Laqueur was writing on the development of the one-sex versus two-sex model of the body.[1] A lot of folks there, grad students as well as faculty, were interested in the history of the body. I lurked on the fringes of the "Med-Heads" reading group, a nexus for a whole generation of scholarship on histories of medicine and science about the body. It was a really rich intellectual environment.

At the same time, I was coming into a still rather under-the-radar involvement in San Francisco's queer, trans, and kink communities. I was definitely exploring that by the mid-'80s. One foot in the ivory tower and the other foot in the dungeons and drag bars—a very precarious position to try to hold! I was thinking and theorizing academically and also learning about some of the things I thought about in a more embodied sense. I was learning a methodology of thinking through the flesh. San Francisco in the '80s was an intense place for doing that, with a very political and edgy radical sexuality underground.

Even though San Francisco in the '80s was already expensive, it was not nearly as expensive as it became later. There was still an underground art scene. There was still a counterculture. The AIDS crisis gave queer politics an urgency. It was just an interesting place to be. And then the '90s: with the Gulf War, with the collapse of the Soviet Union, the rise of the internet, with what Alan Greenspan at the Fed was calling the "irrational exuberance" of the stock market, the heady early days of a new kind of global capitalism, the premillennial fantasies that people were having about the fin de siècle—life felt productively unsettled and full of potential because of the depth of change, as well as full of new challenges. I remember both utopian fantasies and a lot of reasons for continued outrage in the early '90s. I mean, the AIDS crisis was still utterly unchecked; this was before the antiviral cocktails. But it seemed to me personally that I had an opportunity to bring together parts of my life that had been separated, divorced from one another, that could be rearticulated in some better way.

That was certainly my experience in trying to navigate a new way of being trans, in relation to subcultural spaces and the academy and the street. The experiences one might have in dungeons and drag bars, or with the community of people you're having sex with, were not exactly what you would talk about in the classroom. Nor, on a date, would you necessarily talk about poststructuralist gender theory, or Foucault's notion of *counter-conduct*—though dates where you did were especially fun.

There was a collapse of boundaries in the '90s that I still look back on with great fondness. This was the moment when queer theory was coming into the academy, and I was already thinking: queer theory gets us certain ways down the road, but it doesn't deal with trans issues in quite the right way. That's when I started thinking: What might the intellectual project of a trans studies be?

I don't want to be nostalgic and say that when I was young, those were the best days, the golden age. But there was something that I found quite special happening in "my" San Francisco between say, 1990 and 1995, that I did not see happening elsewhere. I certainly saw potentials there that didn't manifest, that did not become what they could have been, but there was a lot else going on that I see as having a profound and lasting impact, a kind of Guattarian "molecular revolution" that rearranged the material conditions of life.[2] That sense of attending to what was at stake, having a sense of what changed, what persisted, what fell by the wayside is one of the things that made me interested in your curation of some of my work focusing on that period. I think you have your own perspective on that period, something to triangulate from, when you pick and choose some of my pieces from that time. You're attuned to some of those things that I was seeing and trying to write about.

MW: We are close contemporaries in cis-birth years, even though I came out so much later. I found that an interesting pair of perspectives to bring, as someone who was raised as a trans woman by millennials, but who is your contemporary in numbers of times we've been 'round the sun.

A thing I want to ask you about those pieces from the '90s has to do with, as you say, having one foot in dungeons and drag bars and one foot in Berkeley. There's a way that the writing as form has to negotiate between those spaces. You could call what you were writing autofiction or autotheory, if one wanted. The dual situations were putting pressure on the form. And so there is this "I" that's present in the texts, but it's not memoir or confession or anything like that. It's a kind of multiply situated prose. I wonder what you were reading that headed you in that direction and how you felt about writing?

SS: If I had to say what was an inspiration, I really think it was Chicana feminisms. It's Gloria Anzaldúa, it's Cherríe Moraga.[3] Something about that phrase "theory in the flesh," it was a light bulb that went off in my head. That's what feminism is about for me, writing and thinking and acting from a position of embodied difference vis-à-vis an oppressive norm—in this case androcentrism. Same with writing from a position of racial minoritization or writing about disability, there's this whole—I don't want to say genre—but a whole cluster of academic fields, or fields of literary production and politics, that revolve around how you take the knowledge generated by how you move your body through the world. Then there's more formally legitimated academic, discursive forms of disciplinary knowledge. Finding a way to toggle between those two ways of knowing just really seemed like the problem to be solved when I was trying to write and think *as* trans, *about* trans.

There were things I was learning in community that felt very intellectually and politically and aesthetically exciting. Ways of being with people in subcultural spaces that, for me, were taking place alongside a more formally legitimated academic kind of knowledge.

I was very self-conscious about trying to write and publish in venues that might not seem like they would go together: queer porn zines like *Taste of Latex*, and in the pages of a then-new queer theory journal called GLQ. I wanted to write about similar kinds of things in each space, in different vernaculars and idioms, tweaked slightly more in one direction than another, depending on the audience. I wanted to say the unsaid things, whatever was usually unsaid in a given space.

I did have an embodied and experiential sense that being trans involved a change of form that could shift one in a different genre or gender—what the historian Leah DeVun has recently called a "shape of sex," or a phenotype, that has a relationship to social categorization—meaning one can change physical shape to change social place.[4] Trying to express that in writing, it just seemed like a no-brainer to use words in ways that put pressure on form, that shift genres or that stitch together things that are usually considered incongruous or anomalous or incompatible or incommensurable with one another. I had a lived sense of being a shambolic assemblage of things, of trying to hold together parts that don't usually go together. That was just very much what it felt like to be me at that time.

MW: Putting pressure on forms is exactly what a transition is. And we're also theory in the flesh—or vice versa. You use the device of journal entries sometimes. I'm curious if that's a device or if you actually kept journals.

SS: I do keep journals. And I do draw from them in my published writing. But I also give myself permission to revise and extrapolate and fictionalize for rhetorical effect.

MW: There's a shift in the work as we move toward the later '90s and into the early part of this century. In the middle part of the book, I put together a series of pieces that have more formal academic venues. You're addressing historians, you're addressing gay and lesbian studies, addressing feminism. There's arguments for where trans-ness fits in relation to each of those discourses that excluded us or made us tokens. How do you feel about the change toward more frequently appearing in that sort of discursive space?

SS: To me it felt like the early '90s was a moment of explosion, and that I was writing in more of what you'd call an autotheoretical or autofictional style as a way of trying to capture it all more or less on the fly. It felt very exploratory, experimental, and open-ended. I was indeed very self-consciously playing with form. I was going through my public and medicalized transition in those years. I'd been active in gender-bent leather subcultures since the '80s, but didn't start publicly transitioning until 1991–92. That's when I was first coming out, dealing with what it means to be perceived as trans, what that means for my working life and daily life, and not just how I occupied subcultural spaces.

By the later '90s, I was in a different position in life. I kind of joke about it and say, 1991 to 1998 was my seven-year unpaid residential fellowship in transgender studies. By around 1998, I was starting to get some grant funding for some of my research. My finances improved a little bit, my working life improved a little bit. I was taking things that I had learned from "livin' *la vida loca*" for a number of years, and then starting to situate that in more academic contexts. How is trans experience related to feminist studies, or how does it relate to queer theory? How does it relate to other fields of inquiry?

I was very "elbows out" about it. I felt I needed to clear a space for conversations about trans-ness (whatever we want to call trans-ness, whatever we say it means or does) that were not co-opted within antithetical power/knowledge formations or other discursive regimes. I'm very ecumenical—like, if you call it trans, great, it's trans, let's have big-tent trans! But then let's have a conversation among us about what's at stake, in dialogue with whomever wants to join in, about what trans-ness is. My goal was to make space for conversations that centered trans experience, trans lives, trans perspectives, trans theories, without subordinating that to some other perspective.

That was the next phase of my working life. I had an opportunity to build on my privileges. Having come from a working-class rural white background, I never had class privilege, but I certainly had racial privilege, and I had the opportunity to access higher education; I took full advantage of that. Higher education put me in a different place in life, regardless of how marginalized my trans-ness made me. Because of that privilege, I felt like I was able, by the end of the '90s, to access a platform for doing a kind of trans work that is still not always available to trans women. I started doing the work of building a trans studies in the academy, and I thought of this as political work, in that it intervened in the power/knowledge formations that directly impacted trans lives and could help foster practices of *knowing differently*.

I undertook that field-building work very deliberately. I don't think the institutionalization of new fields is the be-all end-all. I know the importance in my own life of the kinds of politics and cultural production that takes place outside the academy, but the academy can still be a very well-resourced place, a place that allows academic workers to intervene sociopolitically in the kinds of formally legitimated knowledges that get made, which in turn inform the lives that people live. I do see working to foster a trans studies as creating more life chances for trans people and more trans people in the academy. The academy, and how it puts a stamp on what it deems possible to know, and how best to know, and what counts as better or worse ways of knowing, is an arena for social struggle. I mean, it's not the revolution, to get the full professorship at an Ivy League university, but if you *can* do that, and you can access some of the resources attached to that, and you can use it for the cause, well, more power to you. All hail the "undercommons" of the Enlightenment.[5]

MW: I choose to start the second section with an appreciation you wrote for Gayle Rubin. I love the detail where you meet Gayle in a gay bar.

SS: I was at a fundraiser at the Eagle, a gay leather bar, for the Beat Jesse Helms Flog-A-Thon. She was the DJ and I was like, "Who is that cute butch, just like spinning this cool industrial kinda stuff?" I started chatting her up between sets, and suddenly realized who she was. And it was like, "Oh, hey, you're Gayle Rubin! I've read the 'Traffic in Women' and 'Thinking Sex.' Nice to meet ya!" We became good friends.

Gayle had the same kind of professional life that I did. She had made these incredible contributions to feminist scholarship, gender and sexuality scholarship. But she could not find a job to save her soul. That's how we knew each other in San Francisco. We were in reading groups together, we shared research, we hung out in the same circles, and neither of us was employable right at that moment. You can be doing important intellectual work, and that just doesn't translate into having an academic job.

MW: It's so often that's where the interesting stuff comes from. Someone has an intellectual practice that they need to live, rather than from the seminar, but it's good to be able to have access to the academy and create access. It's a general question I wanted to ask actually. The specific bit of it is: Did we lose the thread of what was there to be learned from BDSM worlds in things like trans studies? Or stated more generally: Did we lose things from the kind of more, kind of open, avant-garde bohemian worlds that many of us came up through?

SS: You know, that's kind of what I feel. I feel like by around '95–96 there was this new word—well to me, *transgender* was already an old word. It first appears around 1965 as far as anybody can tell, but it really begins to take off as a popular term in '92–93. It was seen as something that replaced *trans-*

sexual. It was initially something that meant something much more like *genderqueer* or *nonbinary* when it was popularized in the early '90s. It was a thing of expansive possibilities, not constrained by medicalized psychotherapeutic gatekeeping.

As the term *transgender* took deeper root, it began to index a shift toward, or co-optation by, a neoliberal politics of minority identity and diversity. It came to be seen as something that was highly assimilable, just another candy-colored rainbow flavor. It came to be seen as depoliticized. It became a concept that was useful for the biopolitical management of the population, an identity category that could be expanded or contracted based on some exterior political rationale rather than a radical sociocultural formation for blowing shit up. Which is what it felt like to be in the early '90s. So yeah, I do think something was lost in that transition.

I have not been one of these trans people of late who will say: "Oh, we have to use the word transsexual, not transgender, because that's how we acknowledge our sexuality and avoid depoliticizing trans-ness and evacuating it of all danger." For me, transgender in the '90s was an intensely politicized and sexualized erotic space. Not necessarily in a way that was eroticized or sexualized from the outside in an oppressive way. Just a sexy AF space to be in. It felt alive and vital; cruisy and flirty and playful, with lots of hookups and clusterfucks. It felt like throwing off the traces of the culture that you had inherited and inventing something new and feeling the release of a lot of libidinal energy. And that felt great. I do think that sense has been lost. I think some of it has been lost, honestly, because most people don't live in tightly knit urban communities of self-styled radical exploratory, bohemian, people who want to touch, taste, lick, smell, and poke, or get poked by other people in as many ways as possible. I think it's harder to find your way to those places and work your way into them. I think there are fewer such communal and collective spaces, because internet-based sex is so channelized and privatized.

There's a lot more people who now identify as trans now than in the '90s, and they all bring their own sense of what trans-ness means to them to that identity label, derived from the context in which they've come up and where their sense of self has been shaped. There's been a lot of mainstreaming of trans-ness, a lot of capture.

Of course, there's also still a lot of repression. We in the US live in a country where reactionary political forces are actually making it a thought crime to talk about trans-ness and a felony to provide trans health care to the young. After a period of relatively expansive increases in trans civil rights, it's becoming possible again to exclude more and more trans people from more and more walks of public life. Increased trans visibility in recent decades has led to increased antitrans violence, disproportionately directed at trans women of color. When you live in such a world, do you have as much time for the kind of radical, experimental, drug-fueled, party-oriented, late-night subcultural exploration of ways of being different that I can easily romanticize about the early 90s? Maybe "kids today," besides having come up as trans in very different circumstance, are needing to pay attention to survival in a different kind of way.

It feels very sobering right now, the political environment not just in the US, but globally, with the rise of authoritarian, ethno-nationalist, neofascist movements, with the war in Ukraine, with the environmental situation we live in. It's all pretty dire. I would hope that out of trans experience, analysis, and life we can find resources for living there that we can not only cultivate among ourselves, for ourselves—but that are shareable with other people. I hope there can be a revitalized sense of radical trans cultural production and intervention. Back in the '80s in San Francisco, we talked about *culture jamming*.⁶ I'd love to see a little more culture jamming and hacking of systems of oppression that can be informed by trans experience. I hope that's coming, that it's happening. I'll do my part—

MW: I hadn't intended we have this conversation on the "day of trans visibility," but given that we are: there is this argument that visibility turned out to be not only a two-edged sword, but maybe a bad thing, particularly for trans people of color. And I wonder if you had thoughts on that.

SS: I think visibility is a place to struggle. I always think about that dichotomous form of argument: "Topic x: good or bad?" Well, topic x is just a place where a struggle is happening. It's a terrain, not a side. And so, yes, at one level: transvisibility is good. Positive representation in mass media is good; it's how trans people know that trans people exist, and see validation and possibilities for themselves. On the other hand, if that visibility just puts a target on your face, or on your sister's face, it's bad. It really has everything to do, I think, with the social positionality of what is being made visible and the intentions enacted by the people who see something.

I gave a talk recently that drew a considerable amount of transphobic feminist attention. I was giving a keynote at a lesbian studies conference whose theme was "solidarity"; but a lot of so-called TERF-y, gender critical, transphobic feminist stuff got pointed at me on social media. The organizers and I were getting harassing phone calls and emails and social media postings and all that. In such situations, it feels like I don't want to make any noise; it's like being in a zombie movie, where any bump, any noise, and they'll know right where to go and get you. So, you want to be imperceptible, or you want to talk just to the people you want to be with, without drawing anybody else's attention.

Looking ahead, I think that strategy of imperceptibility, or of strategic visibility, is going to become increasingly important. When the world pays attention to trans right now, it's usually not a good thing. So how do we become imperceptible to hostile forces, while continuing to live our lives and finding each other? That to me feels like a really important question.

MW: Since you mentioned zombies, I get to segue to one of your most famous pieces of writing, "My Words to Victor Frankenstein." In the third part of our book, I've put together several reflections on its reverberations that you've written since it came out. It's kind of like this rhythm. I wanted to ask you in 2022 how you're thinking about that text.

SS: Who knew it was gonna become that thing that it became? Not me. I thought it was a one-off, and it almost didn't get published. And now it's an inveterate global traveler. I've put a Google alert on it, and news of it shows up from time to time in my inbox. "Oh, look, a radical vegan collective in Northern Italy wants to translate it because they're seeing in it this interspecies posthuman veganesque ethos at work." "Oh, look, a Scandinavian glitter punk band has set it to music, and they're screaming it at their audience in some basement club in Stockholm." The work gets out there and circulates in ways I never would have imagined when I wrote it.

It sometimes feels like I'm like one of those old school, one-hit wonders, who's doing the musical variety showcase on a PBS pledge drive: "Here's Susan Stryker performing her classic hit from 1994, 'My Words to Victor Frankenstein,' let's give the little lady a big round of applause!" But it's kind of interesting to see what now feels dated, as well as what still feels prescient in that work. And to reflect on the fact that it is still something that gets cited a lot.

Duke University Press recently sent me a new book by Nicole Erin Morse, *Selfie Aesthetics*; they use my Frankenstein piece as a way of framing their questions about the aesthetics of trans self-representation in digital media.[7] Who knew that would be a use that somebody would make of that article in 1994?

The development that has surprised me the most, though, is the way it's being increasingly put in conversation with black feminisms, particularly around the question of a primordial, prediscursive, outside of representation, cosmological sense of nonbiological generativity. What Zakiyyah Iman Jackson has called "theorizing in a void."[8] Or what Hortense Spillers is writing about.[9] This sense of a generative or insurgent ground that is the wellspring of everything. I felt like in my "Frankenstein" piece, I was following what trans experience was teaching me about feeling thrown outside of human community. And about the kind of affective work that's necessary to take that sense of abjection and make it something transformative that refigures not just you yourself but the world you're in, something that moves toward life by refusing the terms that subordinate you, that threaten to kill you, whether that's gender or something else.

When you refuse an ontological framework that excludes the possibility of your existence and tries to erase you so the framework will be true, what does that refusal then throw you into? To me, that space of refusal and possibility felt like the void of interstellar space, or the cosmological spacetime before the big bang or something.

That space felt like it manifested itself to me, held me within itself as a possibility. And told me that a profound difference was possible from the existing order of things, that the social systems that rank and hierarchize and order life, that diminish some life and elevate others—that there's nothing ontologically given about that. It's something that people make up and do. There are other ways of being.

I felt like I got that from my own white trans experience, but I see similar ideas coming out of black feminist traditions. And I've been really interested in how a new generation of scholarship is putting gender-trans-ness and the "trans-ness of blackness" into conversation. Certain passages in my old "Frankenstein" piece are functioning as switch-points that allow conversations that have taken place in two different locations to start being more in dialogue. That's the thing that has surprised and thrilled me the most about a piece I wrote as a one-off, almost thirty years ago.

MW: Starting in the '90s, your writing is taking trans-ness out of the hands of doctors and psychiatrists. You're finding all of these different languages to rewrite it. There's political language, obviously, cultural language, aesthetic language, language of affect—it's famously about rage. There's also a spiritual language here that emerges from time to time. And can we say a little bit about that?

SS: It goes back maybe to the dissertation work, but I have always sensed these affinities about how, without sharing the beliefs of the people that I wrote my dissertation on, I was impressed and moved and informed and inspired by the sense in early Mormon history of a transformative potential for being-in-the-world, available to people through so-called religious experience, or ecstatic experience. That those experiences can be a way of *re-worlding*.

It's the same thing I like in science fiction, in speculative fiction, that sense of feeling the freedom to really imagine how things can be otherwise. I like to pay attention to the affective dimensions that link one's own experience, not just to other people, but to the nonhuman and more-than-human cosmos that we live in. That same sense that I have seen expressed in a religious or spiritual language, I feel is also part of trans experience.

We live in the late Anthropocene. The Eurocentric world order that has emerged out of the legacies of colonialism and racial chattel slavery, the epistemology of scientific modernity that is part of the control and command structure of a global capitalist economy, is a particular, historically contingent way of being that is deadly for ourselves and the planet. We have to find our way out of it. The modernist framework contains a secular/spiritual dichotomy that deadens us.

If you're really paying attention to how feeling works, to how ontology works, you have to pay attention to what gets called, for lack of a better word, the spiritual. It's part of recognizing the connections between those of us who are trying to worm our way out of the belly of the beast of Eurocentric modernity toward things that were known in premodern times, things that are part of non-Western cultures, things that are part of indigenous worldviews, things that are part of a speculative and experimental orientation toward the future.

Attending to what gets called the spiritual is part of the political work we need to be doing, to actually be reworlding. I think at an even deeper level, that to phrase things that way implies a sense of hopefulness for the future. This is the future that we're going to build. But I want to be really mindful of the fact that we might not make it as a species or as . . . well, we might not make it much longer as a species, let's just leave it at that.

And there's the question of death. I mean, we all die individually. But are we also going to die collectively, in the not-too-distant future? It's a real question. Dealing with that question of how you confront death, and make meaning in life, is really important. Trans people are often associated with death. Death sticks to us in these *necropolitical* ways—to some of us more than others.[10]

I think a lot of transphobia is rooted in the sense that trans is somehow a destruction of life. That trans-ness can involve physically sterilizing reproductive capacities, depending on what genital modification you might pursue. It could certainly be connected with a refusal of biological reproductivity through your affectional choices, even if you are a biologically reproductive trans person. Acknowledging the proximity of trans-ness and death can be a source of power, not to be disavowed—it can be a form of transcultural production, and knowledge-formation. We confront what it means to make meaning in life, without denying the reality of death. That's a body of experience-based knowledge that is useful to other people as well as to ourselves. Can we think about trans people as having a special capacity or ceremonial function, to serve as death doulas for our culture, ritualizing and celebrating the inevitability of transitions?

MW: Oh, yeah. I totally feel you on that.

SS: I use psychedelics, I'm pretty open about that. There was something that came to me in an experience once, where I saw this banner in my mind's eye that said: "The meaning of life is to experience joy as we move toward death." I came back from that trip, and I thought: that's a pretty good one sentence philosophy. I'm gonna stick by that one. Thank you, chemical teacher.

Notes

1   Laqueur, *Making Sex.*
2   Guattari, *Molecular Revolution.*
3   Anzaldúa, *Borderlands/La Frontera*; Moraga, *Native Country of the Heart.*
4   DeVun, *The Shape of Sex.*
5   Moten and Harney, *The Undercommons.*
6   DeLaure and Fink, *Culture Jamming.*
7   Morse, *Selfie Aesthetics.*
8   Jackson, "Theorizing in a Void."
9   Spillers, "Mama's Baby, Papa's Maybe."
10 Mbembe, *Necropolitics.*

Acker, Kathy. *Bodies of Work: Essays*. London: Serpent's Tail, 1996.

Agamben, Giorgio. *Homo Sacer: Sovereign Power and Bare Life*. Stanford, CA: Stanford University Press, 1998.

Ames, Jonathan, ed. *Metamorphosis: An Anthology of Transsexual Memoirs*. New York: Vintage, 1999.

Anzaldúa, Gloria. *Borderlands/La Frontera: The New Mestiza*. San Francisco: Aunt Lute, 1987.

Armstrong, Elizabeth. *Forging Gay Identity: Organizing Sexuality in San Francisco, 1950–1994*. Chicago: University of Chicago Press, 2002.

Armstrong, Elizabeth, and Suzanna Crage. "Movements and Memory: The Making of the Stonewall Myth." *American Sociological Review* 71 (2006): 724–51.

Awkward-Rich, Cameron. *The Terrible We: Thinking with Trans Maladjustment*. Durham, NC: Duke University Press, 2022.

Bachelard, Gaston. *The Poetics of Space*. Translated by Maria Jolas. 1958. Boston: Beacon Press, 1994.

Baer, Hannah. *Trans Girl Suicide Museum*. Los Angeles: Hesse Press, 2019.

Barad, Karen. "TransMaterialities: Trans*/Matter/Realities and Queer Political Imaginings." *GLQ: A Journal of Lesbian and Gay Studies* 21, nos. 2–3 (2015): 387–422.

Bell, Shannon. "Fast Feminism." *Journal of Contemporary Thought* 14 (Winter 2001): 93–112.

Benjamin, Harry. *The Transsexual Phenomenon*. New York: Julian, 1966.

Bergson, Henri. *Matter and Memory*. New York: Zone Books, 1990.

Bettcher, Talia et al., eds. "Trans/Feminisms." Special issue, *Sinister Wisdom* (Spring 2023).

Bey, Marquis. *Black Trans Feminism*. Durham, NC: Duke University Press, 2022.

Bey, Marquis. "The Trans*-ness of Blackness, the Blackness of Trans*-ness." *TSQ: Transgender Studies Quarterly* 4, no. 2 (2017): 275–95.

Billings, Dwight B., and Thomas Urban. "The Sociomedical Construction of Transsexualism: An Interpretation and Critique." *Social Problems* 29 (1981): 266–82.

Blackwood, Evelyn, and Saskia Wieringa, eds. *Female Desires: Same Sex Relations and Transgender Practices across Cultures*. New York: Columbia University Press, 1999.

Bloom, Harold. Afterword to *Frankenstein, or The Modern Prometheus*, by Mary Shelley. New York: Signet, 1965. Originally published as "Frankenstein, or The New Prometheus," *Partisan Review* 32 (1965): 611–18.

Bombardier, Cooper Lee. *Pass with Care: Memoirs*. New York: Dottir Press, 2020.

Boyd, Nan Alamilla. *Wide Open Town: A History of Queer San Francisco to 1965.* Berkeley: University of California Press, 2003.

Brooks, Peter. "What Is a Monster? (According to *Frankenstein*)." In Peter Brooks, *Body Work: Objects of Desire in Modern Narrative* 199–220. Cambridge, MA: Harvard University Press, 1993.

Broshears, Raymond. "History of Christopher Street West—SF." *Gay Pride: The Official Voice of the Christopher Street West Parade '72 Committee of San Francisco California*, June 25, 1972.

Burgin, Victor, James Donald, and Cora Kaplan, eds. *Formations of Fantasy.* London: Methuen, 1986.

Butler, Judith. *Bodies That Matter: On the Discursive Limits of "Sex."* New York: Routledge, 1993.

Butler, Judith. "Contingent Foundations: Feminism and the Question of 'Postmodernism.'" In *Feminists Theorize the Political*, edited by Judith Butler and Joan W. Scott, 3–21. New York: Routledge, 1992.

Butler, Judith. "Critically Queer." GLQ: *A Journal of Lesbian and Gay Studies* 1, no. 1 (1993): 17–32.

Butler, Judith. "Decking Out: Performing Identities." In *Inside/Out: Lesbian Theories, Gay Theories*, edited by Diana Fuss. London: Routledge, 1991.

Cache, Bernard. *Earth Moves: The Furnishing of Territories.* Cambridge, MA: MIT Press, 1995.

Califia, Patrick. *Macho Sluts.* Vancouver: Arsenal Pulp Press, 2009.

Califia, Patrick. "San Francisco: Revisiting the City of Desire." In *Queers in Space: Communities, Public Spaces, and Sites of Resistance*, edited by Anne-Marie Bouthilette, Yolanda Retter, and Gorden Brent Ingram, 177–96. Seattle: Bay Press, 1997.

Cameron, Loren. *Body Alchemy.* San Francisco: Cleis Press, 1995.

cárdenas, micha. *Poetic Operations: Trans of Color Art in Digital Media.* Durham, NC: Duke University Press, 2022.

Carlisle, Madeleine. "Anti-trans Violence and Rhetoric Reached Record Highs across America in 2021." *Time Magazine*, December 30, 2021.

Carter, David. *Stonewall: The Riots That Sparked the Gay Revolution.* New York: St. Martin's, 2004.

Chen, Jian Neo. *Trans Exploits: Trans of Color Culture and Technologies in Movement.* Durham, NC: Duke University Press, 2019.

Cohen, Cathy J. "Punks, Bulldaggers, and Welfare Queens: The Radical Potential of Queer Politics?" GLQ: *A Journal of Lesbian and Gay Studies* 3, no. 4 (1997): 437–65.

Cugini, Eli. "The Troubled Golden Age of Trans Literature." *Xtra*, September 15, 2021. https://xtramagazine.com/culture/trans-literature-troubled-golden-age-208560.

Daly, Mary. "Boundary Violation and the Frankenstein Phenomenon." In Mary Daly, *Gyn/Ecology: The Metaethics of Radical Feminism.* Boston: Beacon, 1978.

Davis, Whitney. "History and the Laboratory of Sexuality." Paper presented at Foucault at Berkeley: Twenty Years Later symposium, Townsend Center for the Humanities, Berkeley, CA, October 16, 2004.

DeLaure, Marilyn, and Moritz Fink, eds. *Culture Jamming: Activism and the Art of Cultural Resistance*. New York: NYU Press, 2017.

Deleuze, Gilles. "Coldness and Cruelty." In *Masochism: Coldness and Cruelty and Venus in Furs*, edited by Gilles Deleuze, Leopold von Sacher-Masoch, and Jean McNeill, 9–123. Cambridge, MA: Zone.

Deleuze, Gilles, and Félix Guattari. *Anti-Oedipus: Capitalism and Schizophrenia*. London: Penguin, 2016.

D'Emilio, John. *Sexual Politics, Sexual Communities: The Making of a Homosexual Minority in the United States, 1940–1970*. Chicago: University of Chicago Press, 1983.

DeVun, Leah. *The Shape of Sex: Nonbinary Gender from Genesis to the Renaissance*. New York: Columbia University Press, 2021.

Dinshaw, Carolyn. "A Kiss Is Just a Kiss: Heterosexuality and Its Consolations in Sir Gawain and the Green Knight." *Diacritics* 24, nos. 2/3 (1994): 204–26.

Dolphijn, Rick, and Iris van der Tuin. *New Materialism: Interviews and Cartographies*. London: Open Humanities Press, 2012.

Duggan, Lisa. *The Twilight of Equality? Neoliberalism, Cultural Politics, and the Attack on Democracy*. Boston: Beacon, 2003.

Echols, Alice. *Daring to Be Bad: Radical Feminism in America, 1967–1975*. Minneapolis: University of Minnesota Press, 1989.

Enke, Finn. *Finding the Movement: Sexuality, Contested Space, and Feminist Activism*. Durham, NC: Duke University Press, 2007.

Feinberg, Leslie. *Transgender Liberation: A Movement Whose Time Has Come*. New York: World View Forum, 1992.

Feinberg, Leslie. *Transgender Warriors*. Boston: Beacon, 1997.

Fitzpatrick, Cat. *The Call Out*. New York: Seven Stories Press, 2022.

Fleishmann, T. *Time Is the Thing a Body Moves Through*. Minneapolis: Coffeehouse Press, 2019.

Foucault, Michel. *History of Sexuality*. Vol. 1, *Introduction*. New York: Vintage, 1978.

Foucault, Michel. "Sexual Choice, Sexual Act: An Interview with Michel Foucault." *Salmagundi* 58/59 (1982): 10–24.

Foucault, Michel. *Society Must Be Defended: Lectures at the Collège de France, 1975–1976*. Translated by David Macey. New York: Picador, 2003.

Fournier, Lauren. *Autotheory as Feminist Practice in Art, Writing, and Criticism*. Cambridge, MA: MIT Press, 2021.

Freud, Sigmund. "'A Child Is Being Beaten': A Contribution to the Study of the Origin of Sexual Perversions" (1919). In *Standard Edition of the Complete Psychological Works of Sigmund Freud*, edited by James Strachey, 17:175–204. New York: W. W. Norton, 2000.

Friedman, Mack. *Strapped for Cash: A History of American Hustler Culture*. Los Angeles: Alyson, 2003.

Galarte, Francisco J. *Brown Trans Figurations: Rethinking Race, Gender, and Sexuality in Chicanx/Latinx Studies*. Austin: University of Texas Press, 2021.

Gallo, Marcia. *Different Daughters: A History of the Daughters of Bilitis and the Rise of the Lesbian Rights Movement*. New York: Carroll and Graf, 2006.

Galofre, Pol, and Miquel Misse, eds. 2015. *Politicas trans: Una antología de textos desde los estudios trans norteamericanos*. Barcelona: Editorial Egales.

Gamson, Joshua. "Must Identity Movements Self-Destruct? A Queer Dilemma." *Social Problems* 42, no. 3 (1995): 390–406.

Gasparini, Philippe. *Autofiction: Une aventure du language*. Paris: Le seuil, 2015.

Gilbert, Sandra, and Susan Gubar. "Horror's Twin: Mary Shelley's Monstrous Eve." In *The Madwoman in the Attic: The Woman Writer and the Nineteenth-Century Imagination*, 213–47. New Haven, CT: Yale University Press, 1979.

Gillis, Stacy, Gillian Howie, and Rebecca Munford, eds. *Third Wave Feminism: A Critical Exploration*. London: Palgrave, 2007.

Gill-Peterson, Jules. *Histories of the Transgender Child*. Minneapolis: University of Minnesota Press, 2018.

Gill-Peterson, Jules. *A Short History of Trans Misogyny*. New York: Verso Books, 2023.

Gilmore, Ruth. *Golden Gulag: Prisons, Surplus, Crisis, and Opposition in Globalizing California*. Berkeley: University of California Press, 2007.

Gleeson, Jules Joanne. "How Do Gender Transitions Happen?" *Boston Review*, June 4, 2021. https://www.bostonreview.net/articles/how-do-gender-transitions-happen/.

Gordon, Avery. *Ghostly Matters: Haunting and the Sociological Imagination*. Minneapolis: University of Minnesota Press, 1997.

Gossett, Che, and Eva Hayward. "Trans in a Time of HIV/AIDS." *TSQ: Transgender Studies Quarterly* 7, no. 4 (2020): 527–53.

Gossett, Reina, Eric A. Stanley, and Johanna Burton. *Trap Door: Trans Cultural Production and the Politics of Visibility*. Cambridge, MA: MIT Press, 2022.

Green, Richard, and John Money, eds. *Transsexualism and Sex Reassignment*. Baltimore: Johns Hopkins University Press, 1969.

Gregg, Melissa, and Greg Seigworth. *The Affect Theory Reader*. Durham, NC: Duke University Press, 2010.

Grosz, Elizabeth. *Volatile Bodies: Towards a Corporeal Feminism*. Bloomington: Indiana University Press, 1994.

Grosz, Elizabeth. "Women, Chora, Dwelling." In *Space, Time, and Perversion: Essays on the Politics of Bodies*, 111–24. New York: Routledge, 1995.

Guattari, Félix. *Molecular Revolution*. New York: Penguin Books, 1984.

Guillaumin, Colette. "Race and Nature: The System of Marks." *Feminist Studies* 8 (1988): 25–44.

Halberstam, Jack. *Female Masculinity*. Durham, NC: Duke University Press, 1998.

Halberstam, Jack. *In a Queer Time and Place: Transgender Bodies, Subcultural Lives*. New York: NYU Press, 2005.

Haraway, Donna. *The Companion Species Manifesto: Dogs, Humans, and Significant Otherness*. Chicago: Prickly Paradigm Press, 2003.

Haraway, Donna. "A Cyborg Manifesto: Science, Technology, and Socialist-Feminism in the Late Twentieth Century." In *Simians, Cyborgs, and Women: The Reinvention of Nature*, 149–81. New York: Routledge, 1991.

Haraway, Donna. *Simians, Cyborgs, and Women: The Reinvention of Nature*. New York: Routledge, 2013.

Harney, Stefano, and Fred Moten. *The Undercommons*. Wivehoe: Minor Compositions, 2013.

Hausman, Bernice. *Changing Sex: Transsexualism, Technology, and the Idea of Gender*. Durham, NC: Duke University Press, 1995.

Heaney, Emma. *The New Woman: Literary Modernism, Queer Theory, and the Trans Feminine Allegory*. Evanston, IL: Northwestern University Press, 2017.

Heyes, Cressida. "Feminist Solidarity after Queer Theory: The Case of Transgender." *Signs: Journal of Women in Culture and Society* 28, no. 4 (2003): 1093–120.

Hill, Robert. "A Social History of Heterosexual Transvestism in Cold War America." PhD diss., University of Michigan at Ann Arbor, 2007.

Hinchy, Jessica. *Governing Gender and Sexuality in Colonial India: The Hijra, c. 1850–1900*. Cambridge: Cambridge University Press, 2019.

Homans, Margaret. "Bearing Demons: Frankenstein's Circumvention of the Maternal." In *Bearing the Word: Language and Female Experience in Nineteenth-Century Women's Writing*, 100–119. Chicago: University of Chicago Press, 1986.

Horn, Stacey. *Cyberville: Clicks, Culture and the Creation of an Online Town*. New York: Time Warner, 1998.

Horowitz, David. *The Professors: The 101 Most Dangerous Academics in America*. Washington, DC: Regnery, 2006.

Irvine, Janice. *Disorders of Desire: Sex and Gender in Modern American Sexology*. Philadelphia: Temple University Press, 1990.

Jackson, Zakiyyah Iman. "Theorizing in a Void: Sublimity, Matter, and Physics in Black Feminist Poetics." *South Atlantic Quarterly* 117, no. 3 (2018): 617–48.

Jacobus, Mary. "Is There a Woman in This Text?" In *Reading Woman: Essays in Feminist Criticism*, 83–109. New York: Columbia University Press, 1986.

Jean, Qween, Joela Rivera, Mikelle Street, and Raquel Willis. *Revolution Is Love: A Year of Black Trans Liberation*. New York: Aperture, 2022.

Jorgensen, Christine. *A Personal Autobiography*. Jersey City, NJ: Cleis Press, 2000.

Kahler, Frederic. "Does Filisa Blame Seattle?" (San Francisco) *Bay Times*, June 3, 1993, 23.

Kendall, Mikki. *Hood Feminism: Notes from the Women a Movement Forgot*. New York: Penguin, 2022.

Kessler, Suzanne J., and Wendy McKenna. *Gender: An Ethnomethodological Approach*. Chicago: University of Chicago Press, 1985.

Killian, Kevin, and Dodie Bellamy, eds. *Writers Who Love Too Much: New Narrative Writing 1977–1997*. Brooklyn, NY: Nightboat Books, 2017.

Kittler, Friedrich. *Gramophone, Film, Typewriter*. Stanford, CA: Stanford University Press, 1999.

Kristeva, Julia. *Powers of Horror*. New York: Columbia University Press, 1992.

Laclau, Ernesto, and Chantal Mouffe. *Hegemony and Socialist Strategy: Towards a Radical Democratic Politics*. 2nd ed. London: Verso, 2001.

Laqueur, Thomas. *Making Sex: Body and Gender from the Greeks to Freud*. Cambridge, MA: Harvard University Press, 1992.

Levinas, Emmanuel. *Humanism of the Other*. Urbana-Champaign: University of Illinois Press, 2005.

Liberazioni. 2015. "Monstri (e) Queer." *Liberazioni: Rivista di critica antispecista*, no. 21 (2015).

Lugones, Maria. *Pilgrimages/Peregrinajes: Theorizing Coalition against Multiple Oppressions*. Lanham, MD: Rowman and Littlefield, 2003.

Lyotard, Jean-François. *The Differend: Phrases in Dispute*. Minneapolis: University of Minnesota Press, 1989.

Malatino, Hil. *Side Affects: On Being Trans and Feeling Bad*. Minneapolis: University of Minnesota Press, 2022.

Marx, Karl. *Wage-Labor and Capital*. Translated by J. L. Joynes. New York: International, 1971.

Massey, Doreen. "A Global Sense of Place." In *Studying Culture: An Introductory Reader*, edited by Anne Gray and Jim McGuigan, 232–40. New York: Edward Arnold, 1993.

Mbembe, Achille. *Necropolitics*. Durham, NC: Duke University Press, 2019.

Meeker, Martin. *Contacts Desired: Gay and Lesbian Communications and Community, 1940s–1970s*. Chicago: University of Chicago Press, 2006.

Members of the Gay and Lesbian Historical Society. "MTF Transgender Activism in San Francisco's Tenderloin: Commentary and Interview with Elliot Blackstone." *GLQ: A Journal of Lesbian and Gay Studies* 4, no. 2 (1998): 349–72.

Merleau-Ponty, Maurice. *Phenomenology of Perception*. 1945. New York: Routledge Classics, 2002.

Meronek, Toshio, and Miss Major. *Miss Major Speaks: The Life and Legacy of a Black Trans Revolutionary*. New York: Verso Books, 2023.

Meyer, Morris. "I Dream of Jeannie: Transsexual Striptease as Scientific Display." *Drama Review* 35, no. 1 (1991): 25–42.

Meyerowitz, Joanne. *How Sex Changed: A History of Transsexuality in the United States*. Cambridge, MA: Harvard University Press, 2002.

Meyerowitz, Joanne. "A New History of Gender." Paper presented at the conference Trans/Forming Knowledge: The Implications of Transgender Studies for Women's, Gender, and Sexuality Studies. Center for Gender Studies, University of Chicago, February 17, 2006.

Mikuteit, Debbie. Letter. *Coming Up!* February 1986, 3–4.

Miller, Korin. "Why Are Women Putting Wasp Nests in Their Vaginas?" *Women's Health Magazine*, June 1, 2017.

Mock, Janet. *Redefining Realness*. New York: Atria Books, 2014.

Monir, Carta. *Napkin*. Ann Arbor, MI: Diskette Press, 2019.

Moraga, Cherríe. *Native Country of the Heart: A Memoir*. New York: Picador, 2020.

Morgan, Lynn M., and Evan B. Towle. "Romancing the Transgender Native: Rethinking the Use of the 'Third Gender' Concept." *GLQ: A Journal of Lesbian and Gay Studies* 8, no. 4 (2002): 469–97.

Morse, Nicole Erin. *Selfie Aesthetics: Seeing Trans Feminist Futures in Self-Representational Art*. Durham, NC: Duke University Press, 2022.

Muñoz, José Esteban, Jinthana Haritaworn, Myra Hird, Zakiyyah Iman Jackson, Jasbir K. Puar, Eileen Joy, Uri McMillan, Susan Stryker, Kim TallBear, Jami Weinstein, and Jack Halberstam. "Dossier: Theorizing Queer Inhumanisms." *GLQ: A Journal of Lesbian and Gay Studies* 21, nos. 2–3 (2015): 209–48.

Najmabadi, Afsaneh. *Professing Selves: Transsexuality and Same-Sex Desire in Contemporary Iran.* Durham, NC: Duke University Press, 2013.

Namaste, Viviane. *Invisible Lives: The Erasure of Transsexual and Transgendered People.* Chicago: University of Chicago Press, 2000.

Nanda, Serena. *Neither Man nor Woman: The Hijras of India.* Belmont, CA: Wadsworth, 1990.

Nietzsche, Friedrich. *Untimely Mediations.* Cambridge: Cambridge University Press, 1997.

O'Hartigan, Margaret D. "I Accuse." (San Francisco) *Bay Times*, May 20, 1993, 11.

Pasolini, Pier Paolo. *Petrolio.* New York: Pantheon Books, 1997.

Perkins, Roberta. *The Drag Queen Scene: Transsexuals in Kings Cross.* Sydney: HarperCollins, 1983.

Peters, Torrey. *Detransition, Baby.* New York: Oneworld, 2021.

Pollack, Rachel. *The Body of the Goddess: Sacred Wisdom in Myth, Landscape and Culture.* Rockport, MA: Element Books, 1997.

Preciado, Paul B. *Testo Junkie.* New York: Feminist Press at CUNY, 2013.

Prodger, Charlotte. *Selected Works.* Berlin: Walther Konig, 2022.

Prosser, Jay. *Second Skins: The Body Narratives of Transsexuality.* New York: Columbia University Press, 1998.

Puar, Jasbir. *Terrorist Assemblages: Homonationalism in Queer Times.* Durham, NC: Duke University Press, 2017.

Raymond, Janice G. *The Transsexual Empire: The Making of the She-Male.* Boston: Beacon, 1979.

Repo, Jemima. *Biopolitics of Gender.* Oxford: Oxford University Press, 2015.

Rocero, Geena. *Horse Barbie.* New York: Dial Press, 2023.

Rocque Ramirez, Horacio N. "A Living Archive of Desire: Teresita La Campesina and the Embodiment of Queer Latino Community Histories." In *Archive Stories: Facts, Fictions, and the Writing of History*, edited by Antoinette Burton, 111–35. Durham, NC: Duke University Press, 2005.

Roen, Katrina. "Transgender Theory and Embodiment: The Risk of Racial Marginalisation." *Journal of Gender Studies* 10, no. 3 (2001): 253–63.

Roscoe, Will. "Priests of the Goddess: Gender Transgression in the Ancient World." Paper presented at the American Historical Association meeting, San Francicso, CA, January 9, 1994.

Rubin, Gayle. *Deviations: A Gayle Rubin Reader.* Durham, NC: Duke University Press, 2011.

Rubin, Gayle. "Thinking Sex: Notes for a Radical Theory of the Politics of Sexuality." In *The Lesbian and Gay Studies Reader*, edited by Henry Abelove, Michèle Aina Barale, and David M. Halperin, 3–44. New York: Routledge, 1993.

Rubin, Gayle. "The Traffic in Women: Notes on the 'Political Economy' of Sex." In *Toward an Anthropology of Women*, edited by Rayna R. Reiter, 157–210. New York: Monthly Review Press, 1975.

Rubin, Gayle. "The Valley of the Kings: Leathermen in San Francisco, 1960–1990." PhD diss., University of Michigan, 1994.

Rubin, Henry Samuel. "Transformations: Emerging Female to Male Transsexual Identities." PhD diss., Brandeis University, 1996.

Russo, Vito. *The Celluloid Closet: Homosexuality in the Movies*. New York: Harper and Row, 1981.

Salamon, Gayle. *Assuming a Body: Transgender and Rhetorics of Materiality*. New York: Columbia University Press, 2010.

Sandoval, Chela. 2000. *Methodology of the Oppressed*. Minneapolis: University of Minnesota Press.

Sante, Lucy. *Low Life: Lures and Snares of Old New York*. New York: Farrar, Straus and Giroux, 2003.

Sante, Lucy. *The Other Paris*. New York: Farrar, Straus, and Giroux, 2016.

Schulman, Sarah. *Let the Record Show: A Political History of ACT-UP New York, 1987–1993*. New York, Farrar, Straus and Giroux, 2021.

Schulman, Sarah. *Rat Bohemia*. Vancouver: Arsenal Pulp Press, 2008.

Sedgwick, Eve Kosofsky. "Queer Performativity: Henry James's *The Art of the Novel*." *GLQ: A Journal of Lesbian and Gay Studies* 1, no. 1 (1993): 1–16.

Sedgwick, Eve Kosofsky. *Touching Feeling*. Durham, NC: Duke University Press, 2003.

Shapiro, Judith. "Transsexualism: Reflections on the Persistence of Gender and the Mutability of Sex." In *Body Guards: The Cultural Politics of Gender Ambiguity*, edited by Julia Epstein and Kristina Straub, 248–79. New York: Routledge, 1991.

Shelley, Mary. *Frankenstein, or The Modern Prometheus*. 1817. New York: Signet, 1965.

Shermatta, Benjamin. "Mission Armory." Master's thesis, University of California, Berkeley, 2001.

Silverman, Victor, dir. *Commies, Coloreds and Queers*. Center for Independent Documentary, forthcoming, Documentary film.

Silverman, Victor, and Susan Stryker, dirs. *Screaming Queens: The Riot at Compton's Cafeteria*. Frameline, 2005. Documentary film.

Snorton, C. Riley. *Black on Both Sides: A Racial History of Trans Identity*. Minneapolis: University of Minnesota Press, 2017.

Solnit, Rebecca. *Infinite City: A San Francisco Atlas*. Berkeley: University of California Press, 2010.

Sophia, Zoe. "Container Technologies." *Hypatia: A Journal of Feminist Philosophy* 15, no. 2 (2000): 181–219.

Spigel, Lynn. *Make Room for TV: Television and the Family Ideal in Postwar America*. Chicago: University of Chicago Press, 1992.

Spillers, Hortense. "Mama's Baby, Papa's Maybe: An American Grammar Book." *Diacritics* 17, no. 2 (Summer 1987): 64–81.

Steinmetz, Katy. "The Transgender Tipping Point." *Time Magazine*, May 29, 2014.

Stiegler, Bernard. *Technics and Time 1: The Fault of Epimtheus*. Stanford, CA: Stanford University Press, 1998.

St. John, Graham. *Technomad: Global Raving Countercultures*. London: Equinox, 2009.

Stoller, Robert. *Sex and Gender*. Vol. 1, *The Development of Masculinity and Femininity*. New York: Science House, 1968.

Stoller, Robert. *Sex and Gender*. Vol. 2, *The Transsexual Experiment*. London: Hogarth, 1975.

Stone, Sandy. "The 'Empire' Strikes Back: A Posttranssexual Manifesto." In *Body Guards: The Cultural Politics of Gender Ambiguity*, edited by Julia Epstein and Kristina Straub, 280–304. New York: Routledge, 1991.

Stryker, Susan. "At the Crossroads of Turk and Taylor: Resisting Carceral Power in San Francisco's Tenderloin District," *Places Journal*, October 2021, https://placesjournal.org/article/transgender-resistance-and-prison-abolitionism-san-francisco-tenderloin/.

Stryker, Susan. "Biopolitics." *TSQ: Transgender Studies Quarterly* 1, nos. 1–2 (2014): 38–42.

Stryker, Susan. "The Compton's Cafeteria Riot of 1966: The Radical Roots of the Contemporary Transgender Movement." *Critical Moment*, no. 12 (2005): 5, 19.

Stryker, Susan. "(De)subjugated Knowledges: An Introduction to Transgender Studies." In *The Transgender Studies Reader*, edited by Susan Stryker and Stephen Whittle, 1–18. New York: Routledge, 2006.

Stryker, Susan. "How the Castro Became San Francisco's Gay Neighborhood." In *Out in the Castro: Desire, Promise, Activism*, edited by Winston Leyland, 29–34. San Francisco: Leyland Publications, 2002.

Stryker, Susan. "My Words to Victor Frankenstein above the Village of Chamounix: Performing Transgender Rage." *GLQ: A Journal of Lesbian and Gay Studies* 1, no. 3 (1994): 237–54.

Stryker, Susan. "The Riot at Compton's Cafeteria: Coming Soon to a Theater Near You!" *Transgender Tapestry*, no. 105 (2004): 46–47.

Stryker, Susan. *Transgender History: The Roots of Today's Revolution*. New York: Seal Press, 2017.

Stryker, Susan. "The Transgender Issue: An Introduction." *GLQ: A Journal of Lesbian and Gay Studies* 4, no. 2 (1998): 145–58.

Stryker, Susan. "Transgender Studies: Queer Theory's Evil Twin." *GLQ: A Journal of Lesbian and Gay Studies* 10, no. 2 (2004): 212–15.

Stryker, Susan, and Aren Aizura, eds. *The Transgender Studies Reader II*. New York: Routledge, 2013.

Stryker, Susan, and Talia M. Bettcher. "Trans/Feminisms." Special issue, *TSQ: Transgender Studies Quarterly* 3, no. 1 (2016).

Stryker, Susan, and Stephen Whittle, eds. *The Transgender Studies Reader*. New York: Routledge, 2006.

Sullivan, Caitlin, and Kate Bornstein. *Nearly Roadkill: An Infobahn Erotic Adventure*. New York: High Risk Books, 1996.

Sullivan, Nikki. "Transmogrification: (Un)becoming Others." In *The Transgender Studies Reader*, edited by Susan Stryker and Stephen Whittle, 552–64. New York: Routledge, 2006.

Tea, Michelle. *Valencia*. New York: Seal Press, 2008.

Till, Gretchen. "Space of Reception." Master's thesis, University of California, Berkeley, 2006.

Tracy, James. *Dispatches against Displacement*. Chico, CA: AK Press, 2014.

Treut, Monika, dir. *Gendernauts: A Journey through Shifting Identities*. Hyena Films, 1999. DVD, First Run Features, 2006.

Valentine, David. "The Categories Themselves." GLQ: *A Journal of Lesbian and Gay Studies* 10 (2003): 215–20.

Valentine, David. "I Went to Bed with My Own Kind Once: The Erasure of Desire in the Name of Identity." *Language and Communication*, no. 23 (2003): 123–38.

Vance, Carol S., ed. *Pleasure and Danger: Exploring Female Sexuality*. London: Routledge Kegan Paul, 1984.

Volcano, Del LaGrace, and Judith [Jack] Halberstam. *The Drag King Book*. London: Serpent's Tail, 1999.

Wark, McKenzie. "The Cis Gaze and Its Others." *e-flux journal*, no. 117 (April 2021). https://www.e-flux.com/journal/117/387134/the-cis-gaze-and-its-others-for-shola/.

Wark, McKenzie. *General Intellects*. Brooklyn, NY: Verso Books, 2017.

Wark, McKenzie. "Trap Metaphysics." *e-flux journal*, no. 122 (November 2021). https://www.e-flux.com/journal/122/429125/trap-metaphysics/.

Weaver, Harlan. "Monster Trans: Diffracting Affect, Reading Rage." *Somatechnics* 3, no. 2 (2013): 287–306.

Weheliye, Alexander. *Habeas Viscus: Racializing Assemblages, Biopolitics, and Black Feminist Theories of the Human*. Durham, NC: Duke University Press, 2014.

Weheliye, Alexander. *Phonographies: Grooves in Sonic Afro-Modernity*. Durham, NC: Duke University Press, 2005.

Williams, Raymond. *The Long Revolution*. London: Chatto and Windus, 1961.

Williams, Walter. *The Spirit and the Flesh: Sexual Diversity in American Indian Culture*. Boston: Beacon, 1986.

Wittig, Monique. "The Mark of Gender." In *The Straight Mind and Other Essays*, 76–89. Boston: Beacon, 1992.

Wojnarowicz, David. *Close to the Knives: A Memoir of Disintegration*. New York: Vintage, 1991.

Wölfe Hazard, Cleo. *Underflows: Queer Trans Ecologies and River Justice*. Seattle: University of Washington Press, 2022.

Zalewski, Marysia. "A Conversation with Susan Stryker." *International Feminist Journal of Politics* 5, no. 1 (2003): 118–25.

Zigarovich, Jolene, ed. *The TransGothic in Literature and Culture*. New York: Routledge, 2018.

Index

Beatty, Christine: *Misery Loves Company*, 36
Beauvoir, Simone de, 124
becoming transgender, 5
Bell, Shannon, 62
Bergman, Ingmar, 77
Bergson, Henri, 64–65
Berkeley, CA, 59, 94, 114, 143, 166–67, 169
Bérubé, Allan, 95
Bettcher, Talia, 166
Bey, Marquis, 17, 162
Big Berks (Berkshire Conference on the History of Women, Genders, and Sexualities), 123
Billings, Dwight B., 108n4, 149n10
biological determinism, 112
biology, 9, 99, 101–2, 112, 143, 158, 178
bio-materiality, 84
biopolitics, 16, 60, 129, 157–58, 161, 163, 173
bisexuality, 10, 17, 46, 77, 103, 106, 110, 111, 113–14, 118, 121n7, 136, 151
Black and Blue Tattoo, 60, 88
Black feminisms, 175–76
Blackness, 130; and trans-ness, 17, 162
Blade Runner, 57, 87
Bloomer, Amelia, 100
body alteration/modification, 7, 15, 42–44, 67–68, 112, 126, 157. *See also* hormones; sexual surgeries
body performance artwork, 42
bohemian spaces, 2, 4–5, 7, 17n3, 26, 79, 172–73
Bombardier, Cooper Lee, 7, 58, 87–89; *Pass with Care*, 8
bondage, 24–26, 51
Bornstein, Kate, 35
Brandeis University, 148n3
Brat Attack, 34
Brooks, Peter, 137, 149n7
bulldykes, 30
Burning Spear, 72
Bush, George W., 153
butches, 11, 56, 79, 115, 148n3, 172; butch bottoms, 54; stone, 121n5

butch-femme cultures, 56, 115, 148nn3–4
Butler, Judith, 9, 15, 46, 114, 146, 151, 160, 167

California Academy of the Arts, 35
California State University, San Marcos, 133
Cameron, Loren, 42; *Our Vision, Our Voices*, 35
caning, 26, 31
capitalism, 2, 59, 73, 88, 102, 149n10, 168, 177; racial, 17
cárdenas, micha, 85
castration, 39, 43–45, 47
Catacombs, 60
Chen, Jian Neo, 17
Chesapeake Bay Tidewater, 83
China, 2
chora, 69
Christianity, 47, 135. *See also* Mormons
Christopher Street Liberation Day, 128
Church of Jesus Christ of Latter-day Saints. *See* Mormons
cis gaze, 6, 14
cisgender people, 15, 17, 87. *See also* non-transgender people
cisnormativity, 15, 160
cis sexism, 155
citizenship, 10, 99
Civil War (US), 37, 59, 107
The Clash, 72
Clinton, Bill, 111
the closet, 3, 78, 128, 139
Club Confidential, 88
Cohen, Cathy, 159
Cold War, 88
colonialism/imperialism, 9, 88, 154, 157, 162, 177; neo-, 129
coming out, 1–4, 7, 17, 18n15, 95, 127, 151, 152, 169, 171
Compton's Cafeteria riot, 11, 116–19
Connell, R.W., 18n7
consciousness-raising, 101
Constantinou, Sophie: *Trans*, 35

counter-conduct, 168
counterculture, 26, 117, 168
cowboy subculture, 115
critically transing, 156
critical race studies, 101
cross-dressing, 1, 74, 96, 100, 110, 112, 128, 130. *See also* transvestite (identity)
Crossing the Line (exhibit), 35
culture jamming, 174

Daly, Mary, 134–35
Daughters of Bilitis, 115
Dear Abby, 74, 124
death, 3, 68, 88, 114, 125, 140; and trans-phobia, 13, 15, 130, 136, 156, 177–78
Deleuze, Gilles, 14, 67
Democratic Party, 94
Denali, 141–42
Deneuve, 34
depathologization, 42
Derrida, Jacques, 157
DeVun, Leah, 170
diagnosis, 42, 45, 126
Diagnostic and Statistical Manual of Mental Disorders (DSM), 42, 126
Dinshaw, Carolyn, 71n23
disability, 10, 104–5, 120, 128, 169
disability studies, 101, 153
disciplinarity, 95, 169; and homonormativity, 109–21; normativizing, 11, 119
discrimination, 10, 37, 105, 114, 117–18, 125
dive bars, 5, 55, 88
Dodge, Harry, 60, 88
Dodge Brothers, 88
drag, 54, 101, 110, 121n7, 148n4; academic, 10; genderfuck, 134; street, 115
drag bars, 54, 94, 168–69
drag kings, 58, 121n5
drag queens, 116–17
Dr. Phil, 36
Duggan, Lisa, 109
Duke University Press, 175
dungeon intimacy, 7, 58–70

dungeons (s/m play spaces), 94, 112, 168–69
dyke (term), 48, 136
dykes, 77, 134, 147; bulldykes, 30; butch dykes, 11, 54, 56, 79; diesel dykes, 121n5; dyke spaces, 34–35, 60, 88; femme dykes, 11, 56; leatherdykes, 13, 94, 135, 143. *See also* lesbians
Dyke Tactics, 128

Eagle, 8, 94, 172. *See also* Beat Jesse Helms Flog-A-Thon
East Bay, 59
ecosexual post-porn art activists, 85
848 Community Art Space, 35
Elliot, Beth, 128
embodied knowledges, 61, 120
Employment Nondiscrimination Act, 111, 129
Enke, Finn, 128
Enlightenment, 138, 149n7
epistemology, 11, 102–3, 119–20, 137
Equal Rights Amendment (ERA), 101, 125, 128
essentialism, 9, 103, 152
estrogen, 13, 44, 135
eunuchs, 44, 130
Eurocentrism, 9, 11, 99, 102, 106, 120, 128, 161, 163, 177

fascism, 47, 61, 135, 174
Fassbinder, Rainer Werner, 77
Feinberg, Leslie, 10, 15, 110, 121n5, 152
female impersonation, 54, 115
The Feminine Mystique, 125
femininity, 14, 44, 74, 100–101, 104, 115, 125–26, 138. *See also* femmes
feminism, 112, 120, 138, 149n7, 163, 169, 172; Black, 175–76; Chicana, 169; cis sexist, 155; cultural, 100, 108n4, 148n3; feminist philosophy, 83, 157; gender critical, 174; and generationality, 124–30; "good-girl," 8, 96;

Kimo's, 36

kink, 8, 26, 68, 95, 112, 168. *See also* s/m

kink.com, 68

kinship, 80, 84, 86, 102, 142, 154, 161, 162, 166; queer, 84–85, 141–43

Klaus, Veronica, 35

knowledge, 7, 62, 70n5, 93, 100, 140, 166; disciplinary, 95, 169; embodied, 10, 12, 61, 107; erotics of, 25, 29; politics of, 4, 9, 12, 119–20, 169–72; power/knowledge, 171; subcultural, 63; trans, 5, 8, 44, 96, 105–6, 115–16

Koskovich, Gerard, 121n7

Kovic, Kris, 35

Kramer, Joseph, 85

Kristeva, Julia, 69

The Lab, 45, 88

Lacan, Jacques, 66

language reclamation, 48, 136

Laplanche, Jean, 62

Laqueur, Tom, 149n7, 167

Law of the Father (Lacan), 147

leather bars, 8, 51, 94, 172. *See also* Eagle

leather culture, 54–55, 60, 94, 115, 171–72; old leather, 63. *See also* s/m

leatherdykes, 13, 94, 135, 143

Lesbian Avengers, 127

lesbian bed-death, 80

lesbian feminism, 11, 60, 121n7, 123, 126–28, 130, 148n3

Lesbian Resource Center, 136

lesbians, 121n7, 136, 148n4, 151; gender-normative, 109; and homonormativity, 10–11, 110–21; lesbian generations, 123–30; middle-class, 81; trans lesbians, 36, 54, 73–74, 78, 95, 113, 123–30, 135, 143, 148n3, 167; and trans people, 11, 13, 17, 47, 48, 60, 106, 152; working-class, 148n3. *See also* butches; dykes; femmes

lesbian separatism, 100–101, 128

lesbian studies, 170, 174

Levinas, Emmanuel, 157

Levine, Richard, 34

"LGB without the T" politics, 10

liberalism, 2–4, 10, 104, 113, 125, 153

liberation, 6, 11; gay, 60, 117–18, 128–29; trans, 19n39, 34, 42, 110

Lilly, John, 1

LINKS s/m play parties, 59–60, 62–64, 67

Los Angeles, CA, 6–7, 45, 51–57

Love, Heather, 93

Lyotard, Jean-François, 16, 157

Macquarie University, 157

Madonna, 2

male gaze, 14, 125

March on Washington for Lesbian and Gay Rights, 111

Marin County, CA, 35, 59

Marx, Karl, 14, 93

masculinism, 120

masculinity, 13, 24, 54–55, 74, 109, 115, 127, 137, 161. *See also* butches

Massey, Doreen, 61

materiality, 32, 67, 84, 138, 145, 157, 161

Mattachine Society, 115

Maupin, Armistead, 11

media theory, 16

medical colonization, 6, 38, 140

medicalization, 7, 104, 149n10, 171, 173

memoir, 12, 19n44, 169. *See also* autobiography

memory care, 85

mental health, 10

mental illness, 5, 7, 104. *See also* pathologization

Merleau-Ponty, Maurice, 157

Meyer, Morris, 149n10

Michigan Womyn's Music Festival, 111

middle-class people, 3, 13, 26, 43, 81, 100, 117, 148n3

Middle Passage, 38

millennials, 2–3, 168–69

misogyny, 104–5, 121n7, 125, 152

Mission Dolores, 59–60

Mock, Janet, 18n15

passing, 15, 56, 79, 127
pathologization, 141; of homosexuality,
42; of trans people, 37, 42
patriarchy, 9, 100, 104, 130, 135; hetero-,
129
Paul, 141–42
performativity, 9, 15, 43, 103, 133, 159
Perkins, Roberta, 18n7
Persian Gulf Wars, 2, 153
personhood, 96, 136, 153–54; gendered,
98, 100–101, 147
phallocentrism, 69
phallogocentrism, 147
phenomenology, 6–7, 52, 62, 73, 157
Philadelphia, PA, 101, 128
piss play, 27–28, 63
Plato, 69
poetics, 58–70
Pollack, Rachel, 19n51
Pontalis, Bertrand, 62
pornography, 7–8, 44, 68, 75, 96, 170;
ecosexual post-porn activists, 85
pornsophy, 62
posthumanism, 103, 158–59, 163, 175
postidentitarian queerness, 152
postmodernity, 102–3, 152
poststructuralism, 44, 69, 102, 108n7, 127,
168
post-transsexualism, 152
Presidio, 59
Prince, 2
prisons. See incarceration
privilege, 61, 103, 137, 148, 151–54; heterosexual, 78, 110; and homonormativity,
112, 120; racial, 102, 124, 171
Prodger, Charlotte, 7, 84–86
professors, 70, 80, 95, 156, 167, 172. See
also academia
proletarianization, 3
psychiatry, 11, 39, 42, 44–45, 104–5, 126,
136, 176. See also American Psychiatric Association
psychoanalysis, 6–7, 43–44, 47, 62
psychobiography, 99

psychology, 38, 49, 62, 75, 101, 125
Puar, Jasbir, 10
public history, 118–19

queer (term), 7, 48, 63, 78, 136, 148n4, 153
queer communities/networks, 15, 17, 113,
136, 160
queer crip critique, 160
queer culture, 6, 101, 111, 112–14
queer desire, 54
queer ecology, 15
queer gender play, 15
queer geography, 70n5
queer history, 114, 118
queering the woman question, 9,
98–107
queer kinship, 84–85, 141–43
Queer Nation, 110–11, 121n7, 127, 134, 152
queerness, 4, 71n23, 83–84, 127, 166; and
feminism, 96, 105–7, 129; and the in-
human, 155–58, 160–61; and trans-
ness, 10, 64, 97, 105–7, 110–18, 128–29,
139, 146
queer of color critique, 160
queer of color feminisms, 162
queer people, 2–3, 8, 15, 29, 78–79, 88;
orientation queers vs. gender queers,
111. See also bisexuality; butches;
dykes; femmes; gay men; gay people;
homosexuality; lesbians
queer politics, 12, 101, 110–12, 127, 133, 153,
160, 168
queer reproduction, 67
queer studies: and transgender studies, 3,
9, 15, 99, 151–54, 159–60, 168
queer theory, 16–17, 61, 99, 161–63,
170–71; and transgender studies, 3, 9,
15, 99, 151–54, 159–60, 168
queer writing, 16
queerzines, 34, 170

race, 6, 37, 61, 150n16, 157, 169, 177; and
trans-ness, 101–7, 113, 119, 153, 161–62.

See also Blackness; critical race studies; whiteness

racial capitalism, 17

racial discrimination, 37

racialization, 17, 161

racial privilege, 102, 124, 171

racism, 94, 105, 156, 162. *See also* white supremacy

Radical History Review, 118–19

Radical Queens, 101, 128

radical sexuality, 94, 127, 168

Raelyn, 59

Rage across the Disciplines conference, 133

Raphael, Sally Jessy, 36

raves, 14

Raymond, Janice, 100, 126, 128–29, 134–35, 151

the real (Lacanian), 66

"real gender" discourse, 12

Red Dora's Bearded Lady Cafe, 60, 88; Over and Out, 35

religion, 6, 94–95, 106, 165, 167, 177. *See also* Christianity; Mormons

Renaissance, 6–7, 34–40

reparative reading, 6

Rethinking Sex conference, 93–97

revisionist history, 101, 117

re-worlding, 177

rhythmoanalysis, 62

Richards, Renée, 76

Rivera, Geraldo, 36

Rivera, Sylvia, 128

Rocero, Geena, 18n15

Rocky Horror Picture Show, 77

Roen, Katrina, 16, 161

Rubin, Gayle, 8, 13, 127, 150n16, 172; role in gender and sexuality studies, 93–97; "Thinking Sex," 93–94, 96; "The Traffic in Women," 93–94. *See also* Rethinking Sex conference

Rubin, Hank, 35

Rubin, H. S., 148n3

Rupp, Leila, 123–24

sadomasochism. *See* s/m

Saint Andrew's Crosses, 64

Salmacis Society, 128

Sandoval, Chela, 162

San Francisco, CA, 2, 18n24, 23, 26, 45, 49, 61, 70n5, 81, 83–84, 86, 87, 94–95, 114–15, 133, 143, 152; in the 1990s, 2, 4–5, 60, 63, 68, 78, 88, 110–11, 127, 167–74; Bernal Heights, 58–59, 68, 85; Castro District, 60, 83; Miracle Mile (Folsom St.), 60; Mission District, 59, 88; Potrero Hill, 59; South of Market, 56, 59, 60; Tenderloin, 11, 27, 55, 57, 116–17; trans art scene in, 34–40; Valencia Street, 88. *See also* Trans SanFrisco

San Francisco Bay Area, 4–5, 7, 15, 34–40, 45, 83, 114, 127, 167. *See also* Berkeley, CA; Oakland, CA; San Francisco, CA; Trans SanFrisco

San Francisco Human Rights Commission, 112

San Francisco International Gay and Lesbian Film Festival, 35

San Francisco National Guard armory, 59

Santa Cruz, CA, 86, 162

Sante, Lucy, 17n3

science fiction, 87, 159, 177

Scotland, 83; Aberdeenshire, 84

Scott, Ridley, 87

Screaming Queens: The Riot at Compton's Cafeteria, 118

Seattle Bisexual Women's Network, 136

Sedgwick, Eve Kosofsky, 160

sexed body, 9, 17, 101, 103, 111

sex/gender/sexuality relationship, 111, 148n4

sex/gender system, 9, 99

sex-positive feminism, 96

sex radicals, 95

sex trouble, 10

sexuality studies, 93, 96–97, 103, 151

sexualization, 9, 96, 173

sexual language, 8

trans artists, 34–40, 42

trans autobiography, 5–6, 18n15, 38–39, 86–87, 123, 151

TransCentral, 88

trans erotics, 7

Trans-Exclusionary Radical Feminism (TERF), 9, 174. *See also* gender critical feminism; transphobia

transgender (term), 2, 7, 10, 64, 79, 102–7, 110, 121n5, 127, 148n4, 152–53; origins of, 172–73

transgender activism, 11, 34, 36, 99–101, 110–19

transgender feminism, 10, 98–107

transgender history, 1, 6, 11, 166–67; and homonormativity, 109–21

Transgender History, 1

transgender knowledges, 8, 106, 118–19

transgender lesbians, 36, 54, 73–74, 78, 95, 113, 123–30, 135, 143, 167

transgender liberation, 19n39, 34, 42, 110

Transgender Nation, 111, 133–34, 152

transgender politics, 12, 104, 110, 113–14

transgender rage, 4–5, 12–13, 27–28, 48, 133–48, 151–52, 160–61, 176

transgender spaces, 55

transgender studies, 16, 80, 95–96, 103, 156–57, 161, 171–72; and feminism, 106–7, 127, 129; and queer studies, 3, 9, 15, 99, 151–54, 159–60, 168

The Transgender Studies Reader, 1

transgender theory, 8, 11–12, 73, 103, 113, 152, 161, 171

transgender time, 1–4

transhomosexuality, 125

transitioning, 7, 13, 55, 78–79, 114, 146, 167, 171; as art of the body, 12; into a community, 127; language of, 5; mentors in, 2; obstacles to, 17; as putting pressure on forms, 170; racially classed, 6; in trans autobiographies, 38; trans expertise in, 178. *See also* hormones; sexual surgeries

trans lesbians, 36, 54, 74, 78, 95, 124, 127–28, 135, 148n3, 167

trans men, 11–12, 111, 127. *See also* FTMS

trans-ness, 4–5, 16, 89, 165, 167, 170, 173, 176–78; and abjection, 11–12, 15, 126, 137, 143, 146, 152, 155, 157, 162, 176; and feminism, 10, 44–45, 78, 98–107, 108n1, 152, 171; and gay people, 17, 47, 109–21, 135, 151–52; and queerness, 10, 64, 97, 105–7, 110–18, 128–29, 139, 146; and race, 17, 101–7, 113, 119, 153, 161–62; and sexuality, 8–10; and s/m, 7

transnormativity, 10, 19n39

trans people in academia, 8

trans people of color, 3, 174

transphobia, 11, 79, 88, 100–105, 127, 130, 134–35, 149n10, 174, 177. *See also* Daly, Mary; gender critical feminism; Morgan, Robin; Raymond, Janice; Trans-Exclusionary Radical Feminism (TERF)

trans rage, 12–13, 27–28, 48, 133–48, 151–52, 160–61, 176

Trans SanFrisco, 4–5, 7–8, 12, 14, 88, 167

transsexual (identity), 15, 17, 27, 36–37, 52, 74–79, 95, 104–5, 110, 113, 119, 121n5, 136, 149n8, 150n13, 152–53, 156, 159, 161; and feminism, 9–10, 100–101, 108n4, 123–30, 134–35, 148n3, 151, 155; and generationality, 123–30; and sexual surgeries, 30, 36, 41–49, 53, 129, 149n10; and transgender rage, 133–48

transsexual (term), 2, 64, 75, 79, 96, 110, 128, 148n4, 172–73

transsexual erotics, 51–70

transsexual lesbians, 36, 54, 74, 78, 95, 124, 127–28, 135, 148n3, 167

transsexual pride, 37

trans studies. *See* transgender studies

trans theory. *See* transgender theory

trans tipping point, 6, 18n15

Transvestia, 98–99

transvestite (identity), 10, 75, 100–101, 116, 121n5, 148n4
transvestite (term), 2, 110, 128. *See also* cross-dressing
trans women, 1–3, 5, 8, 13, 17, 111, 167, 169, 171; of color, 15, 174; and feminism, 9, 11, 123–30; and lesbian culture, 11; and sexuality, 7, 9. *See also* MTFS
trans writing, 11–12, 16
Treut, Monika, 35; *Gendernauts*, 58
Tribe 8, 60
tricks, 5, 23–29, 32, 52
"true sex" discourse, 42
TSQ: Transgender Studies Quarterly, 1
Twitter, 159, 165
2010s, 3

Ukraine, 174
undocumented labor, 10, 104–5
United Kingdom, 72
University of California, Berkeley, 94, 114, 143, 166–67
University of California, Santa Cruz: History of Consciousness, 162
University of Pennsylvania, 93, 95
University of Wisconsin–Madison, 128
unnaturalness, 12, 48, 52, 103, 134, 136–39, 159
Urban, Thomas, 108n4, 149n10
US Embassy in Tehran, 129

vaginoplasty, 6
Vanguard, 117
Venice Biennale, 84
Vietnam War, 88, 128
Vimeo, 84
virtuality, 14, 61, 65, 67
Vistima, Filisa, 136
Volcano, Del LaGrace: *The Drag King Book*, 58

Walker, Willie, 95
Washington, DC, 101, 111, 128
Weheliye, Alexander, 161
Weinstein, Jami, 157
West Coast Lesbian Conference, 128
Whale, James, 139, 149n11
white men, 129
whiteness, 4, 9, 13, 37, 102, 105, 117, 124, 129, 176; classed, 171; and colonialism, 83, 162; and critical race studies, 107; critical studies of, 157; and normativity, 10, 120, 161; and sexual surgeries, 43; of trans networks, 16
white supremacy, 47, 135. *See also* racism
white women, 9, 13, 129
Williams, Montel, 36
Williams, Raymond, 13
Wilson, 141–42
Wilson, Flip, 76
Wolf, Max, 35
woman (category of), 8, 98
womanhood, 9, 11, 13, 15, 52, 98, 100, 128–29
womanness, 46
the woman question, 9, 98–107
women of color, 11, 15, 174
Women's Building (San Francisco), 135
women's movement, 60, 101. *See also* feminism
women's studies, 8, 98, 102–3, 106–7
working-class people, 9, 11, 100, 115, 148n3, 171
World War I, 59
World War II, 60, 99, 114, 116
WTO, 2

Yerba Buena Center for the Arts, 35

zines, 4, 34, 170